Aurea Vidyā Collection*

——— 22 ———

* For a complete list of titles see page 333.

AWAKENING

This book was originally published in Italian as

Fuoco dei Filosofi

Fuoco di Ascesi

Fuoco di Risveglio

Translated from the Italian by Arthur Farndell

ISBN 979-8-716953-07-9
Library of Congress Control Number 2021913761

Front cover: Fire of Awakening, © Aurea Vidyā

Raphael

Āśram Vidyā Order

Awakening

Aurea Vidyā

'If you wake up to your immortality, which is beyond time, space, and causality, you resolve, at a stroke, all your existential problems; or rather, the problems are not resolved: they vanish like mist in the wind. The problem exists only in the transitory nature of becoming, but in the non-temporal there are no problems, just as in the sun there is no dualistic problem relating to sunrise and sunset.'

Raphael, *The Threefold Pathway of Fire,* I, 51

'We are speaking and writing in order to point towards It, to awake from the sleep of words to the wakefulness of Vision. The teaching may concern only the way and the road, but the vision is wholly the personal work of one who desires to contemplate.'

Plotinus, *Enneads,* VI, 9, 4

CONTENTS

Fire of Ascent

Fire of Awakening

INTRODUCTION

by Arthur Farndell

This book is a collection of topics which Raphael has presented in the form of short articles over a number of years. Although the topics vary, they are all concerned with the subject of traditional Knowledge, and they have been brought together with the aim of being useful to all of those who take a practical interest in the Way of Realisation. In the course of the book there are repetitions, but since we are dealing with writings which stimulate self-comprehension, the repetitions, seen from a traditional perspective, have their place.

The three sections of the book – Fire of the Philosophers, Fire of Ascent, Fire of Awakening – refer to 'Fire', and since Raphael often speaks of the 'Way of Fire' in his writings, it is good to emphasise that we are not dealing with a new teaching or with something personal or individual, or with a syncretistic teaching, but with the 'universal Way' to realise our own Essence, because, fundamentally, every traditional Branch reveals itself as a 'pathway of fire'. Let us quote some words of Raphael: 'He who is writing, having received the *Asparśa* and *Advaita Vedānta* teaching, at a certain point during his *sādhanā* was told to light the Fire, to burn himself with the Fire and to resolve himself into Fire.' We also find a reference to this Fire in the *Kaṭha Upaniṣad* (I, I, 13-14): 'O Yama, thou who knowest the Fire which leadeth to Heaven, do thou reveal it unto me, who am full of faith.' 'I shall teach thee that Fire, O Nachiketas, which will exalt thee to Heaven.'

We shall not dwell on the individual topics dealt with in this book, but we leave it to the reader to intuit and meditate upon the Teaching they express. What we would like to emphasise, however, is a feature which we cannot fail to note as we turn the pages, a feature which we meet in most of Raphael's books.

In the *kali yuga*, it seems that he wishes to present us, especially in the West, with the traditional Teaching from a purely metaphysical point of view, and so we may note his insistence on speaking in terms of unity of the Tradition, a unity which only a metaphysical Vision can comprehend and express.

In a world where the various traditional or initiatory Branches clash with each other through blind incomprehension, Raphael indicates how to transcend all types of 'dogmatic sectarianism' by helping us to recognise that the different Branches are nothing but formal expressions of a single Reality which underlies every genuinely traditional Teaching. The outward diversity of the Teaching can be resolved only through a metaphysical Vision, a vision which synthesises the apparent facets which operate exclusively at the level of the sensible world.

This vision, especially in the West, is deficient for a number of reasons which it would take too long to explain. We would simply say that the West in general is more empirical, pragmatic, dogmatic, and so more individualistic, paying little attention to the Sacred and extensively developing the discursive or dianoetic mind. This extreme individualism can be noted in various fields such as those of politics, literature, and religion. In the West – with some exceptions – it is a very difficult undertaking to get three people to agree with each other; and if one were to succeed, it would immediately give rise to 'currents' or factions, alternatives with so much 'innocence'.

It is only through a metaphysical conception in which all possible points of view are synthesised that the West would be able to rediscover agreement, tolerance, and the possibility of effecting the influence of the Greater Mysteries, or *paravidyā*, the lack of which has caused the 'fall' into the *cul-de-sac* of materialism.

When a society becomes detached from the Principle, which is the 'unmoving Mover' around which all individual contingencies have to rotate, that society gradually declines to the point of finding itself nothing but 'mass', 'matter' (*prakṛti*/χώρα), darkness: it is the *kali yuga*, the dark age, where all are against all, and division reigns.

The metaphysical conception thus excludes the descent into mere syncretism (which seeks to reconcile even the formal aspects of the various Teachings) and also helps us to comprehend the difference between the Lesser and the Greater Mysteries, between *aparavidyā* and *paravidyā*, lower Knowledge and supreme Knowledge. To give an example concerning ritual aspects: the Christian Mass is not the Hindu *pūjā* or a Buddhist ritual, for every ritual, however different it may be in its formal aspect, in the traditional sense is a *means* for attracting spiritual Influence (or Grace) from the intelligible or supra-sensible world. If the ritual does not have this value, it is not at the traditional level, but is a mere ceremony of an individual order.

To make a branch of the Teaching exclusive is, sooner or later, to face a potential enemy in combat. To think that only the Alchemical Branch – or the Qabbalistic, the Platonic, the Vedāntic, the Buddhist, or any other Branch – is able to resolve the *avidyā* or ignorance of the fallen being is merely to intensify the pomposity of party pride and sectarianism.

That most people are under the rule of 'opinion' is an evident fact, just as it is clear that they are desperately seeking to make that opinion absolute. But for a disciple in search of supreme Knowledge to consider, for example, that only the West or only the East holds a monopoly of the Truth is symptomatic of opinion and not of pure Knowledge, which by its own nature is one, beyond all sectarianism, beyond time and space and all possible constrictions.

Since disciples differ in their initial qualifications, their culture, their mental attitude, their particular psychological conditions, and so on, the different traditional Branches provide for their various needs and their specific states of consciousness. For example, in the East there is only one *yoga*, but it has various nuances, names, and different techniques for meeting the requirements of the aspirants, and yet this is always with the same purpose: union with the divine counterpart.[1] Where this purpose is missing, there is degradation of *yoga* and a movement away from the Tradition.

Wishing to unite, at the merely emotional level of theism, the many spiritual and religious currents or the different initiatory schools which are found only in the realm of mental and 'spirited' processes is a pointless task – we would say it is undoubtedly illusory and even pathetic. Only by means of a vision which transcends the 'part' and the single 'current' can one comprehend the *Whole* (as Plato says); only from a higher perspective can one include and comprehend that which is lower or individual, and this perspective can be none other than the metaphysical perspective which embraces Being and non-being by going beyond both, with all the consequences which this inclusion and simultaneous transcendence can produce.

Thus, by placing himself in the metaphysical Vision, Raphael is able to verify that Parmenides, Plato, Plotinus, Gauḍapāda, and others have expounded the same nucleus of principles of the single Teaching, the same goal which the individual must attain, and frequently the same analogies and the same idioms. And why is this? It is because traditional Knowledge cannot but be one, just as there is only one Truth which gives rise to it. The traditional East is more synthetic, the Teaching being condensed into a few *sūtras* or aphorisms and directed exclusively at intuition and the awakening of awareness, whereas the West, in general, being more dianoetic and related to the empirical mind, is discursive, analytical, and detailed, so that it stimulates and fosters the analytical mind.

---

[1] For more on this theme, see *Essence & Purpose of Yoga* by Raphael. Aurea Vidyā, New York.

This is why in the West, with a few exceptions, we speak a lot about Tradition and little about realisation.

However, to reach metaphysical Knowledge one needs to transcend not only the individualised state (which is obvious), where unilateralism and contradictions are irreconcilable, but even the principial, universal state. In fact, the theists oppose one another because each of them is defending his own God to the detriment of the God of the others. To follow a metaphysical pathway one has to place oneself in a condition which is completely without form, qualification, and quantity.

Raphael often says that each should pursue his own Teaching, provided that it is universal and not the result of the 'originality' of the mind to make a show of distinction and seem different at all costs, thus emphasising the needs of individuality. Every Branch of the Teaching, if followed honourably and seriously, leads to the same goal.

The One-Good of Plato, the One of Plotinus, the Being of Parmenides, the *Ain Soph* of *Qabbālāh*, the *Nirguṇa Brahman* of *Vedānta*, and so on, are the same thing, because they designate the same Principle, or rather the root of the Principle, even if in the course of time – it has to be said – many disciples and scholars have added superimpositions to the point of producing deformations, and they have made unilateral interpretations in order to be 'original'.

Another typical peculiarity of the ego is to exalt the *person* who is transmitting the Teaching rather than the Teaching itself. This gives rise to the absurdity of over-emphasising the means at the expense of the end. Adherence to the form or body dies hard.

Parmenides, Plato, Plotinus, Gauḍapāda, Śaṅkara, and others, following the requirements of *dharma*, have been precise transmitters of the Tradition, frequently paying attention to particular aspects of the Teaching.

Parmenides particularly emphasised Being, inasmuch as it *is* and does not become. Plato spoke at length about both

Being and becoming. Plotinus raised his consciousness to the transcendent One. Gauḍapāda and Śaṅkara highlighted especially the supreme state of the *Brahman* (*Advaita, Asparśa*), while others put the emphasis only on becoming (the Lesser Mysteries). But the Tradition embraces both the Greater and the Lesser Mysteries, that is, supreme Knowledge and lower knowledge.

If great numbers of disciples, rather than attaching themselves to names or people, were to give their attention to the Teaching, many points of misunderstanding would certainly disappear, and among the various schools or disciples, there would be greater comprehension and more productive co-operation.

But to transcend names, even the names of the great mediators, such as those we have mentioned, means to betake oneself into that metaphysical Vision where the many become One and opinion becomes supreme Truth.

A further consideration is that in the traditional Knowledge, which re-establishes the link with the Holy Mysteries of the West and the Sacred Tradition of the *Vedas* (to mention just two Branches of the single Source), the theoretical and practical aspects of realisation are always connected and present together. Philosophy, as the expression of this Knowledge, therefore develops along a double track, which can give the figure of the traditional Philosopher or Knower his specific characteristic: that of presenting a vision and embodying it.

It is commonly said that the thought of a dianoetic philosopher has its development or evolution in the sense that it gradually matures and assumes a structure, eventually reaching its full expression. Sometimes this development occurs with retractions, reconsiderations, and even implicit denials of earlier phases. But this does not happen with the traditional Knower, for he appears on the world-scene complete with a full vision of Knowledge. And this cannot be otherwise, because he has 'seen', with the eye of Consciousness, the Truth in its entirety and its unity. Parmenides, Plato, Plotinus, Gauḍapāda, Śaṅkara, and others have, from the very beginning, offered the Knowledge with the certainty of someone who has indeed 'seen'.

In their writings there are no phases, no developments, no processes of maturing, but the constant and unchanging exposition of that Vision from many angles. And most of all, that Vision is carried into act, lived consciously, so that we may say of these great ones that they were Masters not only of Knowledge but also of Life.

This characteristic, so rare nowadays, surfaces anew in its fullest form in the writings of Raphael. In this book, too, as in all his works, Raphael puts side by side with notes of pure Knowledge (see, for example, the chapters 'Realisative Metaphysics', 'Being, free will, liberation', and 'Being/the Constant') suggestions for their practical implementation, demonstrating an integrated knowledge of what he calls – with an awareness of this word's profound significance – individuality. This gives rise to the articles 'Brotherhood' and 'The disciple's aboulia', which reveal the traps into which a spiritual seeker can fall.

Raphael's books – and those who have followed his writings know this – are not essays in which to make a display of mental ability or erudite knowledge, but, on the contrary, they are synthetic and essential, aiming more at the reader's 'heart' than at his mind, and 'heart' is not sentimentality but comprehensive intelligence, Dante's 'Intellect of Love', the *buddhi* in *Vedānta*, the *noûs* in Plato, and as such it is not of an analytical or discursive order but is synthetic and universal (see the chapter 'Heart and Love'). They all indicate a goal, that goal which is the true end of man: awakening to what one really is, the act of awareness of one's own Reality and Truth. And it is only by effecting this type of awakening that man will eventually find true peace within himself.

To all those readers who 'truly and sincerely aspire to be free' let the following words be an invitation from Raphael:

'Awake! Arise! Be filled with hope. Do not crystallise yourself in false sophistry or sadden that heart of yours which yearns for fulfilment. Spread forth the wings of Knowledge/Awareness. Kindle the mercurial radiant Fire and take flight towards Harmony and Beauty, those destroyers of strife and ignorance.'[1]

[1] Raphael, *The Threefold Pathway of Fire*. Aurea Vidyā, New York.

Fire of the Philosophers

Awakening to Traditional Truths

METAPHYSICS

Aristotle describes metaphysics as 'science or knowledge of causes and first or highest principles'.

The cause (αἰτία) and principle (ἀρχή) of a thing are none other than the why of the thing itself, its *raison d'être*; they are *that on account of which* the thing is and is what it is. Causes and principles, therefore, can be defined as the *conditions* or the *fundamentals* of things, inasmuch as they are that on which the things are founded and conditioned; if the causes and principles are removed, the things themselves are instantly removed, too. If the threads of a piece of material or cloth are removed, the material itself disappears. The atom is the foundation of matter. But in the definition given by Aristotle we spoke of first or highest principles.

When we possess knowledge of the causes and principles of something (as in the examples given), we certainly possess the *science* of the thing, but not necessarily metaphysical science; we have 'metaphysical science' when *assured* causes and assured principles are known. Which ones? Precisely those which are *highest*, *first*, or ultimate.

Again, if we study the principles of number and numerical relationships, we shall have arithmetical science; if we study the causes and rationale of celestial phenomena, we shall have astronomical science; if we study the causes and principles of atmospheric phenomena, we shall have meteorological science; when we study the emotional, mental, and instinctive phenomena of the individual, we shall have psychological science. Then when shall we have metaphysical science? Not when we study, and become acquainted with, the causes and principles which are valid only for particular 'zones' of reality or only for groups of things and thus within the limits of circumscribed 'sectors' of being; but – and this is the decisive point – when we study and determine what the causes and principles are of *all* things without distinction, of the whole of reality without restriction, that is, of all beings. These are the 'first' or 'highest' causes and principles which are the specific subject of metaphysics: the causes and principles which condition all reality whatsoever and are therefore the causes and principles on which all beings in their totality are based.

Thus metaphysics is the science of the ultimate cause of all things, the science of the *supreme reasons* of reality, and for this reason, as Aristotle says, 'it is the science which is higher than all the other particular sciences'[1] which propound particular truths and not universal truths.

Another definition of metaphysics given by Aristotle is this: the science of being as being, and of that which belongs to being as such.

Here are Aristotle's words:

> 'There is a science which studies being as being, and the properties which belong to it as such. It is not identified with any of the particular sciences: indeed none of the other sciences considers being as such in its universality, but, having delimited one part of it, each science studies the characteristics of that part. This is what mathematics does, for example.'[2]

This shows that today's specialisation turns out to be anti-metaphysical, which implies getting lost in the particular.

> 'The particular sciences, therefore, restrict themselves *to a determined part of being*; they isolate it from the rest and investigate its properties and characteristics. Metaphysics, on the other hand, has reality as the object of its enquiry, not as

---

[1] Aristotle, *Metaphysics*, edited by Giovanni Reale, Volume I. Loffredo, Naples.

[2] Aristotle, *Metaphysics*, G, 1.

this or that determined reality considered as such, reality as reality, total being as total being, whole and absolute (τὸ ὄν ᾗ ὄν). The "highest" or "first causes" are valid for the whole of reality and the whole of being, and conversely, the causes of reality as reality or of being as being cannot but be the *first* or *highest causes* and certainly not particular causes: if this were not the case, they would be valid only for this or that sector of being, and not for being as such.'[1]

Many philosophers have tried to give theoretical, rational proof of this supreme Cause, this Absolute; or rather, like countless materialists, they have maintained that all that is not amenable to rational proof is unknowable. We can say that if the supreme Reality could express itself in a duality, thus losing its identity of Unity, then such a dual reality could be proved rationally. The mind, operating in terms of subject and object, would thereby find it possible to know something other than itself, that is, the second or the object of knowing. But since Reality is one and only one, all these philosophers, although they have been able to expatiate on it, have been unable to know it or prove it.

If we admit Being as absolute unity, we shall have to agree that it cannot be known or proved by a mind that is dualistic or relational.

But if Being cannot be proved and yet is held to exist as undivided Unity, then it can only be realised. Non-realisation of the being within unity would imply the admission of duality (I and Being), and this would invalidate our previous assertion.

On the other hand, everything that manifests itself, being a second or something other than Being, can be subject to proof; and if truths of the 'subtle' or supra-sensible order have not yet been proved it is because the human being, in his present state, has not opened, within himself, other windows of perception which he potentially possesses.

[1] Aristotle, *Metaphysics*, edited by Giovanni Reale, Volume I. Loffredo, Naples.

The intelligible world is to be perceived, comprehended, and expressed through means of a supra-sensible order, and this is obvious. Only the world or realm of the material or physical sensible can be perceived and known through physical, material means, and through the five sensory organs.

We can therefore speak of ultimate truth only in terms of Realisation of consciousness, because ultimate Truth is concerned with the *Entirety of Being*, totality, since it re-integrates apparent multiplicity in the Unity without a second.

It must be made clear, however, that there are different levels or aspects of Realisation. The word 'realisation' means 'making active, effecting'; and so we can speak of psychological realisation, which implies *actualising* the mind/psyche/body[1] harmony or unity of the sensible being; we can speak of the realisation of the intelligible, which implies *actualising* or *effecting* unity with the intelligible or supra-sensible; we can speak of ontological realisation, which implies *actuating* the principial One or Being as the first expression of the One-without-a-second; and finally, we can speak of metaphysical Realisation, which brings into actuality Non-Being or the Absolute or the One-without-a-second or the Infinite[2], beyond the physical and concrete sensible and beyond the formless intelligible. This is Plato's One-One.

We know that there are different levels of initiation, levels which correspond to different states of realisation of total

---

[1] The purpose of the forward slash [/] in this text is to show the relationship of the two or more items either side of it. Thus it may indicate a single concept seen from two different perspectives or a concept of unity or wholeness. However, it is left to the intuition of the reader to appreciate the specific nuance imparted by the use of the slash each time it occurs.

[2] We need to look carefully at these two terms: 'infinite' and 'indefinite'. 'Infinite', in its purest meaning, is 'beyond all limit, series, beginning, and end; beyond all conditioning, number, point, line, and constraint'. The 'indefinite' is a *series* of data which, although they may extend indefinitely, are nevertheless finite and under the law of necessity. Thus a series of numbers, which can be combined indefinitely with each other, is still *finite*. See page 54 of *Tat tvam asi* by Raphael. Aurea Vidyā, New York.

Being. Every traditional Branch has its own level, which may, of course, differ from those of other traditional Branches, especially in number.

It is certain that the metaphysical is the highest initiatory level and involves, on the part of the neophyte, not only transcendence of the formal sensible but even transcendence of the principial intelligible or ontological Being or the 'World of Ideas'. In other words, such realisation transcends (as is commonly said) the world of men, the world of the gods, and even the world of the principial God/Person (*avyakta*).

THE ONE-MANY

We often hear the unity of Life spoken of, not only in spiritual terms, but even in scientific terms. We are told that the complexity and the differentiation of material forms originate from a single substance; one physical atom differs from another only by the *number* of electrons/protons. But although this truth strikes us as evident, all the same we approach life, and therefore the different relationships of every order and level, in terms of duality, differentiation, and strong opposition.

And yet, in theory, no clear thinker would admit that two individuals have a nature so opposed and separate as to be two absolutes. On the other hand, if they were such, how could they communicate? Religions maintain that we are children of the same Father. Science, as we have seen, accepts the unity of life; the ecological view holds that all beings are inter-related and not absolutely distinct and it thus acknowledges the interdependence of the various realms of nature, including the human realm.

At this point we may ask ourselves, 'How does the Philosopher who is aspiring to Realisation understand the unity of Being, *Brahman*, and God?' The names have little importance, but what is important is to understand what the names connote. Being, God, *Brahman*, and so on cannot be multiple: several Gods would be mutually exclusive. Nor can we admit the possibility of an absolute duality between Being and the world itself. To speak of the world and God in terms of opposition means to annul that unity which has been proposed and been considered acceptable. On the other hand, if the world is a phenomenon it must find its valid cause in something else.

To state that the being and life are merely the offspring of God means to refer to the whole, to the divine unity, so that between God and the being, whatever it may be, there is no difference or dichotomy. Again, to say that one thing is God while another is the being, or its effects, is to propose an absolute and unacceptable duality: one must necessarily come from the other. Moreover, something living, because it is an effect, cannot but have the nature of its cause, and this precludes diversity and opposition. There are no effects which are not potentially with their cause. Ice is nothing but solidified water. The aspiring Philosopher, therefore, while proclaiming the unity of Being, may find himself living multiplicity and differentiation at the practical level, and even opposition and unconscious confrontation. But what does he see in the other to provoke confrontation and create conflicting duality?

Given what we have just said, we shall still have to put forward one consideration: if we look at the problem with an 'empirical eye', we shall have to acknowledge also that the 'many' exist and that differentiation seems to be self-evident to our 'perception', which means that this consideration contradicts what we have stated about the unity of Being. In short, we find quite a difficult problem on our hands, and we shall need to meditate on how it can be solved. Our reason cannot but find it anomalous and contradictory: on the one hand, we declare unity, while on the other hand we also have the supposition of duality/multiplicity.

The problem of the One and the many was first posited by Plato, but the *Upaniṣads* propounded it, too; or rather, some words in the *Māṇḍūkya Upaniṣad* would seem to offer some clue to guide our discussion.

> 'This is the explanation concerning generation: the *Ātman* is considered in the form of a *jīva* (spark of the *Ātman*), like the space enclosed in a vessel and even in composite objects similar to vessels, and so on.'

Just as with the destruction of the vessel [jars, jugs, etc.] the ether confined within the vessel merges into the [universal] ether, so do the *jīvas* [merge] into the *Ātman*.'[1]

From meditating on these words we can extract a sequence of pointers which we could expound in the following way:

1. We have ether and we have pots or jars.
2. What ether is and what jars are.
3. What the jars may represent compared to the ether.
4. Are ether and jars an absolute duality?
5. What may be their rightful relationship?
6. Can the ether persist without the jars and the jars without the ether?

The *Upaniṣad* suggests to us that within every jar/pot there exists an entity called ether, hence Spirit, Soul, *ātman*, *noûs*; the terms have little importance. The text also points to something very important, that the ether in a jar is of the same nature as the ether outside the jar. This implies that the ether inside the pot is *identical* to the ether inside other pots, apart from being indistinguishable from the universal ether which transcends both the ether in the jar and the jar itself. In other words, the *Upaniṣad* gives us to understand that there is a single Reality/ether which pervades the many jars, since, as we were able to note earlier, the ether within the jar is of the same nature as that outside the jar.

According to the vision of the *Upaniṣad*, we may consider the pot as a 'window' through which the manifest or individualised ether perceives a system of life. This means that this ether makes use of a jar as an instrument by means of which it operates in an existential context; in this way, again, in comparison to the ether, the jar constitutes a mere 'object', an accidental factor of service.

[1] Gauḍapāda, *Māṇḍūkyakārikā*, III, 3-4.

Let us continue and ascertain whether the two aspects, ether and jar, are a duality. A jar/body is always an effect, belonging to the world of becoming and contingency. A jar/body, whatever kind it may be, is born, has its life-span and then declines and is resolved into its essence or elementary substance. If it is an effect, it cannot be an ipseity, and so it must have a cause. Everything that is determined is so by reason of an efficient and undetermined principle. And what could this principle be? In the context of our exposition we are left with nothing but the ether, as we do not have any other elements or data, so that we must necessarily admit that the jar/body is born from the ether itself. We have to acknowledge that nothing is born from nothing. But how can it be born from the ether? We are helped by our dreams at night. Yes, our dreams, the ones that we have every night (although we also day-dream; do we not frequently say, 'I have fulfilled my *dream*'? But, for the moment, this is outside the scope of our essay).

Let us therefore take this analogy and ask ourselves: Who is it that creates dreams?

We may answer: our mind, which in fact has the capacity/possibility of manifesting/projecting the sleeping subject and also the dream object so fully that it experiences what it itself has created. If we wish to consider this deeply, dream is an extraordinary event because it allows us to understand so many things. The mind creates the events and, according to the situation, through the events it enters into a relationship of suffering, happiness, or indifference. It may seem strange, but the joy and the suffering, as well as the good characters and the bad, are created by the mind: we ourselves are the creators of it all. And yet within all this multiplicity of events, people, things, and so on there exists the unity, which is the mind, because the mind is undoubtedly one: we do not have two or three minds. We may also say that if the mind is one, its object is multiple. If we hold to this analogy, we have to conclude that the ether/*jīva* creates the jar/body and embodies itself within it – of course, with just a part of itself. In the *Bhagavadgītā* there is a *śloka* which speaks of 'An eternal fragment of Me, having appeared as a living soul in the world of mortals.'[1] The entire universal 'jar', moreover, is said to have been born from *Mahat*, the Great, the universal Intelligence, so that Being, and Being alone, can say, 'The universe is nothing other than My dream.'

Plotinus, especially in the fourth *Ennead*, expounds the principle that the sensible world (the 'Down here') is brought forth by the Soul, so that we may rise from 'Down here' to the intelligible world, where there is the true homeland of the Soul.

The word 'fragment' in the *śloka* is not to be understood to imply that Being splits and creates a fracture within itself; what takes place is nothing but a specification, the irradiation of a mere aspect, a reflection of universal Being, for Being is not a quantity but pure essence devoid of extension. Being/One and the many are just two sides of the same coin, although the many are dependent on the One.

> 'In every atom, in every molecule, in every cell of matter, there live, hidden and operative – without others realising it – the omniscience of the eternal and omnipotence of the infinite.'
>
> (Teilhard de Chardin).

The philosopher Jean Guitton writes[2]:

> 'I do not think that we have been created in the image of God. We are the very image of God.'

And again, we are:

> ' ... a little like a holographic plate, which contains the whole in each of its parts, every human being is the image of the divine totality.'

Moreover the *apparent* multiplicity has not been born in time under the impulse of a 'plan', a schedule, or a decision

---

[1] *Bhagavadgītā*, XV, 7, edited by Raphael. Aurea Vidyā, New York.

[2] Jean Guitton, *Dieu et la science*. Éditions Grasset, Paris 1991.

made by the Being/One, as is the case with human beings, who, to carry out a task, must first will, then ideate, and finally materialise. Within timeless Being there is no 'first' or 'then', no discriminative 'thinking', to express the multiplicity of beings, and not even a predetermined goal.

When it is said (as we read in some texts), 'Being thought and the worlds came forth', that word 'thought' can be a source of doubts, since it is related to the human realm; in dreams we have the immediacy of the being and of the existence of the projected data, or of the subject and object. We can simply maintain that Being is pure act in the eternal present.

Let us approach the question from a different angle: the pots/bodies are 'compounds' (according to the *Upaniṣad* we have quoted), but a compound of any kind presupposes the simple. This is not only Plotinus' thesis but also Kant's (thesis of the second antinomy). If we rise from the compound to the simple, or from the pot to the ether, we discover the unity of Being.

And since particular Souls (*jīvas/psyches*) are of the same nature as universal Being – for they are its irradiation – the task of all the traditional Teachings is to awaken the soul's awareness to its identity with That, or to lead the reflection of consciousness back to its Source.

> 'Here is the thesis in brief: Souls originate from one alone, and these many Souls, originating from one alone, such as Intelligence, are divided and undivided; the Soul which perdures is the single word of Intelligence, and from it originate particular and immaterial words, as it is up above [in the intelligible world].'[1]

Therefore we cannot speak of absolute duality, just as we cannot say that the subject and the object of dream are a duality, for they are born from the same matrix (the mind), just as universal multiplicity is born from the same, single, divine Matrix.

---

[1] Plotinus, *Enneads*, IV, III, 5.

However, an apparent duality could also subsist; for example, in dreams, if the mind *forgot* that the subject and object are its products, or – which is the same thing – if it *identified* itself with the dualistic dream to the point of shrouding itself in darkness. The ether inside the jar can, of its own free will, conceive itself to be wholly jar, to the point of forgetting that it is ether and, at the same time, the creator of the jar. However, this is always an apparent duality; we shall say that it is a duality produced by ignorance (*avidyā*). We come back, as we can see, to the myth of Narcissus or the *self-oblivion* of the Platonic Teaching. We note that in this way there is no longer a proper relationship between cause and effect, ether and jar. The values are successively changed and inverted: a correct relationship between dreamer and dream arises when the dreamer recognises firstly his own nature and then the nature of the dream and the nature of what is dreamt (and *vidyā*, traditional knowledge, seeks to discover precisely the profound nature of Being rather than the nature of phenomena); only then can he take account of the full extent of his creative possibilities of being able to manifest dreams at night or during the day that are conformable to his will, or, indeed, of being able not to dream, since the dream depends on him and he does not depend on the dream: the effect depends on the cause and not *vice versa*, as we have seen. This means that he is able to resolve any dream which he has been able to project, for it belongs to him and to no one else.

From our exposition so far we can conclude that there exists a single, all-pervasive ether ('Nothing else is or will be outside the ὄν'[1], says Parmenides) and there are many jars of different forms, qualities, and sizes. Thus, if we look with the eyes of the jar, being identified with it, we see multiplicity, with all the consequences that arise from this; if we look with the eyes of the ether, we observe unity, τὸ ἓν , and only unity, be it with

[1] Parmenides, *On the Order of Nature*, fragment 8, lines 37-8, edited by Raphael. Aurea Vidyā, New York.

the ethers inside the jars or with the ether which transcends, or is outside, the jars. These are also the two ways (ὀδὸς) of Parmenides: that which leads to Truth and that which leads to error; it is one thing to see with the eye of the pure Intellect (*noûs*), through which the ὄν (that which Being is) reveals itself, and it is another thing to see with the physical eye the πράγματα; in other words, the becoming of the things which are not, or the representation which we make for ourselves of the things Intelligible. Here is Plato again:

> '... and I was afraid that my Soul had become blind by looking at things with my sensible eyes and trying to gather them together with each of the other senses. For this reason, turning in the other direction, I considered it necessary to take refuge in the words and consider in them the truth of the things which are (τῶν ὄντων).'[1]

'All of those things that mortals have decided, convinced that they were true, will be names (ὄνομα).'[2] This brings us to an extremely important consideration: there being no reciprocity between the subject and its 'projection' excludes the pantheistic conception of Being. Being is one. The many, seen by the One, are only 'appearances', names which, although they participate in the reality of Being, are not Being. We do not accept the statement made by some to the effect that the Being of Parmenides is of a pantheistic nature.

When the Soul turns its attention to the *particular*, it particularises 'or rather, it becomes the object itself ... and lets itself be shaped by the object contemplated'; this process, however, is not absolute; '... we must not speak of change when, by thinking, we pass from the things Intelligible to our own ego, or when we pass from our ego to the things Intelligible: the two aspects are a single thing.'[3]

---

[1] Plato, *Phaedo*, 99e.

[2] Parmenides, *On the Order of Nature*, fragment 8, lines 38-9, op. cit.

[3] Plotinus, *Enneads*, IV, IV, 2.

If we acknowledge that the whole of the sensible, or the world of experience, is the expression of the universal Soul or the Intelligible, of which the human soul is a moment of consciousness, then in order to return to the Source, we shall have to:

1. Become *aware* of our true nature.
2. Stop identifying ourselves with the physical sensible.
3. Create identity with the Intelligible, or the universal Source, which happens naturally if 'separation' is actuated.
4. Put the sensible in its rightful place and, when wishing to experience it (not that this is still necessarily inevitable), consider it as a mere means and not as an end, thus avoiding the attribution of an absolute nature to that which is not absolute.

'The universal Soul, remaining within itself, creates, while the things created go towards it, but the other souls [proceed] towards the things and thus go further into the abyss; or rather, their main part goes right down towards the bottom and takes with it even the souls with their thoughts into the lower regions.[1]

Mahat, equated to the *saguṇa Brahman* (or *Īśvara*) of *Vedānta*, is the universal Intelligence (*noûs*) described by Plotinus or Plato's world of Ideas; the same things are expressed with different names.

The *saguṇa Brahman* represents the universal causal Body, which constitutes the principial Seed that unfolds the multiple possibilities expressive of the entire manifestation.

Just as in the seed of a plant there is perfect unity within the variety of its determinations, so in the Intelligence/Being there are indefinite ways of manifesting on the part of the indivisible unity.

[1] Plotinus, *Enneads*, IV, III, 6.

Mahat, divine 'thought', is not sundered from Being. The Ideas of *Īśvara* are not other than *Īśvara* himself seen from the perspective of identity; they are not products, the fruit of 'projective reflection', but are of the same nature as his universal being, since within him they are *simultaneously present and actual*, for they represent Intelligence in its totality.

Manifestation of living being is generated from inside towards the outside of the causal Body (although these two terms can give rise to misunderstandings) through a spontaneous and immediate act, without the need for any second, just as the possibilities of a seed arise from that same seed as its spontaneous development.

Śiva, *Viṣṇu*, and *Brahmā* (the Hindu *Trimūrti*) are none other than principles expressive of *Īśvara*: it is always *Īśvara* under the aspects of the unfolding and maturing of nature and its re-integration into his breast. It is his sensible 'part', non-being or becoming, which has not, however, come forth from his 'aura', there being no concept of space within Him.

Space and time are representations of reference for the individual being, which, not being able with its dianoetic instrument to immediately embrace that totality of which, in its unconscious principle, it is a part, must necessarily experience one datum at a time.

The world of *Īśvara* represents the One-Many of Plato's *Parmenides*, just as the One-One or the One-Good, devoid of determinations, is identical to the *nirguṇa Brahman* of *Vedānta* (*nirguṇa* means 'devoid of qualifications or determinations'). *Īśvara*, therefore, as Unity/differentiation, resolves himself into the *nirguṇa Brahman* or *Turīya* because he is not an absolute, just as the One-Many of Plato resolves itself into the One-One or the One-Good.

From this framework we can deduce the following *identities*: Being = Intelligence (*cit*); Being/Intelligence = everything living. Being is therefore identical to all and to each in particular, because differentiation is contained within Being as indivisible

Unity; or, again, Being is the metaphysical foundation of the formal and phenomenal sensible.

Thus, as Parmenides gives us to understand, if we wish to have Knowledge or true Science of things, we need to grasp that first factor which ensures that things are; within the multiplicity of phenomena we need to recognise that which *is*, by means of which phenomena appear. Becoming, or the world of names and forms, can be thought of only by postulating unity, and this has been verified even by modern physics.

The realised Philosopher is the one who has known how to re-integrate himself into the ether/essence, so that he sees nothing other than unity, while the unrealised philosopher is the one who sees with the eye of the pot/body, thereby discovering multiplicity, quantity, contradiction, opposition, strife, and evil.

From what is the Liberated Man liberated if not from the false representation of multiplicity, of 'variety' as Kant calls it, or of the 'different' (θάτερον) to use our Plato's term? There is no other difference between the two beings – Liberated and unliberated – but it is of no small account when we consider the enormous implications that must necessarily follow.

PHILOSOPHER, LOVER OF WISDOM

'The *philosophos* of Plato is not a professor of philosophy or a university scientist who boasts such a title for assiduously cultivating his tiny patch of learning.

'Even less is he an "original thinker", because it would not be possible, at a single time and in a single place, for so many thinkers to be born as would be needed for Plato's republic.

'The "philosopher" that Plato has in mind is a man of tenacious memory, quick understanding, and great desire to know. A stranger to all pettiness and trifling, his eye is always turned to the whole in everything and has grown accustomed to looking from on high at formal existence, time, and space. He does not set high value on life and cares little for external goods. His every act breathes dignity and greatness, coupled with friendliness. He is the friend and companion of truth, justice, courage, and temperance. As for the possibility of this type of man manifesting, Plato believes that it happens when there is a concurrence of early and continuous selection, the best education, and maturity of years. The essential point for Plato is *harmony* between intellect and character. This is why he also refers to his philosopher simply with the comprehensive expression of *kalokagathós*.'[1]

> 'And would it not perhaps be an adequate defence if we were to reply that he who truly loves wisdom should, through his own nature, draw everything towards Being, and without being content with the multiplicity of isolated objects – which are nothing other than matters of opinion – he should go straight

---

[1] W. Jaeger, *Paideia. Die Formung des griechischen Menschen*. Vol. II.

ahead, without losing his spirit or neglecting his love, until he has first grasped the nature of everything in itself together with that part of the Soul whose activity is concerned precisely with gathering the essences – having itself the same substance –, and having, with this part of the Soul, come close to and united himself with Being in itself, he should, by begetting intellection and truth, succeed in knowing indeed, live a true life, have true nourishment, and thus, but not till then, cease suffering the pangs of childbirth?'[1]

It seems appropriate to quote another passage, this time taken from Plato's *Theaetetus*:

'Before all else, true philosophers, from their childhood, have been unacquainted with the way to the Agora; they do not know where the law-courts are, or the council, or any other places of public assembly in the city; they neither read nor hear the laws and decrees, written or proclaimed. The intrigues of political cliques to acquire public offices; gatherings, banquets, and parties in the company of flute girls: these are all things which, even in dreams, have never entered their minds ... and the truth is that his body [the philosopher's body – editorial note] is in the city, but not his soul, which, considering all these things of little value, and indeed of none, and holding them in great disparagement, flies about in all directions, as Pindar says, now descending to the depths of the earth, now measuring its surface, now rising up into the heavens to view the stars, and all the while, and at every point, investigating the nature of all beings, each in its universality, without ever abasing itself to anything in particular of whatever is close to it ... Because, in truth, the philosopher not only is unaware of what is near him or of what his neighbour is doing but doesn't even know, we may say, whether it is a man or some other animal. However, if it is a question of re-discovering what man is or what befits the nature of man – in contrast to other beings – to do and to suffer, to this he will devote all his attention.'[2]

---

[1] Plato, *Politéia*, 490b.

[2] Plato, *Theaetetus*, XXIV, 173-4.

He is a true philosopher who investigates the ultimate Reality of things, that is, the 'Whole', and who *accommodates* himself to the Truth that has been discovered.

A philosopher is not one who only speaks of Principles, but one who penetrates and realises these Principles within himself. It is from this perspective that we can say that the Realised Man is a Philosopher.

LOVE IS A PHILOSOPHER

If *devotio* is a sacrificial offering, and *religio* is holiness, then Love is essentially *devotio* and *religio*. The first implies peacefulness at all levels; the second, total self-consecration. And both are identified in the figure of the Roman *sacerdos*, the universal *father/mother*. One needs, in fact, to have transcended the ego to be able to know and express that higher note which has nothing to do with the feeling known to us.

Love is not a pious weakness towards other people's weaknesses. It is *pietas* in the Latin sense, and because of this it is extremely creative. It turns to *gold* whatever it touches, and in its unceasing consuming of itself lies the measure of its greatness.

Love is *beauty*, *composure*, *dignity*. But not the kind of beauty, composure, dignity which the mind defines and recognises. Indeed, it could reveal itself to the ego as quite the opposite of what it knows, for Love in no way corresponds to those conceptual, ethical, and aesthetic canons in which the ego usually recognises the *beautiful*.

Love disorientates the ego. Because it is something new. Because it does not belong to the world of the ego. Because Love wounds the ego and, if it is the right moment, annihilates it.

But what is important for Love is that the 'seed' germinates, that it does not remain a seed. And it stimulates the seed enough to split it. Because, as Plato maintains, *Love is a philosopher. Love has immortality as its object. Love is a daimon ... And it is love of Beauty. And if Beauty is whatever has consonance of harmony with the Divine*, that being is Beautiful which manifests in unison with Idea, Will, Love, and Wisdom.[1]

[1] To go deeper into this topic, see *The Science of Love, from the desire of the senses to the Intellect of Love*, by Raphael. Aurea Vidyā, New York.

SÔMA (body) = SÊMA (tomb)

> 'And what if Euripides were right when he said, "Who can know whether living is not dying and dying living?" and if our life is indeed like death? In fact, I once heard from the Wise that we are now dead and that our body (σῶμα) is a tomb (σῆμα) for us.'[1]

> 'But Beauty still shone complete before our eyes when, with the choir of the Blessed, we following Zeus, others a different god, we enjoyed a view and a beatifying spectacle, and we were initiated – it is permissible to say – into the most blessed of the initiations which we celebrated, when, perfected and impervious to the ills awaiting us in the future, and being initiated into the most profound Mysteries, we enjoyed those perfect, simple, calm, and happy visions, in a pure light, ourselves being pure and not buried in this tomb which we call a body and which we drag around with us, imprisoned in it like oysters in their shells.'[2]

Someone reading these passages of Plato could – unless he is inside these initiatory matters – be disconcerted and troubled. Our physical body, with which we identify ourselves and which we probably believe we *are*, becomes for Plato a tomb in which we are buried and which we drag around and in which we are imprisoned, like oysters in their shells.

Even some disciples intent on Liberation may find these words so disturbing that they are driven to a desperate search for valid reasonings to re-evaluate their bodily/formal experiences. Let us leave aside all those who have had direct experience, outside the body, of the 'shining Beauty' and the beatific vision (*samādhī*) of which Plato speaks, for they need no reasonings

---

[1] Plato, *Gorgias*, 492e.

[2] Plato, *Phaedrus*, 250c.

of any kind. Let us also leave aside all those who, while not having direct experience of this Beauty, feel deep in their hearts that it is true, not from a mere belief of faith but from an innermost unshakeable certainty, as of a distant *recollection*.

Plato says, 'Let all this be said, then, as a tribute to recollection, of which, from our yearning for the things of that time, we have spoken at some length.'[1]

Why can the 'form', the bodily compound, constitute an imprisoning shell from which, according to Plato, we must escape as soon as possible and fly to other shores? To answer this question we shall have to analyse the constitution of the being according to Plato's Teaching and the hierarchy which he applies to the level of values.

We shall also have to say that the Platonic Teaching, the part which he was able to expound – for he had to observe initiatory silence about certain matters – is of a traditional order and, with regard to the question which we are examining, corresponds to the esoteric Orphic Teaching, as he himself gives us to understand.

The being, in its composition, is tri-partite, consisting of *noûs*/pure intellect, *psyche*/soul, and *sôma*/body. *Noûs* is the 'pilot' of *psyché*, and *psyché* is the 'pilot' of *sôma*. The scale of values corresponds to the following scheme: in the first place there are the Gods, a totally universal and spiritual value; next comes man's Soul, which represents his highest part and whose fundamental qualification consists of knowledge, which comes from *noûs*, the truly divine factor within us; then comes the body/*sôma* with its requirements and its biological needs; finally there are riches or external things in general. The Soul is immortal, while the body/*sôma* is mortal and therefore subject to corruption and every possible ill. The Soul is incorruptible, although one of its reflections, commingled with the body, undergoes the influences of the contingent sensible.

---

[1] Plato, *Phaedrus*, 64a.

> 'Of all the goods which each possesses, the most divine, after the Gods, is the Soul, which is the innermost good. In every man there are two parts: the higher and better, which commands, and the lower and less good, which serves. Now he should always honour the part within him which commands, in preference to that which serves.'[1]

> 'Two birds united in friendship fly around the same tree: one of them eats the sweet fruit of the pippala, while the other looks on without eating.'[2]

The latter is the higher, transcendent aspect; the former is its reflection incarnated in the body. The Soul has all the virtues and knowledge itself innate within it; it contemplates the World of Ideas, of the Beautiful, and of the Good. The body is a mere instrument devoid of autonomy, heavy, and resistant to the influence of the divine Good: it cannot exist without the participation of the Soul, while the Soul, being immortal, has no need of the body in order to be; rather, it becomes numb when it assumes a body.

> 'It seems that there is a mysterious pathway which leads us, through reasoning, directly to this conclusion: in truth, as long as we have a body, and our soul is commingled with such an evil, we can never adequately reach that for which we yearn: the truth.'[3]

According to Plato and the Tradition, we are not the body: *we are the Soul* with the *ability* to take, or not to take, a body for ourselves on the sensible plane, according to whether we wish to ascend or descend in the multiple states of Being. According to the Athenian Master, true Philosophy is the 'practice of death'[4], which implies that the death of the sensible, in its various expressions, gives rise to the life and re-birth of the Soul. Hence the philosopher is one who yearns

---

[1] Plato, *Laws*, V, 726a.

[2] *Śvetāśvatara Upaniṣad*, IV, 6.

[3] Plato, *Phaedo*, 66b.

[4] Plato, *Phaedo*, 64a.

for authentic Knowledge/Beauty/Good, for the true intelligible life, and does not seek the corruptible world of shadows. We are *luminous beings*, but the sensible – including the *sôma* – renders us opaque, obtuse, shadowy.

> 'The body causes us unending confusion, incessant turmoil ...'[1]
>
> 'This body is the product of food, and it constitutes the food-sheath. It lives on food and dies if deprived of it. It is an amalgam of skin, flesh, blood, bones, and other relative items. Thus it can never be the eternally pure *ātman*, which owes its existence to none but itself.'
>
> 'Before its appearance, it could not exist, and after its disappearance it will never be able to be; its span is but a lightning-flash. Its qualities are uncertain; by nature it is subject to change; it is composed of parts, inert, and, like a pot, is a mere sensory object. Can such a body ever be the *ātman*, the imperishable Witness of all phenomenal changes?'
>
> 'One who is devoid of sense identifies himself with this collection of skin, bones, flesh, and so on, but the aspirant who is equipped with discrimination acknowledges the *ātman* as the only reality.'[2]

Will one who contemplates the dazzling beauty of the sun ever be able to turn to the weak rays of the moon? This is what Śaṅkara asks. If by direct experience, by super-conscious intuition, or by 'recollection' and so on, we recognise that we are pure Soul, pure Idea, or *ātman*, then we shall acknowledge that these two great Masters of the Tradition are right. If our true homeland is the intelligible world, then we can look upon the realm of the sensible as a mere precipitation, devoid of absolute principle and actuated by the Soul in its descent.

The *sôma* (σῶμα) becomes *sêma* (σῆμα) only for the Philosopher; for someone who has not yet comprehended, be-

[1] *Ibid.*, 66c.

[2] Śaṅkara, *Vivekacūḍāmaṇi*, 154, 155, 159. Translation from Sanskrit and commentary by Raphael. Aurea Vidyā, New York.

ing identified with, and assimilated into, what is not, the body becomes merely the cause of pleasure/pain, attraction/repulsion, illness/health, resignation/exaltation, and so on. On the other hand, how can we consider that which appears and disappears to be *real*? The body (and not only the coarse physical body) is an aggregate of atoms and molecules which appear on the horizon of the Eternal and disappear without leaving a trace. Plato urges us to acknowledge that which is *real* in us: the constant, the permanent, the immortal. All the ills of the world come from not knowing how to comprehend ourselves as Soul free from imprisoning qualities. This is the surest message for resolving conflict and suffering in the world of men.

In the *Phaedo* we read:

> 'Does that being in itself, which, by questioning and answering, we propose to define, always remain identical to itself, or does it change from time to time? The equal in itself, the beautiful in itself – in short, the being – does it ever admit even the smallest change? Or is each of these absolute realities, being uniform in itself, always and in the same way identical to itself, never admitting any change in any way, shape, or form?'
>
> And Cebes replied: 'Socrates, it must necessarily always, and in the same way, be identical to itself.'
>
> 'But what, on the other hand, shall we say of the countless things such as men, horses, garments, and all the others that are equal to them, or beautiful, or at any rate distinct, with names derived from those *essences*? Are these perhaps always identical to themselves or indeed – unlike those realities – within themselves or among themselves are never, so to speak, in no way the same?'
>
> 'Just like that,' said Cebes, 'they are never in the same condition.'[1]

If the Soul is the constant and has within itself, and only within itself, all the powers, such as Intelligence, Will, Virtue, and so on, while the body/*sôma* is just a 'garment' to put on,

[1] Plato, *Phaedo*, 79d-e.

thus giving space to time/space, devoid of determination or the faculty of discrimination; if the Soul, by removing that garment, can better express its powers, then the body is just something superfluous which can be resolved and transcended. If we accept the premises of the Platonic Teaching, the consequences are inevitable and un-opposable. But just as inevitable are the consequences of the Vedāntic Teaching: the being is *ātman*, absolute Consciousness, pure Spirit, which can clothe itself with a body/limit, and just as easily not clothe itself with a body. It can enter a world/prison created by itself, just as it can take flight into the countless 'states' of Being, where time/space is completely annulled. It can also remain recollected within itself, because it is *causa sui*, its own foundation. What is it that creates multiplicity? Bodies/volumes, and hence time/space/causality. According to Plato, when the spirited (*rajas*) and the appetitive (*tamas*) complexes of energy are mastered and transcended, the Soul regains its wings and flies towards that universal state from which, through 'recklessness', says Plotinus, it has descended.

According to *Vedānta*, when *rajas* and *tamas* are transcended, the Soul flies towards the dazzling sun of the *ātman*-without-a-second. The same thing is expressed in different language – but not that different – for the Tradition is one, although adapted for different peoples. In the course of time it can even become overloaded with verbal 'garments', but anyone who knows how to go beyond the world of words and purely dianoetic interpretation can detect in them a single foundation, an identical truth, a substratum which is the noumenal essence.

> 'Everything arcane', writes M. Sendivogius in *De Sulphure*, 'is hidden within the Sulphur of the Philosophers, which is also contained in the entrails of Mercury.'

> 'The bad thing,' states Maximus in *Ignis*, confirming the thought of Sendivogius, 'is that the Sulphur is incarcerated in a very dark prison, and it is Mercury who has the keys to this infernal dungeon. It is therefore necessary first to find it and then to liberate it.'

THE PHILOSOPHER ACCORDING TO PLATO

'It seems to be the case that all the things which people normally consider beautiful or furnished with some other quality, things which are innumerable, circulate in some way *in an intermediate world, between the world of non-being and the world of being in its absolute purity.*'

'This is what we have now found.'

'In any case, we were agreed that, if something like this were discovered, we would have to call it *opinion* and certainly not *knowledge*. That which circulates, in fact, wandering about in the intermediate zone, can be conceived by the intermediate faculty.'

'Yes, we have admitted this much.'

'Well, then, all those who see countless beautiful things but do not contemplate Beauty in its pure objectivity, and being unable even to follow anyone who leads in that direction, and in the same way contemplate countless just things, but not Justice in its objectivity, and so on, in the same way – in short, we shall say that *all these have only opinion, at all times and in all things, but really know nothing* of what they opine.'

'That must be so,' he replied.

'And, by contrast, we shall say that those who contemplate individual things in their pure intelligibility, the things which are eternally unchanging and always the same, therefore know. We shall certainly not say that they have opinion.'

'This, too, necessarily follows.'

'And shall we not say perhaps that the latter turn in joy, through love, towards that of which there is *knowledge*, while the former turn towards that of which there is *opinion*? Or do we not recall our saying that these men love and contemplate beautiful sounds and colours and other such things, but do not even admit that there is Beauty, in the pure objectivity of Ideas and being, or Beauty that can have an existence of its own?'

'Yes, we recall.'

'In conclusion, will it be wrong to call those people *lovers of opinion* rather than lovers of science, that is, philosophers? And do you believe that they will be offended if we call them such?'

'Far from it, and even less if they will listen to me,' he replied.

'Oh! It isn't good to get angry about the truth.'

'On the other hand, all those who turn in joy and love to individual things in the objectivity of their being we shall have to call *philosophers*, lovers of science, and not lovers of opinion.'

'Oh, that's quite right!'[1]

All those on the way of Realisation have often heard talk of realisative Philosophy, perennial or traditional Philosophy, as distinct from dianoetic philosophy or philosophy created just by the projective *manas*, a philosophy which can give an opinion about what things are, but not their reality or essentiality. Noetic knowledge is *knowledge of identity*, so that to know is to be, according to traditional Philosophy (see Parmenides, Plato, Plotinus, and others). This type of Philosophy corresponds to *jñāna-mārga*, the way or *yoga* of Knowledge, according to the Tradition of the *Upaniṣads*.

Plato's Philosophy is mysteric, we could say initiatory; it is metaphysical knowledge (*Politéia*, V, 477) to reveal and *to know* that One as it is (for it does not become), and according to the great Athenian Master:

'*Philosophers are those who have the power to grasp that which is eternal, immutable, and identical to itself.* Those, on the other hand, who do not have this capacity but rather

[1] Plato, *Politéia*, V, 479-480.

stray and wander in plurality and in that which changes in all possible ways, such are not philosophers.'[1]

This definition of philosophers is identical to that given by Śaṅkara:

> 'One must meditate only on the *Brahman* [in its Unity], because [in this way] all these [differentiated aspects] are resolved in That.'[2]

Our readers will, of course, have no difficulty in noting that a philosophical vision, the conception of the actual status of the philosopher and the supreme Reality as expounded by Plato, differ in no way from the expositions given by Gauḍapāda and Śaṅkara. On the other hand, there exists only one Reality, only one Being, and there exists the unity of Life: it is simply that these can be clothed in a conceptual form which differs from one people to another and in time and space. We say that the philosophical/metaphysical Tradition is one and universal but that different adaptations can be found in the course of the different epochs and in accord with the people who express the Tradition.

From passages in Plato we can note that the philosopher does not theorise about the Teaching but lives it, and so it belongs to that Philosophy which is realisative, cathartic, and initiatory, and to which we were alluding earlier. Nor does this conception differ from that given by Śaṅkara.

> 'We are now agreed on this point in relation to the nature of philosophers, that is, that there are lovers of cognition, cognition which can reveal the mystery of that objective *esseity which eternally is*; that esseity which does not stray and wander about in *the cycle of birth and death*.'[3]

---

[1] Plato, *Politéia*, VI, 484b.

[2] *Bṛhadāraṇyaka Upaniṣad*, I, IV, 7.

[3] Plato, *Politéia*, VI, 485b.

Śaṅkara speaks in the same way of realising the One-without-a-second beyond the cycle of births and deaths. The two Masters often use the same language.[1]

The Philosopher writes:

> ' ... *abhorrence of every lie.* ... he hates lies and loves the truth.'
>
> 'Very likely,' he replied.
>
> 'Oh no, my friend, it is more than very likely: it is an absolute necessity. Anyone who is naturally inclined towards love for someone will feel obliged to pursue enthusiastically everything related and close to the beloved.'
>
> 'That's right.'
>
> 'But could you find anything closer to wisdom than truth?'
>
> 'How could I?' he asked.
>
> 'But is it possible for a lover of wisdom, a philosopher, to be of the same nature as a lover of lies?'
>
> 'In no way.'
>
> 'The person, then, who essentially loves to know must, from his earliest years, make his way eagerly towards *Truth in its entirety*.'
>
> 'Yes, undoubtedly.'
>
> 'In any case, we know that within a man whose passion is strongly inclined towards one particular thing, all other desires are weaker, like a stream that is diverted to another place.'
>
> 'Yes, and then?'
>
> 'Then the man, whose passion is like a stream directed to knowing and to that which is similar will, I think, be *wholly directed to the pleasure of the Soul alone for its own sake*. By contrast, the pleasures obtained by means of the body will be diminishing in him, if he is truly and not apparently a philosopher. ... And if he is such, he will also be *attuned in inner harmony, without the slightest thirst for money*. The reasons

[1] See *Initiation into the Philosophy of Plato* by Raphael. Aurea Vidyā, New York.

> for which people go looking for money hold no attraction for the philosopher.'[1]

And again, what intellect should a Philosopher have who is worthy of the name?

> 'Let us therefore look for an intellect which, in addition to the other qualities, is naturally conscious of measure and is full of grace, an intellect which can be guided by a natural temperament and is able to contemplate being in itself within each single thing. ... No one will be able to devote himself to this harmonious use of wisdom unless he is naturally equipped with a tenacious memory which is disposed to study, and unless he is magnanimous, and endowed with grace, a friend and companion of truth, justice, courage, and temperance.'[2]
>
> 'And in your view, who are the true philosophers?'
>
> 'Those,' I replied, 'who love to *contemplate* the truth.'[3]

And what is the Truth, according to Plato (and we shall add, according to Śaṅkara, Gauḍapāda, Parmenides, Plotinus, and so on), that supreme Truth which 'wholly transcends Being in majesty and power?' (*Politéia*, VI. 509). It is the supreme Good, the metaphysical One-One, the essential Reality beyond even the world of Ideas (Being), the absolute Constant, the invariable and the universally valid, identical to itself. The royal Philosopher is the one who, by ascending, *contemplates* this supreme Being to re-discover himself to be Being as such, beyond the 'cycle of birth and death'.

> 'In any case, my friends, for now we should stop pursuing our enquiry into what the Good precisely is. To put into adequate words the concept which I may propose of the Good is an undertaking which transcends, by a long way, all the limits of our powers at this moment. I would like, instead, to speak of him who *manifests* himself to us as the *son* of the Good and

---

[1] Plato, *Politéia*, VI, 485b-e.

[2] *Ibid.*, VI, 486d-487a.

[3] *Ibid.*, V, 475e.

> who is like the Good in all respects. However, if you find the enquiry amenable ... , otherwise I let it pass.'
>
> 'But,' he replied, 'please speak. In the future I shall pay your debt for the account of the Father.'
>
> 'Oh!' I continued, 'I really wish my powers would allow me to offer you this account. Then you could have as much as you like, and not, as now, merely the *son* but the Father himself, too. In any case, receive the one who has been born, by way of compensation, and he is the *son of the* Good. But take note that I do not intend to deceive you. Oh, I would not like to give you an inaccurate account of the one who has been begotten.'[1]

Plato gives us to understand that the metaphysical One-Good cannot be conceptualised. It is difficult to speak of the Son, that is, of Being – imagine speaking of that One whose 'vision' is ineffable.

According to *Vedānta*, too, *Brahman* cannot be expressed in words and cannot be an object of thought. Before the *Brahman* thoughts and words turn back, the *Upaniṣad* declares.

---

[1] *Ibid.*, VI, 506e-507a.

JUSTICE (δικαιοσύνη)

We believe that this word, just like the word 'love', originated with the birth of man himself. It is therefore an extremely important word, of deep significance, but of variable worth if we consider that some – or rather many – have, in the name of this principle, committed outrages, acts of injustice, and even crimes. Since we find ourselves on the dualistic – or rather, polar – plane, justice has injustice as its opposite, and between these two terms there runs just a thread as fine as the edge of a razor.

What is just? And what is unjust? The questions are not easy, and we shall not even try to exhaust the subject, for since it is a fundamental principle for the individual, it is one of enormous complexity and universality.

Let us begin by saying that the idea of justice arises wherever a being, having specific requirements, finds itself face to face with other beings with just as many needs of their own, needs that sometimes even clash. It is clear that, since they have to co-exist, there is the problem of how to *harmonise* the various requirements and the multifarious desires, and of how to decide – in the case of great numbers of people – who should 'govern', for, since individuality is not *causa sui*, there must be precise points of reference and direction.

This means that we shall have to examine the meaning or the principle of justice at both the individual level and the collective level, before seeing who is able or qualified to direct or govern. In short, we shall have to examine the nature of injustice.

When is a being just with itself? For first of all, there is a justice which refers to oneself, collective justice being an extension of individual justice.

In examining this question we may be helped by Plato and his words on the *Politéia* (Constitution). We said that, in collective terms, justice must be able to harmonise – bring into accord – the various requirements of the individuals. The accord and the harmony of qualitative and quantitative requirements are the prerequisites on which the sense of justice has to be based. We shall then see which *faculty* of the being we shall have to attend to in order to effect a just accord, since the harmonisation of qualities requires a directing principle which is actually capable of harmonising clashing requirements and bringing them into accord.

So when can the individual be defined as just? When can the individual be considered to be perfectly upright? In order to understand what it means 'to be just' we have to appreciate the expressive qualities of the being, because justice, as we have said, is the accord of heterogeneous requirements.

We know that the being is formed of a rational sphere (*logos*), an emotional/feeling sphere, and an instinctive/material sphere; that is, an illuminating sphere, a spirited/passionate sphere with a predominance of irrational, one-sided, and distorting qualities, and a sphere that is quite blind, dark, and instinctive, characterised by the law of the jungle. Plato speaks of the noetic sphere, the spirited sphere, and the appetitive/instinctive sphere. *Vedānta* refers to the three qualities of *sattva*, *rajas*, and *tamas*, which are terms that are wholly equivalent to those used by Plato.

If, therefore, we have this tripartite division of qualities, it means that in order to be in perfect justice with itself the being has to find the *right expressive accord*, without which there will be nothing but dishonest dealings, strife, dissension, and disarray among the qualities. If the spirited aspect (*rajas*) prevails, one may find oneself on a plane of self-assertion, domination, hyper-activity devoid of reason, and abuse of power with regard to the other faculties, to the point of neutralising them. If the appetitive activity/quality (*tamas*) prevails, then one will be more of an animal than a human being. If the spirited and the appetitive join forces, then we have a being which in essence is dangerous both to itself and to the community (and humanity has had, and continues to have, great numbers of these). The spirited and the appetitive (*rajas* and *tamas*), by expressing themselves irrationally and in total blindness, cannot but lead to *chaos* and disorder. If these two faculties are chaos and disorder, then the just being is the one who knows how to create within himself a *cosmos*, a principle of order and accord among the manifold sounds. And what is the faculty/quality that can transform *chaos* into a *cosmos*? We shall indubitably have to acknowledge that such a faculty corresponds to the pure noetic intellect (*sattva*), supra-sensible reason, which alone can provide illumination and can *direct*, justly, the two dark qualities, which will therefore have to be subordinated to the noetic quality. Where this subordination does not obtain, we shall have to expect degeneration of the being and thus its death as a human individual.

The greatest tragedy for the individual is that of being limited and constrained within *rajas/tamas* by the exclusion of the supra-sensible sphere. In this way the being has become merely 'dust', 'matter/mass', an organic consciousness trapped in a closed circle. If we exclude the noetic 'part', the intelligible part, we are left with simply an organism that is beleaguered by needs which are utilitarian, contradictory, and often expressed through violence.

The being which does not know how to transcend itself as an organic individual and which does not find knowledge that encourages the awakening of the noetic condition, such a being will not be able to find any Constitution capable of offering harmony and direction to that which by nature is dichotomy and chaos.

'Then it is right for the *rational power* to dominate. It has wisdom and can provide for the soul in its totality. As for the spirited power, it's right for it to be subordinated and allied to the rational power.'

'Undoubtedly.'

'And is it not perhaps true that, as we were saying, a just blending of musical and gymnastic activities will guarantee their appropriate harmonisation? And the first power will be uplifted and nourished through lofty discourse and by means of knowledge, while the other, through gentle persuasion, will be abated and rendered mild by means of harmony and rhythm.'

'It cannot be otherwise,' he said.

'And in this way, both of them, being nourished and instructed through appropriate knowledge and being thus educated, will be able to preside over the *appetitive power*, which is extremely important in everyone and is the most insatiable by nature. And the first two powers must guard the appetitive power, for the latter, by immersing itself in so-called material pleasures, would become extreme and too strong; it would no longer attend to its specific function but would seek to subjugate the other faculties to itself, like slaves, and lord it over them, which is not the natural relationship for them. In this way, the entire life would eventually be thrown into confusion.'

'It certainly would,' he replied.

'And what do you think?' I asked him. ... 'And we call him wise on account of that small part with which that which rules in us declares what should and should not be feared. And this part knows what is profitable to each power and to all three powers together.'

'And hear a little more. Shall we not perhaps be *temperate* by virtue of the *accord* and *harmony* of these same powers? The ruling part and the two parts that are ruled will be convinced that mastery belongs to the rational faculty and that they should not rebel against the rule of the rational part.'

'Indeed, that is true,' he said. 'Moderation is nothing but this – both in a city and in an individual man.'

'And so he will be *just*, as we have been saying repeatedly.'[1]

From the above we can recognise that the Just Man is the one who, through the light shed by *noûs*, knows how to bring the individual qualitative requirements into harmony and how to make subject to the *noûs* the other two powers, which by themselves are, as we have already hinted, devoid of 'light', discernment, and impartial direction. From this we can deduce that:

> 'Injustice must be a discord among these three faculties; an activity unfocused and with too much variation, when one faculty invades another's territory; a real and specific rebellion of one faculty against the whole constitution of the soul, with the aim of acquiring a supremacy which does not rightfully belong to it, for in accordance with its own nature it should be subject to another faculty that is higher and of royal stock. We shall say that from this state of affairs, or something like it, from the confusion and subsequent turmoil, there arise *injustice*, *licentiousness*, *cowardice*, and *ignorance*: in a word, all iniquity.'[2]

And which is that city, *polis*, or community which knows how to live justice or the expression of justice? If a community is formed of a number of individuals, it is also characterised by the qualitative manifestations that belong to the individual being. Of this there is no doubt. Every being is the whole, inasmuch as it reveals the totality within itself. Thus we shall have a heterogeneous mixture of qualities (*guṇas*), needs, desires, and urges, which unless they are directed in accordance with justice, will lead to chaos (and we already have proof of this in our own *polis*).

The community, in its present state of development, is guided by the two qualities/*guṇas* of the spirited and the appetitive, and it includes many rulers. For this reason, until the development of *nóesis*, of the intelligible within us – the highest part of the *logos* – is effected, the community will be

[1] Plato, *Politéia*, IV, 441e-442d.

[2] Plato, *Politéia*, IV, 444b.

completely unable to live the 'sense of justice', for there will always be abuse of power, strife, confrontation, irrational interests, and slaughter. In these conditions the being is outside the community because he is not in his rightful place, and he is not pursuing his own duty (*dharma*) and his own *areté* (ἀρετή). If the two blind powers are obliged by axiomatic necessity to be subservient to that noetic power (*sattva*), then a community can be governed only by those who, in turn, allow themselves to be guided and governed by this luminous power, by those who have already actuated justice within themselves; that is, by just men, the true Philosophers.

> 'And then we shall say, Glaucon, that a man is *just* in the same way that a City, too, is just.'
>
> 'This, too, necessarily follows.'
>
> 'But we have certainly not forgotten that the City is just because each of the three orders [of trade, weapons, and counsel] is attending to its own work.'
>
> 'Oh, I certainly don't think we have forgotten that!'
>
> 'In any case, we must remember that, inasmuch as each of the individual faculties fulfils its own mission, so each of us will be just and each will fulfil his own mission.'[1]

There is no doubt that if the fundamental principles of Plato's *politéia* – leaving aside, of course, some contingent aspects and some details particular to Plato's time – were applied in the context of today's society, there would be a community based on the 'sense of the Just' (the Beautiful and the True).

The *paidéia* of Plato represents, even today, the model of education for the individual and the community: that *paidéia* which is able to provide the means of developing and effecting intellection, *nóesis* (νόησις), as well as order among individuals in opposition to the dark, irrational forces which unfortunately are currently advancing in the human field under the aegis of the sophistry that Plato would have regarded with horror and disdain.

[1] *Ibid.*, IV, 441d-e.

Such a conception of constitution is not utopian, as Plato himself is aware:

> 'If, therefore, some excellent philosophers, either in the limitless course of past centuries or even in our own times – in some distant barbaric land and beyond our immediate knowledge – were constrained to take care of a city or are constrained to do so in the future, we are ready to maintain, with good reasons, that there has been, there is, and there will be such a constitution as we have expounded, when this philosophical Muse asserts her authority on the State, for her existence is not impossible and we are not speaking of impossibilities, though we ourselves are the first to admit that it is difficult to actualise them.'[1]

And why, according to Plato, is such a Constitution feasible, even in future ages? Because whatever proceeds from the 'philosophical Muse' of the supra-sensible, being beyond time and space, is not subject to corruption.

---

[1] Plato, *Politéia*, VI, 499.

INITIATION AND TRADITION

'Initiation' comes from the Latin *in* (within, inner) and *ire* (to go), and therefore means 'going within oneself', 'entering something'. Its more specific meaning is 'entering a new dimension of consciousness'. In Greece the *teleté* (τελετή) was the Initiation into the Mysteries, from the verb *teléo* (τελειόω, 'to make perfect', 'to initiate into the Mysteries').

The aim of initiation is to rise above the human individualised condition, considered in its extracorporeal wholeness, and to allow movement to higher states.

Every initiatory realisation is an essentially *inner* element which transforms the 'inner being', by penetrating and influencing the cause rather than the effect.

Initiation leads to the summit from which it is possible to have the Vision, that Vision of the 'eternal now', in which the past, the present, and the future find expression simultaneously.

Initiation leads to that cave, silent and yet rich with sounds, in which are contained opposites, or multiplicity, and in which the secret of Unity is revealed.

Initiation takes one to liberation, and liberation is the result of realisation, which, in turn, is the effect of the purifying and unifying fire.

The initiatory Way is different from the mystical Way but not opposed to it. On the mystical Way the individual is restricted to receiving merely that which is presented to him and the manner in which it is presented, without having an active part in it himself. On the initiatory Way, the undertaking of Realisation is pursued consciously and persistently. Mysticism is *passive*, while initiation is *active*: in the former, there is abandonment, letting oneself be taken, while in the latter there is an active awareness of being, of resolving, and of self-transcendence.

The mystical way belongs to religion, the initiatory Way to the 'Mysteries', to realisative 'Gnosis'; one is exoteric, and the other is esoteric.

Many follow the former; few follow the latter, and of these few a tiny percentage know how to consciously face 'death' and 're-birth'.

Initiation is not concerned with the 'psychical', for psychical states have nothing to do with transcendence, making them part of the merely individualised condition.

Initiation has nothing to do with clairvoyance, clairaudience, or the exercise of other *psychical* and equally secondary faculties of this kind, even though they be extraordinary.

Initiation could accidentally cause some psychical 'faculty' to manifest, but we need to know how to distinguish.

The Capitoline Geese were clairaudient ....

Those who produce apparently extraordinary phenomena may still be individuals with little endowment at the intellectual/emotional and spiritual levels, and they may often betray pathological signs and hysterical symptoms.

When an individual works exclusively on producing a 'phenomenon', he may become incapable of true vision and cut himself off from the possibility of recognising truth that is of an order other than the one in which he normally operates. The 'phenomenal' may even cause the sentient being to disintegrate, making him incapable of further genuine spiritual development. The Initiate transcends physical forces and that sphere where they appear or originate.

For the Initiate, there is nothing 'occult' or 'magical'. He works from the top downwards, while the psychic moves in the opposite direction.

The Initiate abides in that *non-acting* sphere which is, however, by its character of *non-manifestation*, the very fullness of activity.

Those who remain in the psychical domain will be unable to attain awareness of the spiritual realm. Those who belong to the world of the *great illusion* are precluded from genuine Self-Awareness, which alone can reveal the reality of Being. Initiation leads to knowledge/*gnosis*, to wisdom, to the heart of divinity, to perfection and completeness, to *Pax profunda*, to bliss without an object. Psychism, on the other hand, leads to a merely horizontal extension of the conscious faculties of the individual as a member of the *animalis species*.

Initiation pertains to sacred Metaphysics or the Science of Principles. It transcends the physical (the abode of distorting crystallisations), the subtle (the abode of delusions and mistiness), and the causal (the abode of metaphysical ignorance/*avidyā*/nescience).

Man thirsts for 'powers' pertaining to any kind of sphere or dimension rather than for truth, transcendence, and fulfilment.

In initiatory symbolism, the candidate is considered to be 'voyaging' on the great ocean – which represents the psychical realm that he has to cross – avoiding all its perils, in order to arrive triumphantly at his destination. He can, however, plunge into the ocean, with no choice other than to drown. A distinction has to be made between the higher Waters and the lower Waters.

It is possible to enter upon initiation, pseudo-initiation, or counter-initiation: vigilance is essential; one moment of inattention is sufficient to bring about deflection or death.

Initiation bestows upon the neophyte an 'influence from on High' which quickens the seed in the secret of his heart. It is the responsibility of the person being initiated to transform that geometry in seed-form from potentiality into actuality.

The power of the Fire has carved out and aroused a network of possibilities; it is now up to the disciple to make them fructify, to direct them, and to broaden them.

In order to act, one must be. In order to give, one must have. In order to love, one must possess love. Initiation takes one to the gate of right action, right management, and right relationship.

Initiation involves three conditions:

1. Having the qualification, which consists of particular potentialities required for the neophyte; in other words, one must have that *materia prima* on which the initiatory work will have to find its fulfilment.
2. Receiving the transmission of a spiritual Influence which comes from Above and which at any rate transcends the physical realm and the psychological realm. This transmission grants the possibility of imparting appropriate activation to those conditions which are latent.
3. Proceeding with the inner work, which is also upheld by external *supports* and by which the development will gradually and persistently be accomplished, moving step by step from one recognition to another, right up to the attainment of final Liberation or supreme Identity.

An expansion of stabilised consciousness is a sign of initiation. Synchronisation with the Sublime is the key of initiation.

The initiatory movement releases the Fire which slowly consumes all incompleteness.

Initiation leads to Synthesis. Profane knowledge and erudition, as well as certain teachings – even spiritualist ones – lead to syncretism. What is meant by initiatory synthesis and profane syncretism?

Syncretism represents a differentiated super-imposition of heterogeneous elements gathered together from different sources – we may say, from outside – without being unified by any higher principle or element. Such a disordered heap of elements cannot constitute a complete system or an initiatory

Teaching. There are also philosophical and esoteric theories that are compiled with fragments of other theories. Syncretism, by starting from the outside, stands in contrast to synthesis (which starts from principles, that is, from that which is more inner, from the centre, before moving towards the circumference), and syncretism remains at the circumference or periphery by merely amassing and comparing. Syncretism is more analytical and as such does not penetrate the level of causality, whereas synthesis is noumenal harmony.

The true and traditional initiatory Teaching is, of course, one of synthesis; as its starting-point and essential centre it necessarily has the knowledge of metaphysical or first principles, and its relative development allows it to be applied to different domains, which always presupposes an underlying synthesis.

Behind the traditional Teaching of East and West, there abides the unity which can be perceived through the initiatory *Fiat Lux*. Those who reach this unity will discover that there has always been a *single* initiatory Tradition, with different expressions adapted to time and space.

Syncretism does not lead to unity or to synthesis, but to generalisation and eclecticism, which means that we can get lost in its chaotic fragmentary nature, which is mechanical and based on superficial knowledge. It can lead us into darkness or a blind alley, rather than to unifying Light.

According to the Hindu tradition, there are two contrasting ways of being outside the castes: a lower way and a higher way. One can be an 'outcaste' (*avarṇa*) – that is, beneath all castes – or 'beyond the castes' (*ativarṇa*) because they have been totally transcended. In the same way, one can be within or beyond the various traditions and Tradition itself. The traditional forms are pathways which all lead to the same end: supreme Identity. Once a pathway has been embarked upon, it would be good to pursue it, unless it is discovered that it pertains to a teaching that is comparative, eclectic, or syncretistic.

The pure initiatory teaching receives the Influence from on high, while syncretistic teaching cannot receive it on account of its intrinsically profane nature.

Initiation leads to the effective realisation of 'superhuman' states, while pseudo-initiation leaves the individual in the human state, under the rigid but flattering guidance of samsāric agents.

> 'Syncretism consists in assembling, from outside, elements which are more or less diverse and which, seen from this perspective, have no possibility of being truly unified. In short, it is a question of eclecticism, with all that that means in the way of fragmentation and incoherence – that is, something which is merely external and superficial, whose elements, collected here and there and brought together in a way that is totally artificial, cannot but have the features of things which are improvised and incapable of being effectively integrated into a teaching worthy of the name.
>
> 'Synthesis, by contrast, is effected essentially from within: we mean that it consists precisely in considering things within the unity of their own principle – in the sense of originating from, and depending on, this principle – and consequently in uniting them, or, rather, in becoming conscious of their real union, which is such by virtue of a wholly inner bond relating to what is deepest in their nature. To apply these things to our line of reasoning, we may say that there will be syncretism whenever elements taken from different traditional forms are jumbled together and an effort is made to somehow weld them together from the outside, ignoring the fact that those forms are merely different expressions of a single teaching and are therefore just so many adaptations of that teaching to suit specific conditions of mind in relation to particular circumstances of time and place.
>
> 'Clearly nothing valid can emerge from an agglomeration of this nature; and instead of an organised whole (to give a metaphor that is easily understood) one will have a shapeless jumble of fragments that are useless because they lack that something which could give them a unity analogous to that of a living being or a harmonious building; that is to say, it is character-

istic of syncretism, simply because of its external nature, that it cannot effect such a unity. By contrast, there will be synthesis if one begins from unity itself, without ever losing sight of it in the multiplicity of its manifestations, which means that, outside and beyond the forms, one has attained the awareness of the principial truth which clothes itself in these forms in order to express and communicate itself to the limits of possibilities. From the moment we start from Unity it will be possible to make use of any of these forms, if one is interested in doing so, just as, in order to communicate a particular thought, various idioms can be employed to make oneself understood by the other speakers one is addressing; and this is what some traditions define as the "gift of tongues".

'It may be said that the points of agreement among the various traditional forms represent real synonymities. This is how we consider them; and just as certain things can be explained more easily in one language than in another, so it is more fitting to expound certain truths through one of these forms than through another, as well as making those truths easier to comprehend. It is therefore more than legitimate to make use, from time to time, of the form which seems most appropriate for the point that is being made; and there is no difficulty in passing from one form to another, provided that one really knows their equivalence, which is possible only by starting from their common principle. In this way, there is no syncretism; in fact, since syncretism is a wholly profane viewpoint, it is incompatible with the very notion of "Sacred Science", with which these studies are exclusively concerned.'[1]

Although the goal is always the same (initiatory Realisation), there are different ways of attaining it; but once it has been reached in the transcendent sphere of metaphysics all differentiation comes to an end, vanishes. At first, any concept of the teaching can serve as a support and be helpful on that occasion, but slowly, if there is a desire for true initiation, it is necessary to enter the traditional philosophical current.

---

[1] R. Guénon, *Le Symbolisme de la Croix*. Éditions Véga, Paris 1950.

Those who have love for Truth/Knowledge cannot but move on to inner, transforming *action*, which undoubtedly takes them beyond all dialectical and theoretical frameworks. Truth/ Knowledge is a manifestation of the Spirit, and when this is realised it leads to the abandonment of all mental representations of knowledge itself. The Tradition is to be embodied, not thought about. It is to be lived, not conceptualised in theoretical schemes and philosophical enclosures. Many talk about the Tradition, but few live it and reveal it as a way of Being.

Just as the inner cannot be an effect produced by the outer, the esoteric cannot be formed by the exoteric, the centre cannot originate from the circumference, and the higher cannot be begotten by the lower, in the same way the Influence which flows through the traditional Channel always goes downwards and irradiates from the central Point or Axis and never from the periphery.

R. Guénon writes:

> 'The disputes of the outer world lose much of their importance when they are considered from a point which reconciles all the conflicts which cause them, which is what happens when they are seen from the strictly esoteric and initiatory perspective. Yet it is precisely for this reason that becoming involved in such disputes or, as it is usually put, "getting caught in them" cannot in any way be a characteristic of initiatory organisations, while the various "sects", by their very nature, find themselves enmeshed in these disputes, and perhaps it is precisely this which gives these "sects" their *raison d'être*.'[1]

The meeting of two Hearts is initiation; the meeting of two living rhythms is initiation; the agreement of the lower with the Higher is initiation.

The merely intellectual study of the traditional Texts does not constitute initiation; equally, recalling or memorising those

[1] R. Guénon, *Aperçus sur l'Initiation*. Éditions Traditionnelles, Paris 1980.

Texts does not represent initiation. The erudite person, as such, is not an Initiate, nor is he realised.

A realised person may have read little or nothing and yet has Knowledge; this is explained by the fact that those who have made contact with their own essence have gained the Knowledge of all knowledges.

Reading and studying the traditional Texts can, however, constitute a powerful stimulus for opening particular doors in our psyche which were previously shut. And we need to take account of this; to open the door of super-conscious intuition the corresponding instrument has to be activated.

The Initiated/Realised may also write nothing. Great Realised Beings, such as Buddha and Christ, left no writings. Others have merely sought, for the benefit of their disciples, to elucidate the traditional Texts (*Śruti* or Revelation), with commentaries and notes.

One who is Initiated is not measured by the *number* of words that he writes or speaks. Quantity pertains to the academic scholar and the writer of essays, whose minds are over-imbued with *rajas*.

The sheer *quantity* of concepts may also prove harmful to the initiatory process, because it strengthens the analytical, empirical, and representative mind (*manas*). *Manas* is known to be always seeking conceptual food, but it is not at the level of its expansion and quantisation that the being can find the 'death of philosophers'.

In the same way, the egoic feeling also goes in search of its own food, but if one wishes to reach true initiation one has to know how to die to *manas* and to *kāma*.

It is difficult to make the scholar understand that in order to find true initiation one must die to oneself. The erudite person is often litigious, proud, separative, and motivated by a feeling of superiority which is covered by a false humility, exclusive and vain; and he also makes others feel the weight of his psychical 'power'.

The faculty of *manas* is a psychical power, as is the power of emotion (*kāma*). The scholar makes use of the power of *manas*, while the mystic makes use of the power of *kāma*. Desire/emotion, too, is exclusive and frenzied. It requires a great effort to free oneself from the powers that pertain to individuality.

Love, knowledge, and bliss flow forth from a Heart which is devoid of all superimposition, a Heart which is pure and innocent (not to be confused with the heart of a simple-minded person).

A manipulator of mere words, a 'wonder-worker' of concepts and verbal terms to produce an effect, cannot know the simplicity and beauty of Truth in its essence.

Those who are inclined towards initiation must know that the movement is from multiplicity to unity, from quantity to quality, from psychical power to the comprehension of the Heart, which is the all-pervasive synthesis.

THE QUALIFICATIONS OF THE DISCIPLE

It has to be acknowledged that every worldly/social activity (every profession, and so on) requires a particular attitude, predisposition, and qualification; we could even speak of vocation. For every function, then, an aptitude relevant to that specific sphere is necessary. It may often be the case that professionals or workers are not good, and this is because they do not have the right vocation or aptitude, which can – but not always – be developed, although it may happen that the person is not conscious of having a vocation or aptitude.

The same law holds in the spiritual field, too: a candidate without vocation, predispositions, and qualifications can do very little. Although he may follow a pathway, he will always be a poor aspirant. Furthermore, just as study, time, self-denial, and great seriousness are needed to follow any profession, in the same way great seriousness, self-denial, and a good deal of time at one's disposal are necessary in order to follow a spiritual or initiatory way. It generally happens, however, that the aspirant dedicates himself to Realisation in the left-over bits of time. We may also say that the principal or fundamental occupation is the 'social' one, while the spiritual occupation is relegated to any free time that may be left. There are people who go to initiatory schools once a month, or once a fortnight, and then it all stops there. The other days are obviously dedicated to social relationships, to work – sometimes stressful and troublesome – to the family, and to the inevitable entertainment, all in the belief that one is on the initiatory Way or, indeed, one of the Initiated. Usually one even believes that the Way consists in being better, more ethical, and free from a certain religious conformity, or in keeping the company of people who merely talk of initiatory or esoteric things. It may also be stated that the attention of some is mainly, if not exclusively, given to experiencing a life that is conventional and in the physical world of the senses, even if they continue to speak of spirituality or attend a group that is spiritual, initiatory, or connected to an *āśram*, and so on. A Way, or Path, involves great commitment, as we have already noted, and full availability of heart and mind.

Plato goes as far as to say:

> 'From their childhood [aspiring philosophers] have been unacquainted with the way to the Agora ... Intrigues of political cliques to acquire public office, gatherings, banquets, and parties: these are all things which, even in dreams, have never entered their minds.'[1]

To use alchemical terms, 'separating' and 'fixing' the mercury is not a question of attending a school at regular intervals; to effect this process requires much more. To cross over the Kabbalistic 'abyss', it is not sufficient to sit on a bench in an *āśram* or Freemasons' Hall, or to go to some sort of temple every so often. Only this 'iron' age, or *kali yuga*, can make people believe that this is enough. Although we *are already* Soul, *ātman*, *noûs*, and so on, our *identification* with what we are not is so strong that it is not easy, at a practical, operational level, to realise or to *be* what we are. If, in addition, those qualifications to which we have already alluded are missing, then the situation becomes tragic and also grotesque.

It must be borne in mind that Initiation (*dīkṣā*/μύεσις) requires a genuine revolution in our way of thinking, willing, and acting. In Greece, at the time of the Mysteries, the *teleté* (τελετή), initiation into the Mysteries entailed *metánoia* (μετάνοια/re-thinking/repentance) and, as Plato states, conversion/revolution (περιαγωγή). This involves a new way of life

[1] Plato, *Theaetetus*, XXIV, 173d.

which has nothing to do with the old way of expressing oneself. One who is Initiated, though being in the world, is not of the world.

> 'And the truth is that his body [the body of the aspiring philosopher] is in the city and dwells there, but not so his soul.'[1]

But what can the qualifications be that are required for a right approach to the way of Liberation?

The first qualification – apart from those which can be sensed in what we have already said – is the most difficult to effect: we are speaking of humility. It is presumed that an aspirant comes from a profane social background and has the kind of knowledge that is related exclusively to the world of phenomena and to the field of names and forms. The realisative philosophical Teaching, by contrast, concerns the sphere of Being. To use Plato's terminology, the aspirant comes from the level of opinion (*doxa*), which means that he is in the physical world of the sensible; he knows little or nothing of the state of *epistéme*, which operates through hyper-conscious intuition and grasps the sphere of the intelligible. Thus, finding himself at the level of the individual and particular, he has little familiarity with the universal level. He can offer opinions, but not pure Knowledge; and the more he knows about the material and sensible state, the more difficult it is for him to be detached from the *world of quantity*.

> 'Then we are agreed on this point in relation to the nature of philosophers: that they are lovers of knowledge, that knowledge which is able to reveal the mystery of that objective esseity which eternally is; that esseity which does not go wandering and straying about in the cycle of generation and death.'[2]

At the beginning of the path the aspirant is usually advised to detach himself from the knowledge/demeanour of the collec-

---

[1] Plato, *Theaetetus*, 173e.

[2] Plato, *Politéia*, VI, 485.

tive unconscious, although this is not easy because the aspirant bears upon him, or upon his *aura*, the impress of archetypes which pertain to that order, in addition to the fact that he is still operating within this order. Great humility is required to acknowledge that one is 'ignorant' of certain matters, meaning that one is ignorant of particular types of knowledge. In the ancient Mysteries the candidate had to spend several years in silence, because anything that he might have been able to say had nothing to do with the esoteric and initiatory Teaching. This was also a great help to him in beginning to control his speech, something that is not easy in the individualised world. Here we can recognise the school of Pythagoras, but not only his school.

Another qualification is knowing how to find an accord, an attuning of the consciousness, with the Teaching, because initiatory Knowledge is definitely not like profane knowledge, where all that is needed is sufficient intelligence and, above all, a good measure of memory. At school our teachers taught us particular *notions* about chemistry, physics, mathematics, the *history* of philosophy, and so on, and we memorised them and then repeated them. According to the traditional Teaching, it is not a question of memory, for the traditional Teaching does not consist in quantitative notions, and the function of the Instructor is clearly not that of a teacher in middle school or at university. Their aims and methods are different, and they have different standpoints of consciousness.

The Teaching is directed, not at the brain, but at the Heart; not at *manas*/mind/*diánoia*, but at *buddhi*/ *nóesis*. Its function is to bring forth the Knowledge which is already within us to awaken the consciousness to its true nature. Initiatory Knowledge is like the sun, which awakens the potentialities that are already in the seed. It is a maieutic process. Knowing does not come from outside by means of memorising data about objects: it comes from within, from the essence of which we are woven.

'In fact, the knowledge of these truths cannot in any way be communicated as other branches of knowledge are, but, after many discussions on these subjects and after a period of becoming familiar with them, suddenly, like light blazing from the flashing of a spark, this knowledge is born from the Soul and nourishes itself.'[1]

A further qualification consists in having an attitude that is simultaneously receptive and active and solar. Women, through their particular nature, may be more receptive but less active/solar; men may be more active/solar but less receptive. In either case, in order to *learn/comprehend* there needs to be not only humility and receptivity (not passivity), but also an active and solar standpoint, for the purpose of *fixing* what has been learnt and comprehended, of fixing at the level of Consciousness, rather than at the level of mind, and of doing so *in spite of* all the positive and negative circumstances, within and without, which might manifest. According to Plato, this means 'restoring our wings'[2] and flying back towards our true homeland.

Then there is the qualification of knowing how to live in *silence*, something – as has already been indicated – that is very difficult. It is in the silence of our heart that certain things can happen; or rather, silence is the foundation of every initiatory Way, and this means more than simply not speaking to others: it means to bring to silence that mind which expresses itself through opinion (*doxa*), because someone who is in the process of setting out on a 'new way', a road that is completely opposed to the one followed previously, has little to say or to propose. The Way begins in silence, unfolds, and ends in the great Silence.

According to the *Upaniṣad*, *Brahman* is Silence. According to Plato, the 'Father'[3] of Being is ineffable.

---

[1] Plato, *Letter VII*, 341c.

[2] Plato, *Phaedrus*, 251c.

[3] Plato, *Politéia*, VI, 506d, 507a; VII, 508b, 509c.

A further qualification is knowing how to free oneself from the notion of time/space/causality. Knowledge of a metaphysical order, or Knowledge of the Greater Mysteries (as presented by Parmenides, Plato, Śaṅkara, and others of the universal Tradition), requires the *mens informalis*, which alone knows how to transcend that notion of phenomena which operates exclusively in the realm of the physical and sensible. Realisation is known not to depend on the category of time/space/causality, inasmuch as the Being which we are does not become. It is the conventional life which becomes and which has its own rise and fall. It is the χώρα/*prakṛti* – with its points, its planes, and its forms – that changes itself and becomes.

If, as has previously been noted, Knowledge is already within us, then we need to have that attitude/quality of inner withdrawal (*uparati*) which allows us to connect with the 'voice of Silence' or the voice of our Heart (although it has to be said that this is a little difficult for anyone who is an extrovert).

Although Realisation, or Liberation, is available to everyone, not everyone in this time/space is ready to receive the message; however, it is also true that if we are already Being or *That*, as *Advaita Vedānta* declares, then sooner or later we cannot but reach the point of revealing our real Fullness or Bliss.

TIME/SPACE AND KNOWLEDGE

There is absolute Space, and there is relative space. We may also speak of infinite Space and finite space.

Absolute Space is one, homogeneous, undivided; relative space, on the other hand, is part, division, scission, relationship.

Absolute or infinite Space represents a property/condition of Being, of the principial One, in its totality and completeness; it is the dimensionless point. Relative, or finite, space represents an individual form or body; it is the volume enclosed by a limit. Each body/form occupies a 'space', or rather it is that space, so that several bodies/forms occupy different spaces, distinct spatial volumes.

Supreme space contains within itself all possible objectivised points, lines, and volumes, or circumscribed planes. Thus on *one* of the countless systems of co-ordinates – the physical or gross system – the elementary particle contains within itself the development of all possible atomic nuclei, atoms, and molecules.

Finding out about relative or finite space is the work of our academic science in particular: finding out about the supreme Space is the work of metaphysics and initiatory knowledge.

Relative space is always related to another relative space, so that we could speak of relational space; and the distance between two spaces/bodies represents the relative distance. However, we cannot attribute the 'concept' of distance to supreme Space, because relative spaces, together with their distances, disappear and are resolved within supreme Space. Relative distances are conventions of the empirical sense-based mind designed to assist it in 'locating itself' and having a better conception of itself in its relative process of living. Thus the cardinal points, the concepts of above and below, and so on, are categories invented by man to help him define himself.

Relative space/body is characterised by movement, movement which is relative, of course, to that defined space/body. Or rather, we may say that movement determines the relative space/body, just as the same movement makes it disappear. If the interplanetary space/form exceeds the velocity of light, it disappears into the non-space/body; that is, the space/body vanishes, resolves itself. Mass resolves into energy. Movement is the agency through which relative spaces/bodies can be 'condensed' or 'resolved'. But movement, in turn, is the effect of heat/fire, so that we may conclude that Fire is the cause of movement/space/body.

Fire 'condenses' but also produces 'rarefaction'. But we need to distinguish the heat arising as a result of the friction between spaces/bodies, which we could call the fire/heat produced by friction, from the Fire which we have mentioned and which, of course, does not arise from friction between spaces/bodies, since it pre-exists them. However, there is also a fire to burn up the spaces/bodies.

Relative space is born, grows, and dies or dissolves, and in this expression can be found the 'concept of time'. The 'duration' of a space/body represents the time of that particular finite space. Thus a cloud (a space/body) is born, grows, and vanishes, and the period of time which intervenes between its birth and its disappearance is what we conceive of as 'relative time' or 'finite time'.

Time is always a time of relationship, being relative to that specific system of co-ordinates in which the space/body is located. There is no relative space without relative time, and the converse also holds. The two data are born simultaneously. Trying to abstract relative time from relative space is an impossibility, like trying to abstract humidity from water. One entails the other, just as the subject entails the object, and *vice versa*.

Just as relative space can have no place in the supreme Space, and the finite cannot be infinite, so relative or finite time can find no place there. On the contrary, we shall have supreme Time in supreme Space; we shall have undivided, homogeneous eternity; we shall have the eternal present. Relative time is a 'sense-based datum' within the compass of eternity. According to Plato, time is the moving image of Eternity.[1] To believe that we can make relative time absolute is sheer madness: it is like trying to make the finite absolute. Although we can, for example, lengthen or contract time in relation to the space/body of the individual, we shall never be able to make it absolute, that is, immortal.

Birth/death are part and parcel of relative space/time. We shall be able to expand the time of the physical body/space of the individual to equal that of the sun, but even the sun's days are numbered, for it itself is a relative space/time travelling in the depths of the supreme or infinite Space/Time.

Man's knowledge is always 'knowledge of relationship' (*aparavidyā*), that is, knowledge related to relative or finite spaces/times. Scientific knowledge, as understood today, is knowledge of relationship because it aspires to know the countless numbers of the relative spaces/times with their reciprocal correlations.

An electron is a specific space/time; the human body is another space/time; a planet and a star are relative spaces/times. But although we may come to know all relative spaces/times, together with their interrelationships and their laws, we shall never manage to grasp the supreme Knowledge (*paravidyā*), which is not concerned with relative spaces/times but with the supreme Space/Time.

'Knowledge of relationship' always tends to crystallise Reality into 'knowable finite spaces/times', and the more it persists in making the simple Real finite, the more it estranges

---

[1] Plato, *Timaeus*, 37e.

the individual, preventing him from having contact with other 'knowables' and ultimately with the supreme Space/Time.

No knowledge is worse than that which does not look towards the Infinite. But unfortunately there is a tendency in the human world to imprison or outlaw those who hold any kind of knowledge which looks towards categories that are multi-dimensional or multi-directional.

If relative spaces/times follow their course of birth, growth, and death, then even the 'knowledge of relationship' is not imperishable, but is contingent and subject to modification, because it, too, is a finite space/time.

The knowledge spoken of above is the feature of a specific existential plane or system of co-ordinates pertaining to the human being. If the human being had no other openings or systems of co-ordinates, it could never attain the supreme Knowledge, the supreme Reality, or infinite Space/Time.

There are some – it is more accurate to say many – who do not believe *a priori* in other openings or windows of knowledge for man, and they are therefore obliged to acknowledge that 'knowledge of relationship' is the only system that exists, and to admit, therefore, that only relative and finite spaces/times exist.

'Knowledge of relationship' is a reductive knowledge which restricts the human being, and the non-human being, merely to the presence of finite space/time/volume. And since relative space/time, in the final analysis, is nothing but 'appearance' (it appears and disappears), we may conclude that 'knowledge of relationship' reduces the being to mere 'appearance', to nothing but a 'phenomenon'.

The individual's greatest tragedy has been, and still is, to believe himself to be that which in reality he is not, to think of himself as nothing but a relative and finite space/time/volume.

We may also say that 'knowledge of relationship' is a knowledge of the particular, the individual, the specific, the part; but being (super-human, human, or sub-human) is universal, and the universal is something more than the concept of *generality*.

Someone may ask us, 'What connection is there between this "knowledge of relationship" and the supreme Knowledge? What relationship is there between the relative space/time being and the supreme or principial Space/Time?'

Anyone who asks such questions is undoubtedly enmeshed by the operational dynamic of 'knowledge of relationship', which has it that every thing, every being, can in fact exist only if viewed in relation to other things, other beings, and so on. When this type of knowledge raises the question of the supreme Space/Time – and it is already making a concession to proffer such a question – it frames it in terms of relationship and the gulfs to be bridged in making a relationship of distances in relation to each other. And then how shall we be able to know the Supreme if 'knowledge of relationship' does not allow us to grasp universal Space/Time?

If we wished to become familiar with the planet Jupiter, what would we need to do? If we wish to *know* – not to imagine or guess – what Jupiter is, we shall have to leave the planet Earth, pass through a state of imponderability in which the ordinary physical and cognitive supports or the earthly frames of reference are no longer valid, and *take ourselves* to the planet Jupiter. This is merely an example drawn from the finite world.

In the same way, to know the Supreme requires leaving this system of co-ordinates (knowledge of relationship) and learning how to fly into the imponderable.

When consciousness, which transcends thought, tries to grasp a particular dimension, it has to leave the dimension where it was working before, together with all the frames of reference, including the cognitive ones, which are inherent in it. Here the action is one of ascent, because the consciousness has to follow a vertical line, whereas when one wishes to spread out over a specific existential plane, it is sufficient to develop a horizontal line of cognitive penetration, thus making use of the usual operational instruments. But the vertical ascent requires setting aside a powerful means of support for the human individuality, an instrument on which and by means of which this individuality is built and endures within the range of its existential plane. However, to remove support/aid from the 'child' is to make him afraid and put him in a state of distressful frustration. To cling onto the support/aid, given by 'knowledge of relationship', the individual child is ready to do anything and go so far as to deny not just the reality of other dimensions but even the supposition of other possibilities.

Therefore the supreme Space/Time (we are in the realm of Being) can be known; or rather, to be more exact, it can be *realised.* There are data facing us (duality), and they can be grasped through 'knowledge of relationship', but there is the Datum which is without second or relationship and which thus cannot be an object of sensory apprehension. At this point 'knowledge of relationship', or mediated knowledge, must give way to the actualisation of conscious/existential identity or, to put it another way, Knowledge of identity.

We shall have to admit that relative spaces/bodies are mere effects, and an effect always pre-supposes a cause. Our 'knowledge of relationship' allows us to learn about a world of effects. Every phenomenon is nothing but an effect and although people speak from time to time about discovering the cause of a specific effect, it may be said that the cause, in turn, is the effect of another pre-existing cause. The *universe of relationship* is nothing other than cause/effect/cause/effect and so on. But the Cause of causes transcends the universe of relationship, the world of names and forms, and the world of effects.

Beyond space/time 'appearances' there exists the universal Being, which does not become and does not appear and disappear, just as beyond individual 'general laws' there exists the universal Law, which represents the absolute Constant of all general or relative laws.

Can relative space/time/body, being an 'appearance', be considered as a mere illusion or dream hallucination? Can it be a 'nothing', a 'nothingness', something non-existent?

No genuine knower could support this nihilistic proposition. Some misinformed person might say, for example, that Śaṅkara, the codifier of *Advaita Vedānta*, maintained that relative space/time is a mere illusion, taking this word as it is understood in the West.

Śaṅkara, however, never said this; nor did Parmenides. Śaṅkara says explicitly, 'The universe of names and forms is not like the son of a barren woman, or the horns of a hare.' (See his commentary to the *Māṇḍūkya Upaniṣad*).[1] This means that relative space/time is not a nothingness, a void, an illusion. Ṣaṅkara is pointing out that space/time/*māyā* is just *one* of the aspects of the total Reality: in other words, it represents a simple *level* of truth.

Therefore, to use modern terminology, we may say that finite space/time, which we are experiencing at this moment, is just *one* of the countless systems of co-ordinates. This involves reducing our 'conception' of what is real and of the way we conceive ourselves. It means no longer thinking that our relative time/space has to be unique and absolute or, on the contrary, that the individual has to annihilate himself if he wishes to transcend our relative time/space. And Śaṅkara seeks to demonstrate these mistaken conceptions when he makes the objection that we often 'superimpose' a thick but transient cloud over the resplendent sun.

A space/time/body which 'believes' itself to be absolute becomes alienated. On the other hand, a space/time/body is equally alienated if it 'believes' itself to be merely something relative (relatively real). This is how a human being thinks of himself: either as an 'absolute individual' or as a mere 'body/molecule' destined to be annihilated. And this kind of 'concep-

---

[1] *Māṇḍūkya Upaniṣad*, with Gauḍapāda's *kārikā* and Śaṅkara's commentary. Translated from Sanskrit and edited by Raphael. Aurea Vidyā, New York.

tion' or 'belief' is something he carries over into the field of society, politics, morals, and even religion, with consequences which we all see and experience.

STATES OF CONSCIOUSNESS

When we speak of spiritual Realisation or of initiatory process, we mean the *implementation* of a *state of consciousness*. If Realisation does not foster the awakening of consciousness, it turns out to be a theoretical and dianoetic procedure, an end in itself, which is non-transformative and does not lead to catharsis.

When Initiation (*dīkṣā*/τελετή) is rendered active, it is accompanied by an 'expansion of awareness', a state of being, a revolution in life-style which is complete and in the present moment. On most occasions, unfortunately, it happens that the initiatory or traditional Teaching is merely conceptualised or intellectualised, and, especially for those whose mental development is excessive (the West in general), it assumes the form of a kind of essay. In the West there are theoretical and academic experts of the initiatory Way, those who study traditional thought, but this is not the same as 'following the Way', which involves applying oneself to the *opus*, not theoretically – by collecting ideas (πολυμάθεια) – but practically. It means being 'doers' and not 'hearers', to use St Paul's words.[1] It means that the 'doers' 'have been unacquainted with the way to the Agora ... Intrigues of political cliques to acquire public office, gatherings, banquets, and parties in the company of flute-girls. These are all the things which, even in dreams, have never entered their minds.'[2]

Initiation involves a *new way of being*, not just a new pose. In ancient times, Philosophy was a kind of *jñāna-mārga*, a

[1] Romans, 1:13.

[2] Plato, *Theaetetus*, XXIV, 173-4.

Way of knowledge in order to be, the ”d’j (the Way) which the Goddess teaches Parmenides. It is from this sort of perspective that we often speak of traditional Philosophy or *Philosophia perennis*. The true Philosopher is the one who embodies, lives, and bears witness to the philosophic Vision. According to Empedocles, Philosophy is an art of living and not a pointless academic exercise. In this respect we recall Pythagoras, Parmenides, Plato, Plotinus, and others, to give just a few names. The true alchemists were, and are, great Philosophers, friends and devotees of Hermetic wisdom, doers, ‘distillers’ aiming to transform human lead into divine Gold, and for this operation essays and theoretical reasonings are of little or no use.

The West – of course, with due exceptions, and this needs to be emphasised – is more disposed towards ‘society’, towards profane politics (not the politics of the traditional order or the true *politéia*), towards affirming the empirical ego rather than the ontological ‘I’. It frequently happens that an initiatory group, unworthy of such a name, builds a ‘magnified ego’ for purposes that are more profane than sacred. This represents a clear verification for anyone who is familiar with certain matters.

To transform *avidyā* into *vidyā*, *doxa* into *epistéme* and *nóesis*, and this into pure awareness is no small achievement; it requires a true *vocation*, a commitment that goes beyond the few minutes that people devote to reading after being ‘squeezed’ by profane *karma*. Realisation essentially involves what is defined as ‘initiatory death’, the ‘death of the Philosophers’, that is, the death of the ‘old man’, the death of individuality, as a factor of being sundered from the universal context. Liberation (another word for Realisation) involves freeing oneself *effectively* from the *avidyā* which has obscured us to the point of making us believe that we are what we are not. The being is alienated, sundered. It is a plethora of instincts, feelings, ideations, and yearnings which lead to non-being. It is an assemblage of sounds in unceasing discord. Realisation comes to end the scissure, the multiple sounds, the sub-personalities which fight to gain control of our consciousness. As individualities (and this would seem to be a contradiction, given the meaning of the word), we are *multiplicity*, and initiation, once it is activated or brought into actuality, resolves the multiplicity into conscious Unity.

> 'For Philosophers are those who succeed in reaching *that which remains ever constant*, while those who do not succeed but get lost in the *multiplicity* of the changeable are not Philosophers.'[1]

> 'In truth I am this non-dual *Brahman*, as subtle as ether, without beginning and without end ... the substratum of all phenomena ... eternal ... unchanging ... transcending all differentiations ... constant ... universal.'[2]

What may a state of consciousness represent? We may answer: a dimension of values, an existential condition, belonging to a particular context of life. For example, the vegetable, the animal, and the human are none other than states, dimensions of being, modes of life, systems which operate on specific wavelengths and which exert particular influences. Man, as such, is a mixture of animality, rationality, and divinity. Hence his divisive conflict. He is a figure midway between the sub-human and the divine *states of consciousness*. Sometimes he tends towards animality, and at other times towards egoic rationality, but rarely towards the divine, the intelligible, or the World of Ideas (to use Plato's words). Being compounded of diverse conditions of life, man necessarily possesses a number of vehicles/bodies which can convey him to various states of existence. A vehicle/body is nothing other than a 'window' which opens onto one of life's dimensions. The coarse or gross physical body of the being, for example, is a window which opens onto the physical terrestrial plane, by means of which it can experience and express those possibilities which are inherent in this plane.

According to the traditional Vision of *Vedānta* (although the Tradition is one, with various spatio-temporal adaptations),

---

[1] Plato, *Politéia*, VI, 484b.

[2] Śaṅkara, *Vivekacūḍāmaṇi*, 512 *et seqq*.

the being is composed of five bodies/vehicles/sheaths, which are so many windows that are open or closed, as the case may be, with regard to specific planes or spheres of the sensible and the intelligible worlds.

The multiple states of Being (but multiplicity is apparent) are possibilities for the being which can experience them. We can give a diagram of the vehicles/bodies, behind which there is the Consciousness/Witness of the entire vehicular complex and the actual *qualities* which this complex can express.

	Ānandamayakośa
	Buddhimayakośa
Consciousness/Witness	*Manomayakośa*
	Prāṇamayakośa
	Annamayakośa

Ānandamayakośa is a vehicle (*kośa*) made of (*maya*) bliss (*ānanda*), because it is a window which opens upon a sphere of consciousness whose nature is fullness/completeness/unity. *Buddhimayakośa*, or *vijñānamayakośa*, consists of pure Intelligence, direct knowledge, intuition, or immediate noetic discrimination. *Manomayakośa* is the reflection of the *buddhi* in an individualised condition and is therefore thought which is analytic, discursive, representative/selective; it provides dianoetic knowledge; it is also the sphere of feeling/passion (*kāma*). *Prāṇamayakośa* is the sheath of vital, hyper-physical energy; it is energy/substance in its pure state, whereas *annamayakośa* is the vehicular condition in the state of 'mass'.[1]

[1] For a complete exposition of the constitution of the being according to *Vedānta*, see *Māṇḍūkyakārikā* and *Vivekacūḍāmaṇi*; see also *Bhagavadgītā*. Aurea Vidyā, New York.

The Consciousness/Witness represents the *jīva*/soul as a state of consciousness, and this, in turn, is the reflection of the *ātman*, pure transcendent spirit (it is the same vision of *pneuma*, *psyché* and *sôma* that is found in the Western philosophical Tradition).

Now the reflection of consciousness, on account of the identification which takes effect with a specific vehicle, manifests a particular 'state of consciousness'. In this way, the being, *identified* with the gross physical vehicle, expresses itself as a 'material and corporeal state', as a result of which the whole of its philosophy of life will be characterised by the 'mass' element. Hence the materialistic view of life; and it could not be otherwise. 'Seeing' (with the five senses) through the window of *annamayakośa*, consciousness perceives and really considers that everything is *solid* and only 'mass' exists. When consciousness is identified with the sheath of *kāma*/*manas*, it will have, in accordance with a polarisation that is stronger or weaker, a state of consciousness which is either emotional/passionate or purely mental or, again, a mixture of emotion/passion and mind. On the other hand, we can observe all this through the various ages which the being has *projected*: thus there has been a spiritualistic age, a romantic age, a rational/enlightened age, a materialistic/positivist age, and so on. It is clear that in accordance with the polarisation of the reflection of consciousness within a specific vehicle, the individual will project and manifest qualities that correspond to the sheath. From this we may further note that the various beings can be classified and grouped on the basis of the states of consciousness which they have reached and the corresponding qualities (*guṇas*) which they express.

Man – or the *human state of consciousness* – is characterised by *ahaṁkara* (the sense of ego, and from this comes the scissure and detachment from the universal), by the vehicle/body of *manas*, *kāma* (desire/passion), *prāṇa*, and gross physicality. Considered as a whole, this constitutes individuality in opposition to other individualities, and hence in opposition to the universal context of the intelligible. This is the world of the sensible, of becoming, of the multiple, of *mine* and *yours*. This individuality is the effect of a state of consciousness which is, in fact, essentially human. But we have seen that being is not merely individuality, not merely a 'human' state of consciousness, because it also embraces the divine and the intelligible. Being is also universal consciousness. Its true state is actually universal.

A first step of Realisation involves moving the consciousness from the individualised 'human' to the universal and divine. We say 'first step' because there are other states of consciousness, but for the moment we are alluding to this phase.

An authentic initiation must include that 'new beginning' which takes the individualised consciousness to the realm of universal awareness. And to activate this process, or philosophical alchemy, it is not merely a matter of conceptualising the Teaching or Philosophy. Something quite different is required: the *real death* of a state, by integrating and resolving it into another state of a higher order. In other words, it is a question of solving[1] the individualised 'compound'.

> 'And so, isn't this what is called death: the *solution* and *separation* of the Soul from the body [individuality]?'
>
> 'Exactly,' he replied,
>
> 'And, as we were saying, it is about solving the Soul from the body that those who rightly practise philosophy are always thinking, more than all others; indeed, they alone. And this is precisely the proper study and practice of philosophers: *solving* and *separating* the Soul from the body.'[2]

---

[1] Solution: 1. the action or process of solving; the state, condition, or fact of being solved.

To Solve: 4. to dissolve, put an end to...5. to dissolve, to melt.

The Shorter Oxford English Dictionary, Vol. II. Clarendon Press, Oxford.

[2] Plato, *Phaedo*, 67c-d.

Here we may note the alchemical process of separation and of *solve* and *coagula*: the solution of the Soul from the body/individuality and the fixation of the Soul/mercury within its own nature. We don't need to remind ourselves that Plato was initiated into the Greater Mysteries (the metaphysical way), in addition to receiving initiation, according to Clement, from the Priest Sechnuf in the temples of ancient Egypt.

From this we can infer that what counts is the *state of consciousness*, not the training of a specific vehicle in the belief that this is sufficient for Realisation. For example, there have been, and there are, great Realised ones who have had no mental training; we may say that they were completely devoid of profane notions, of dialectical capacity or *ability*.

And what does it mean to have a universal consciousness? It means that one has nothing ... human, as this state is understood. And if it had to possess a physical body, such a being would have only the 'appearance' of man. Within certain limits, he could express himself in human terms, but his *consciousness* would be elsewhere: 'Being in the world, but not of the world.'

> 'For in truth the Philosopher is not only unaware of what is near him or what his neighbour is doing, but, it may be said, he is not even aware whether he is a man or some other animal.'[1]

To be able to realise the transition from the 'human' to the divine, there are, especially in the East, different paths (*mārga*) to suit each person's disposition. In the West we have the whole Mystery Tradition: Pythagoras, Parmenides, Plato, Plotinus, and so on, which unfortunately has been rendered completely profane by various scholarly interpreters, sophists, and dianoetic philosophers, so that those few who seriously profess the Tradition take good care not to be discovered.

> 'But these men who fail, while those gifts would be equal to the *lofty mission*, leave philosophy alone and abandoned; and for their advantage they lead a life unbecoming to their own

[1] Plato, *Theaetetus*, 174.

nature, an untrue life. Philosophy is therefore orphaned, and those who stay near her no longer have a nature akin to hers. Others infiltrate and make their way in. Unworthy men. They dishonour her and bring shame upon her.'[1]

But the initiatory and philosophical Tradition can never die, because the Principle is the ever-present and eternally valid universal.

'And those who instituted the Mysteries were certainly not fools: in truth, right from ancient times [Orphism] they covertly revealed to us that those who reached Hades without being initiated and without being purified would lie in filth, whereas when those who had been initiated and purified reached there, they would live with the Gods [universal consciousness]. Indeed, the expounders of the Mysteries say that "those who wield whips are many, but the Bacchi [those who have realised the true *epoptéia*] are few." And such, I believe, are none other than those who *rightly* practise philosophy.'[2]

Then we have the Hermetic Tradition and the Kabbalistic Tradition, but the former is often considered from the spagyric/materialistic viewpoint, and the latter from the viewpoint of occultism/magic, both operating exclusively in the realm of the individual.[3]

There is also Freemasonry, unfortunately with its tendencies towards the 'social', tendencies which are sometimes even profane and often individualised, even though its Teaching would approve of 'solving' or breaking the barriers of individualisation. In this initiatory context it should be acknowledged, of course without making generalisations, that true and authentic Masters of the Art are rare, so that it all turns

[1] Plato, *Politéia*, VI, 495c.

[2] Plato, *Phaedo*, 69a-d. For an exposition of Orphism from a traditional point of view, see Raphael, *Orphism and the Initiatory Tradition*. Aurea Vidyā, New York.

[3] For these two Traditions, see *The Threefold Pathway of Fire* and *Pathway of Fire, Initiation to Qabbālāh* by Raphael. Aurea Vidyā, New York.

out to be membership of an élite brotherhood which is often nothing more than a social arrangement.

U. Gorel Porciatti writes:

> 'We would like to refer to an aspect that is not well known and in fact is overlooked [he is speaking of the deeply esoteric and initiatory aspect of Freemasonry], an aspect which in no way affects its social ethic but, rather, fulfils it. This is an aspect which is very different from that which is better known and closer to the traditional purpose which aimed at conferring on the initiate the powers of God and therefore potentialities which could be, and had to be, considered divine. This is why there are scholars who consider that 1717 represents the death of Freemasonry as an initiatory school, because, with its rapid spread and its tendency towards objectives with a social purpose, it diluted and twisted those higher potentialities which were still at its disposal, and its specific inclination towards matters of contingent life made it impossible for the study of knowledge at the heart of Freemasonry to be directed towards a transcendent aim.'[1]

As a result we have the 'turn towards the East', where there is still something good and where there is undoubtedly the concept of Realisation/Liberation for that which must really be: the actualisation of a *Universal state of consciousness*, and of other states besides for those who have the right qualifications; *awakening* to the awareness of the Unity/Good and to the Beautiful in itself, according to the divine Plato:

> 'And someone who believes in beautiful things, but not in Beauty itself, and cannot follow one who is trying to lead him to this knowledge, does he seem to you to be living in a dream or in reality? Look here. Isn't it a kind of dreaming if someone, whether awake or asleep, judges that two similar things are not similar but that one is identical to the other which it resembles?'
>
> 'I', he agreed, 'would certainly say that such a man is dreaming.'

---

[1] U. Gorel Porciatti, *Simbologia Massonica*, Atanor, Rome.

'Then, in the opposite case of a man who acknowledges the existence of the Beautiful in itself and is able to see it in its absolute nature and in the realities in which it participates, and who doesn't confuse the Beautiful with these realities, or these realities with the Beautiful in itself, would you say that he is living in a dream or awake?'

'Awake' he declared. 'Beyond all doubt.'[1]

[1] Plato, *Politéia*, V, 476c-d.

DEATH AND RE-BIRTH OR RESURRECTION

Easter represents a very important event for Christianity. The whole of Christendom gathers in silence around the central focus of the Easter experience.

We say in 'silence' because at this time the Church is in mourning: Jesus is 'dead' and is awaiting the moment of 're-birth', resurrection, glory. This event may be interpreted at two levels of understanding: the first level is strictly chronological, historical, empirical, and in time and space; the second is symbolical, initiatory, esoteric. Other events in the life of Jesus also present these two aspects of truth. On the other hand, it has also to be recognised that the great *Avatāras* expressed themselves at various levels of interpretation. Jesus also spoke in parables, but a parable is a verbal/material symbol of a spiritual, metaphysical truth. Plato, too, by means of myth, intended to reveal ineffable truths.

What may be signified by 'death' and resurrection or re-birth from the esoteric/initiatory viewpoint? If we observe all the phenomena of life which surround us, we notice a large-scale process of life/re-birth: a seed is born, flowers, dies, and from this death a seed is re-born which, in turn, flowers and dies, giving life to another seed, and so on. Within our own organism, too, there is ceaseless evidence of a death and re-birth of cells. This process therefore operates throughout the whole manifestation, for what is born must necessarily die and, as long as the life of the manifestation continues, there will have to be new birth in addition to death. We say that the world of forms renews itself.

As *Vedānta* maintains, forms appear and disappear, only to appear again in an unending game of change (*māyā*). Not even human individuality escapes this phenomenon: it appears in the world of *viśva*, or three-dimensionality, then disappears, and the unresolved qualities/seeds strive to assume a new form by creating another individuality.

However, there is a further process of death/resurrection, which we could consider as a vertical line, while the one we have previously referred to could be defined as a horizontal line. On the vertical line, the process of death/re-birth is presented from the viewpoint of the transcendence of a *state of consciousness*.

On the horizontal line the seed of a flower is born, flowers, and dies, to give life to another flower-seed and not to anything else. In the case of unresolved individuality, it dies in order to restore life to other individualised qualities; we would say that their birth and death always develop along a precise and identical pathway of existence (*saṁsāra*). On the vertical line, by contrast, one 'dies' definitely along that pathway in order to enter upon another that is completely different in all respects. The former is a line that is straight and parallel to the previous one, while the latter is one of *ascent*, transcendence, and rising above the previous state.

In the case of Jesus, we note that He dies and *ascends*, which implies that what happens to Him belongs to an ascending process of death/re-birth, and thus to a vertical order.

Therefore, if we have to ascend, we shall have to die, inevitably and *definitively*, to that which, until now, has represented for us that birth/death which is on the horizontal line. This necessitates coming to a *stop* on the horizontal line and initiating the upward movement. In other words, one must be able to realise the cross. In the development of the cross we note that the vertical arm moves into the horizontal arm at point X; so, to define the vertical arm of the cross, we have to come to a stop at one point of the horizontal arm and rise up along the ascending vertical arm. Real death – the death of the Philosopher – occurs at the precise point of intersection with the horizontal line, which means coming to a stop and ascending simultaneously, thus 'dying' and rising up to a new expression of life.

A Soul's anguish occurs particularly when it has come to a stop without ascending. In such a case, the consciousness is living in a no-man's land, a stalled position, a state of aboulia. But why is this? It is because, having come to a stop, it is no longer following the horizontal line, and by not proceeding up the vertical line it is not heeding the call.

Someone in this state may be afraid of 'death', not realising that, having slowed or stopped his movement along the horizontal line, he is already 'dead', a 'corpse' devoid of interests.

As disciples on the way of Liberation, we have slowed our movement along the horizontal line (the line of becoming) or, rather, we have finally come to a stop and consequently are seeking to erect our vertical arm and are lifting up our cross. This arm extends from *viśva*/earth all the way to *Brahmaloka*, the world of *Brahmā*, that is, from the sensible to the intelligible. Someone may also come to a stop on this vertical line and cut across the horizontal line; in addition to indefinite states of consciousness, the manifestation offers many planes. Someone else may continue as far as the full solution of all states of consciousness, and therefore of all the planes of manifestation, having recognised that the levels/worlds are, as the *Upaniṣad* declares, nothing but accumulated *karma*. 'One becomes what one thinks' in the heart; if we 'think' we are the supreme Being, we shall be the supreme Being, because potentially this is what we already are. If we think we are individual human beings, this is what we shall be; and so on. The power of thought/heart offers us wings to fly to the different worlds/*lokas*, gross or subtle; or, again, to leave them and *ascend* fully to the unqualified and formless God, and this represents the true, authentic, and final death/resurrection.

For us who are advanced disciples, there is no other kind of death, for we have already experienced, and presumably transcended, the other kinds of death. The Teaching of *Vedānta*, like the Western metaphysical Tradition, points to this transfiguration, because it acknowledges, with absolute awareness, that all possible experiences, whether gratifying or not, at the level of the relative and the world of becoming, are nothing but coloured mists which obscure the true fullness of being.

But it is also true that this kind of Teaching requires the right qualifications, psychological maturity, and, most of all, maturity of consciousness.

Easter for the Jewish people was represented by their exodus from Egypt and their journey to the promised land; for Jesus, by the death of the form and the ascension to heaven or the God-Person; for us, it should be a dying to, and transcending of, every conditioned state and a rising to the world of Plato's One-One or the *Nirguṇa Brahman* of *Advaita Vedānta*.

LIBERATION

Every authentic way of realisation involves the idea of Liberation; indeed, we speak of Liberated, Awakened, and so on, to indicate a being that is 'dead' and therefore *born anew*. But dead to what? Liberated from what? To what has this being awakened?

The common opinion is that the human being is merely a 'substantial body' and that the world which surrounds us, the world of indefinite perceptible forms, is also real/absolute. From this there arises a complete view of life based on values that are sensible/perceptible, and from this comes the subjugation to that which has form and the 'worship' of object, of *res*, of thing as a factor of gratification and enjoyment. And this 'thing', this object-datum, becomes such a powerful cause of alienation that it can lead the individual to violence.

If things/events are absolute realities, the only truths that really exist, it is obvious that the being will try to acquire them at any price. If a mere concept or ideal is made absolute, then one will be capable of imposing it by force; but a concept and an ideal are always changeable 'objects' which reveal themselves as appearances or opinions.

The individual, by identifying with the world of things and becoming like it, succumbs so fully as to become petrified and annihilated, given that the nature of this world is one of being born and dying or, rather, of appearing and disappearing. A form, whatever its nature and level – and it may be an idea, a feeling, and so on – is nothing but an emergence from a unitary substratum and a subsequent eclipse.

Things/events, however, are not a nothingness like a 'hare's horns' or 'a sterile woman's son', to use the examples given by Gauḍapāda and Śaṅkara: they are phenomena/movements which present themselves to our senses.

Now all of this is clear; there is nothing new in stating that the becoming process of names and forms is born, grows, and dies; but to say that Being, as such, lies behind becoming and that Being can also be realised may be something new for some people. And traditional Knowledge invites us to realise in practice the revelation of this Being which represents the unitary substratum of all the appearances.

So from what must we free ourselves? We must free ourselves from the false notion that we, as pure beings, are a 'thing', a phenomenon, an object. We must free ourselves from the opinion that the world of names and forms is the only reality. We must free ourselves from the false truth that we, like the world of things, are mortal. We must free ourselves from the ignorance (*avidyā*) which likens us to the realm of that which is merely impermanent.

This Liberation, it should be stated, does not come about through concepts or, more precisely, through conceptualising the idea of liberation, but occurs through the actual and effective elimination of the false representation which we have made of ourselves and of things.

> 'Liberation is the end of *avidyā*.'[1]

> 'To those whose ignorance (*ajñāna*) has been destroyed by knowledge, knowledge, like a brilliant sun, reveals the supreme Reality.'[2]

> 'When the five faculties of perception come to rest, together with the mind, and the intellect is focused, we call that [condition] the supreme Goal.'[3]

---

[1] Maṇḍana Miśra, *Brahmasiddhi*, III, 106.

[2] *Bhagavadgītā*, V, 16.

[3] *Kaṭha Upaniṣad*, II, VI, 10.

'Through union and contemplation of Reality, [practised] constantly, there finally comes about the cessation of *māyā* in the form of the universe.'[1]

From what must we awaken? From the veiling *sleep* which constrains us to mistake the transient for the eternal, the mortal for the immortal, appearances for reality.

To what must we die? To the erroneous conceptions which we have superimposed on what we really are.

With this awakening, Liberation, or 'death of the Philosophers', the Being resumes the fullness of itself within itself, and the things which appear and disappear finally find their rightful places and will no longer be a cause of alienation.

Can those who have discovered the splendour of the sun ever turn back to the weak rays of the moon? Of what do those who live in fullness/completeness (*pūrṇa*) stand in need?

'The worlds whose nature is not divine are certainly permeated by blinding darkness, and to them go those who have forgotten their own Self.'[2]

For the West the Teachings of Parmenides, Plato, and Plotinus are authentic ways of realisation (*jñāna-mārga*), while for the East there are so many ways, to accord with the qualifications of the disciples.

---

[1] *Śvetāśvatara Upaniṣad*, I, 10.

[2] *Īśā Upaniṣad*, II, 3, in *Five Upaniṣads*, edited by Raphael. Aurea Vidyā, New York.

NON-DUALISM AND EQUANIMITY

The Wise look with an impartial eye on a clod of earth and a piece of gold, because for them 'all the different modifications are nothing but distinctions of name and speech.'[1]

Such a view is reached after quite a few identifications with appearances and therefore quite a few conflicts, because attachment to the non-existent brings nothing but tensions, frustrations, uncertainties, and fears. But how can a dualistic consciousness awaken to the recognition that Reality is One-without-a-second? That the distinction between subject and object is merely imagined? That what is perceived is nothing other than an impression transmitted by the senses to the mind, and from the mind to consciousness itself?

Perceptions are erroneous, as has also been proved by science, and yet man continues to 'dream', to believe in what he sees, to let himself be persuaded, to change himself from spectator to actor. And the cinema, this modern symbol of *māyā*, if carefully considered, can be very useful to us in our understanding of this mystery.

The greater the identification with the show, the greater the reality it assumes for the spectator.[2] As a result, to recognise the illusory nature of the form/image one needs first of all to go back into oneself and substitute *knowledge* for *perception* as an end in itself.

---

[1] *Chāndogya Upaniṣad*, VI, 1, 4.

[2] See *Dṛgdṛśyaviveka, A philosophical investigation into the nature of the 'Seer' and the 'seen'*. Translation from the Sanskrit and commentary by Raphael. Aurea Vidyā, New York.

Knowledge allows us to discern whether a datum is real/ constant or unreal. If the real is that which depends on nothing other than itself, because it is *causa sui*, then everything else – which is necessity and generation – is conditioned.

On the other hand, in order to perceive movement something motionless is required, something which is actually aware of the process; otherwise there would not even be the concept of movement. Thus movement/becoming presupposes a cause which cannot change and which represents the final cause of all that 'becomes'. We would say, then, that 'that which is' and does not become is the foundation of all change and every phenomenon. Therefore, behind multiplicity there must be undivided Unity, which represents the *ratio essendi* and the *ratio intelligendi* of everything.

There is, in fact, a sense of continuity behind the impermanent, a presence which never fails when objects fail and desires change, a *self-knowledge* which is not born and does not die, but can only grow weaker, veil itself, cover itself. This is *Self-Consciousness*, the motionless screen on which are silhouetted the indefinite forms/images, both subjective (the various 'egos') and objective (the various 'non-egos'). To be established in this centre means to re-discover a new identity of conscious subjects, no longer conditioned by 'dream' and emotions, free from the enchantment of movement and thus free from attraction and repulsion.

At the level of manifestation, this Subject (*jīvātman*) is identified, at an early phase, with the state of consciousness of *prājña*, where the effect (subject/object) is re-absorbed into the cause, though still remaining latently present. Duality, therefore, is not resolved in *prājña*, which represents the state of potentiality. For this reason, whether it is the dimension of the *jīva* or the individualised dimension that is being dealt with, *Advaita* considers that they both belong to dream/manifestation, to *māyā*.

The Absolute abides beyond all polarity, expressed or unexpressed, and thus beyond all correlation. It will be necessary to transcend movement and non-movement in order to be re-integrated in that, the One-without-a-second; to ascend to the ultimate Subject, which, not being an object of relationship, cannot be perceived or thought, but only realised through pure Awareness.

> 'A form/object is perceived, but it is the eye which perceives. This is perceived by the mind, which becomes the perceiving subject. Finally, the mind, with its modifications, is perceived by the Thinker/Observer, which cannot be the object of perception.'[1]

The first important expansion of consciousness for the disciple is that of resolving multiplicity by reducing the 'diverse' to the One/the Cause, but this requires, above all, the cessation of identification with one's own vehicular complex (*ahaṁkāra*). As long as one remains attached to one's own 'form', it is impossible to acknowledge the illusory nature of other forms. In other words, one cannot unmask the 'non-ego' with the consciousness of the 'ego', just as in dreams it will never happen that the perceiving subject acknowledges the illusory nature of the perceived object, being itself a projection, a non-reality. The attention is therefore moved from the object to the subject, from the 'non-I' to the 'I'.

> 'Who am I? Am I perhaps this body which appears and disappears? Am I the emotion of yesterday, the emotion of today, or that of tomorrow? Or am I my relentless imagination?' And then who is it that is asking these questions?
>
> 'Body, emotion, and thought, external and internal perceptions, not being permanent, cannot be real. Then who am I?' Śaṅkara replies, 'The *ātman* alone is permanent, [while] what is seen is everything that is superimposed upon it.'[2]

---

[1] *Dṛgdṛśyaviveka*, 1.

[2] Śaṅkara, *Aparokṣānubhūti* (Self-realisation), 5. Translation from the Sanskrit and commentary by Raphael. Aurea Vidyā, New York.

This very *ātman* is the substratum of the clod of earth and the piece of gold, and also of individuality itself. We continually pursue ourselves (desire) and reject ourselves (aversion).

Sādhanā affects three moments of consciousness in the life of the disciple: identification, self-awareness, and identity, which correspond to three levels of knowledge.

The first moment is effected with the death of the psychological centre/consciousness, the identification of the *ahaṁkara* – a reflection of the *jīvātman* – with what is perceived. Here perception has an absolute value for the perceiver. One form appears distinct from another, and the distance between them appears insurmountable. At this level, where one object attracts and another doesn't, we certainly cannot speak of *impartiality/equanimity* but only of preference.

The second type of knowledge is realised when consciousness withdraws into itself, re-discovers itself as the *point at the centre*. From this detached position of consciousness, the attractive/repulsive movement in relation to form comes to an end. Awareness prevails over perception. *The Soul sees the Soul.* There is no preference because there is no difference.

Finally, knowledge of identity is realised when Seer and seen merge with the Vision. And it is only at this stage that we can speak of genuine *impartiality/equanimity*, which results not from the equality of two elements but from the very absence of duality. In the former case, impartiality/ equanimity is in relation to what is seen; in the latter case, it is the expression of what one is.

The word *equanimous* derives from *aequus*: having a mind which is equal, unchangeable, indifferent, terms which refer to the consciousness, the primary aspect of being. People are equanimous/impartial if they do not change or undergo any modification of consciousness under any circumstance. The *equanimity*/impartiality or divine indifference of the Sage is the expression, at the manifest level, of someone who has realised himself as Unmanifest, as One-without-a-second. What distinction, therefore, can exist in *That* for which there is no duality? What could it perceive outside Unity, since this Unity leaves nothing outside itself?

> 'In truth, where [there seems] to be duality, there one ... sees another, one hears another, one speaks to another, one thinks of another, one knows another. But when, through Him, everything has become his own *ātman* ... then by means of what will he see, and what? By means of what will he hear, and what? By means of what will he speak, and what? By means of what will he know, and what? By means of what will he know That, by whose grace he knows everything? By means of what, my dear, will he know the knower?'[1]

---

[1] *Bṛhadāraṇyaka Upaniṣad*, II, IV, 14.

GOOD AND EVIL

This planet, on which the 'individualised human state' has existed for many thousands of years, is so permeated by 'evil' that many think that good does not actually exist.

The planetary being has always suffered, suffers now, and will continue to suffer from the power of the evil which tortures it, stuns it, and renders it estranged. The history of humanity has been more or less characterised by internal strife, fratricidal wars, and violence of every kind, so that all traces of reason have been obscured. Some teachings consider this planet of ours to be far from sacred; this means a planet – or rather, its state of consciousness – that is *sundered* from the universal Harmony. It is a realm of suffering because it is ruled by the sense of the ego, of separateness, and the failure to recognise its proper role in nature's bosom.

As long as individuals fail to pause and reflect upon their true existential state, as long as they fail to consider the full and complete vision of their own conscious constitution, they will not be able to comprehend evil, far less resolve it and transcend it. And yet huge numbers of outstanding figures, of vast stature, have sought to give an understanding and even suggestions for eliminating destitution and cognitive and spiritual poverty.

Man has reached the point of such bewilderment as to lie low and be resigned to live that 'part of himself' which expressly manifests ignorance and therefore doubt and confusion, with all their concomitants. Many (and not merely the 'mass' of humanity) view the being as a mere physical phenomenon which emerges from nothing and returns to nothing, and whose contingent appearance brings nothing in its train but contradictions, violence, and evil. At times it may even be thought that evil has become a *real* and inexorable aspect to which we have to submit and come to consider as an integral and lawful part of everyday life. This represents the total annihilation of human consciousness. From this viewpoint, nihilism is man's fundamental philosophy, but it is the darkest, most reductive, and most imprisoning form that the being has ever proposed to itself and to others.

Let us ask ourselves a few questions, aprioristically avoiding an unjustified rejection, and let us seek to provide answers by presenting some extremely useful views which our true Fathers and Teachers have offered us as solutions for understanding and resolving certain matters.

What is the nature of evil?

What is its origin?

Is evil an absolute reality?

Is evil necessary for existence?

To properly comprehend the nature of evil it is useful to first comprehend the nature of the good.

The good – as the supreme accord of the self with itself, and thus with others – is the blissful expression of life at every level and degree. It is that good which *comprehends* the unity of life; which acknowledges multiplicity as the unfolding of unity; which takes all beings back to the supreme Being. It is that state in which the other is acknowledged as inseparable from one's own nature. The good is the condition of having *comprehended* the totality of oneself; it is that expansion of awareness which brushes against the circumference of life. The good is the single and individual foundation of all that exists; and in those who give it shelter, they themselves having become the good, evil can neither germinate nor flourish. This type of good we can refer to the sphere of the supra-rational, the supra-sensible, and the *universal* in its most authentic connotation: the world which is intelligible, commensurate, fulfilled, substantiated by Harmony, as is declared by the greatest Teachers or Sages of the past and the present. In such a world we can find neither the origin nor the nature of evil.

If we accept the nature of the good as we have expounded it, we shall, as a result, comprehend the nature of evil. Evil has the nature of separation, of scissure from the Intelligible, of opposition, of the absolutism of the ego as a factor of distinction. It is dissociation from Being, from Unity. It makes itself into an element of disintegration. It is the state of collapse into total differentiation until even the seed of rationality is lost. The very term 'devil', the personification of evil, derives from the Latin *diábolus* and the Greek *diábolos* (διάβολος from διαβάλλω), words meaning to calumniate, to curse, to be hostile, to provoke discord and therefore separation from that which can unite. Evil is not the real opposite of the good, but the degeneration of a *part* of the being which has sundered itself from the Intelligible so as to establish itself as an autonomous and exclusive reality.

Evil cannot be an absolute reality, because it represents merely a 'debasement'. Even if this is seen as a possibility, it can be said to be an 'accident', to use Aristotle's word. On the other hand, two absolutes cannot co-exist: good and evil. An absolute duality is inconceivable, too, because it is a contradiction, and the two will cancel each other out. Light and darkness, like every duality, do not constitute two realities, one being the absence of the other. Let us also state that the various evils, off-shoots of the original evil, which afflict beings, are uncertain, subject to modification, and can even be eradicated.

But what is the origin of evil?

If intelligible beings express harmony, fullness, bliss, and therefore perfect commensurability among themselves and with themselves, and consequently among themselves and all that exists, this means that at a given 'moment' there was a loosening, a pulling away, as a result of which a scissure occurred, and the being forced itself into the multiplicity of opposition/

repulsion, into 'I' and 'not I', into the generation of the physical with its distinctions.

But can a being which is unity and fullness ever become multiplicity and poverty? Can it ever change its nature? If the nature of something is its permanent state, so that it is what it is and cannot be other than what it is, then the being, having the nature of fullness/bliss, cannot suddenly find itself with a nature that is not only different but downright contradictory.

If evil/poverty/dissipation is in the world of the sensible and not in the world of the Intelligible (phenomenon cannot but pre-suppose the noumenon, the compound the simple, or the inferior the superior), it means that the intelligible being remains identical to itself, and any aspect of it in the sensible world is its 'reflection', its 'shadow', its function, its specificity, a ray that is diffuse and dispersive, an aspect which, while participating in its αρχή, the divine principle, is not the true being in its pure essence (ουσία) and reality.

> 'What is it that has caused souls – which are indeed parts *detached* from above and which really belong completely to the supernal world – to forget God their Father and become ignorant of themselves and Him? Well, the initial root of evil, for souls, was recklessness, and then birth and primeval otherness and the *wish to belong to themselves*. Thus, being visibly intoxicated with that self-determination of theirs and then with the fact that they had made the fullest use of their spontaneous movement, after that great run in the opposite direction, having become so distant, they ended by becoming ignorant of themselves and of their origin.'[1]

In dreams the being can project an *image* of itself which, although substantial, is not real/absolute; and this image, believing itself to be an independent reality, is *sundered* from its source and in an estranged state.

---

[1] Plotinus, *Enneads*, V, 1, 1. (Italics are ours).

The world of precipitation, the world of the sensible and of becoming, is a world in which the inverted image of the true being operates in opposition to other 'images'. This is Plato's myth of the cave. This reflection of consciousness, of the pure intelligible Awareness, is apparently alive but is better described as a wandering corpse, a dream being which appears and disappears from the intelligible horizon. Evil is merely an effect, a product which disturbs the harmony of the world but cannot destroy it.

The scissure, not being absolute, is produced not by the true being but by its reflection, which, believing itself to be autonomous and separate from its source, operates as if it were the only thing in existence, thus disowning its Father: 'detached from above ... with the wish to belong to themselves ...'

This outlines the process of the 'individuation', the 'particularisation' of what exists at the level of the sensible. It is therefore the sensible which detaches itself from the Intelligible. The Intelligible, by encompassing and containing the countless modes of life and by constituting the metaphysical foundation of all that exists at the sensible level, cannot detach itself from anything or anyone. It is wholeness. The being, as reality and unity, cannot split and establish itself as something other than itself, but through its creative faculty it can 'project' an *alter ego* which will be nothing but an appearance, an image which, although consistent, cannot be real, because there is only one reality. One reality cannot produce a second reality if it itself is already real, and it cannot produce a nothingness, which means that things in the sensible world are not like the horns of a hare or the son of a barren woman, to use the examples given by Śaṅkara. What it can manifest can be only a phenomenon (from *phainomai*, 'I appear').

Being (τὸ ὄν), microcosmic or macrocosmic, *is*. According to Parmenides, life at the level of form appears and disappears from the noetic horizon, and this is a proof.

The origin of evil lies in a projecting action of the real being, a projection which determines the equally apparent self-dismembering.

Plotinus speaks of the Soul's recklessness in going out of itself, like a diffusive tendency, an active power dispersed in repeated 'reflections' of form.

But is this process an inexorable necessity for the being? If the intelligible being is absolute fullness, it is also absolute freedom, and in this absolute freedom it can provide determinations for itself; in this way, every determination, being an accident, has the undetermined as its cause. Freedom is not an attribute which may be present or absent; freedom, we would say, is consubstantial with the being, and as such it can do anything except invalidate the nature of the being and therefore the nature of itself.

We acknowledge that human existence at the sensible level can think/project, can identify itself with what is thought, and can refrain from identifying itself; it can also refrain from projecting/thinking. The being also has the freedom not to be, although only in appearance because, of course, it cannot change its nature. Non-being (τὸ μή ὄν), unlike being (τὸ ὄν), is not substantial, but is its 'shadow', its appearance, its illusion, its mirage, which, for the 'dream being', is as substantial and real as being itself.

The being is not in error when it chooses to manifest itself at the various levels of existence, for this is a totally acceptable state of affairs, but it is mistaken when it identifies itself with what it produces, forgetting itself as the reality. This is the myth of Narcissus, which always enlightens us. On the other hand, identification remains one of the being's possibilities, and, in addition, it can see that it is mistaken only when it begins to become aware of its true condition.

It seems paradoxical that such identification – with ideals, passions, material goods, learning, vanity, and so on – can lead man to unbelievable tragedies; and yet it is so. The being which is able to stop identifying itself with its own 'shadow', and hence with what it has produced, can grow new wings and fly towards the state of fullness.

The projecting action of the being is therefore not inexorable, not a necessity. Like evil itself, not being absolute it is not something inevitable. The freedom of the intelligible being necessarily contemplates the indefinite possibility of differentiation, but also that of non-differentiation. The cause of differentiation, however, must be attributed to the 'shadow' which believes itself to be what it is not.

Vedānta speaks of *avidyā*, the failure to recognise what one really is. The empirical or sensible being believes that it is mortal, that it is a body, that it is the only thing that exists in the universe, that it is this or that. All this represents a mere *belief*. In psychological terms, it is the empirical ego which considers itself to be an absolute, a reality as such; but the ego, together with its products, is a *phenomenon* which is silhouetted against the screen of the noumenon, the *noûs*; it consists of continual movement, becoming, and change, as long as it fails to extinguish itself completely by re-integrating itself with its source.

The 'shadow', or the empirical being, receives intelligence, volition, and emotion from the real and immortal being, but these represent merely elements of reflection. Its knowledge is the knowledge one has when facing a mirror; the truths that it discovers are the products of mirror images, and the knowledge is therefore indirect. Plato speaks of *eikasía* and *pístis*, imagination and belief. Things are *represented*, rather than known for what they are.

As empirical compounds, we have the conceptual representation of the tree or of any other physical form, but we do not have the knowledge, or, rather, the awareness of the ουσία of the tree or any other form. This knowledge of identity pertains to the *noûs*.

The diffusive act of the real being is of an a-temporal order, because its power is act, while the events and things which the vital reflection creates belong to time and space, because the reflection operates in the world of compounds and because it itself is formed of compound bodies for its own survival.

The *identification* of the reflection of consciousness with the compounded and not with the Simple (*noûs*) is the cause which promotes evil, darkness, alienation, 'I' and 'not I', opposition, strife, and the supremacy of one over the other; and this can come about simply because one is not. They who are fullness/bliss and self-sufficiency live by their own movement, their own being, their own totality. They who *are* do not give themselves targets because they have nothing to attain. It is the reflection of consciousness which, because it is not, has to give itself targets in order to attain something that it does not have, and hence the strenuous becoming/movement of the empirical being. But although it may become and 'move towards', it will never be able to achieve any aim, especially because the aims are innumerable. By going in the wrong direction, and urged on by desires and anxieties, it is in continual movement, without any real purpose.

But just as the radiation of the real being is not a necessity, so the identification of the reflection of consciousness with the composite is not a necessity; it is just one of its possibilities.

All the philosophical, genuinely realisative Traditions have as their motive the restoration of the embodied reflection to its metaphysical source, which is the most just and natural goal (if one may speak of a goal).

Parmenides, Plato, and Plotinus, however, posit a supreme Reality which transcends not only the conflicting realm of the sensible, but even the realm of Beauty which, with its splendour, makes the whole of the Intelligible beautiful. This Reality, supreme and metaphysical *par excellence*, which transcends evil and even the good and on which all that exists is founded, is known by various names: highest Good, One-One, Being that *is* and does not become, metaphysical One (Plotinus), and, in the words of *Vedānta* as presented by Śaṅkara, *Nirguṇa Brahman* (unqualified *Brahman*), Non-dual (*Advaita*), and so on.

> 'From their very birth, all men make use of the senses before the intellect and, necessarily encountering sensible things from the outset, some, held firm in these, pass their whole life in the belief that these things are the be-all and end-all, and they maintain that whatever is painful or pleasant in these things is evil and good respectively. Thus they think they have enough good and evil, and they spend their life pursuing the one and keeping the other at arm's length. And those among them who pose as philosophers even claim that herein lies wisdom! These resemble ungainly birds who have taken a great deal from the earth and, thus weighed down, cannot manage to fly aloft, although endowed with wings by nature. Others rise a little from the depths, because the noblest part of their soul urges them to move from pleasure to Beauty; but since they fail to see the heights, having no other support on which to rely, they hurtle down, together with their much praised 'virtue', to practical action, which means making a 'choice' among the vile and low things from which they had previously been trying to soar upwards.
>
> 'Lastly, there is a third band: divine people, of greater vigour and keener gaze, who are able to see, as if by means of a supreme visual intensity, the supreme splendour, and they lift themselves up, as if above the clouds and earthly fog, and there they dwell, disdaining all the things of the world and delighting in that place – the authentic good of their forebears – like men who, after endless wanderings, have returned to their homeland, a homeland governed by good laws.'[1]

[1] Plotinus, *Enneads*, V, 9, 1.

FIRE OF THE PHILOSOPHERS

'*Unica ut diximus est operatio, extra quam non est alia quae vera sit.*' 'There is only one operation, beyond which there is none other that is true.'[1]

And again,

'There is only one nature and only one art.'[2]

'The whole of our operation in this art is nothing except being able to extract Sulphur from minerals, by means of which our Quicksilver may coagulate in Gold, and silver in the bowels of the earth; here this Sulphur is understood as the masculine because it is considered nobler, and Mercury is understood as feminine.'[3]

'The artist simply separates the fine from the coarse and puts it in the appropriate vessel.'[4]

The only operation which can concern Hermetic Philosophy is that of

- comprehending the tripartite division of the being into Sulphur, Mercury, and Salt;
- separating the Mercury from the Salt, and then
- fusing the Mercury with the Sulphur through the operation of a 'chemical wedding'; or extracting the Sulphur

---

[1] M. Sendivogius, *De Sulphure.* Taken from 'Short notes on the cosmopolitan'. *Ignis*, 4-5. 1925.

[2] M. Sendivogius, *Novum lumen chemicum.*

[3] *De Sulphure.*

[4] *Novum lumen chemicum.*

> from the Mercury so that the two can unite, fuse together, and become a single thing.

There is a true union when the Queen unites with the King, obtaining a body of immortal glory.

The Gold buried in the dark saline or earthen vessel must be extracted, cleansed with the Water of the Philosophers, and then restored to its original splendour.

We do not have to look far for our 'vessel' because it is close to hand; or rather, it is the 'mud' which we all carry on our backs, very thick and hiding our Gold.

The earth is encircled by dark clouds which conceal the majesty of the Sun; under the pressure of Fire, the clouds are changed into Dew, which, as it falls, bathes and purifies the earth and allows the Sun to shine by making it manifest.

If one strips the beautiful Diana, one can see the parched earth, but the earth is also ready for purification.

Stephen of Alexandria writes: 'We must despoil matter of its quality in order to reach perfection, because the aim of Philosophy is the "dissolution" of bodies and the separation of the Soul from the body.'

And Plato himself, in conformity with the alchemical process, states:

> 'And is this not perhaps what we call death, that is, the loosening and separating of the Soul from the body? ... And this is precisely the aim of philosophers: to loosen and separate the Soul from the body.'[1]

According to Sendivogius, it is easier to liberate the Sulphur than to find it, for it is in a dark dungeon under the control of Saturn. One has to descend into the bowels of this dungeon and rectify in order to obtain the occult stone (*De Sulphure*).

With the regimen of philosophical Fire the golden vapour is fixed in a way that is opposite to what happens with minerals which evaporate.

---

[1] Plato, *Phaedo*, 67d.

The operation is initiated in winter, proceeds through the seasons, and comes to an end in autumn. At the solstice of Saturn, the seed opens because the black has duly mortified the matter of the Sages, and the philosophical infant is extracted.

It needs to be repeated that the radical Moisture is imprisoned – as Orpheus, Plato, and Sendivogius state – in a dungeon from which it cannot escape solely by its own powers: this is where the Art of the Philosophers is employed to make it come forth. Nature is given assistance and support. The Art prepares the rectification by means of the Hermetic Fire, as is done with certain spirits by means of heat. And the Art also involves knowing how to use the regimen of the Fire.

Therefore one must first of all kindle the philosophical Fire, which is in the dark cavern of *Sal petrae*, by using the breath of the bellows. Then, with a well-directed operation – the regimen of the Fire – one must unite Sun and Moon, or King and Queen, in a sweet embrace, so that a Son will be born, who is more wonderful than Father/Mother and who can provide, like a vast tree, countless appetising fruits, one of which is the fruit of immortality.

The operation is conducted with a regimen that is regular and rhythmical, without violence or haste, just the way nature works. The Sun slowly warms the earthly soil, splits the seed, and makes the plant come forth.

The work is easy or difficult, according to the skill of the Artist/Philosopher.

Fire of Ascent

To comprehend, comprehend oneself

GUILT COMPLEXES AND ATONEMENT IN RELATION TO REALISATION

It often happens that some aspirants and disciples – as is the case with many spiritually-minded people in general – are so oppressed by different kinds of contents in their psyches that their *sādhanā* (spiritual discipline/ascent) on the way of Realisation is hindered. Let us consider, for example, the 'guilt complex', which can be an influential factor in the aspirant's life. Without wishing to go into doctrinal and academic disquisitions, we shall try to give some simple account.

What is a guilt complex? After completing an action – ideal or purely material/objective – we may have a *feeling* of guilt; we may believe we have committed an infringement, a sin, or a transgression, with the result that we feel in conflict. For the subject this feeling constitutes an 'offence' given to something or someone; thus one is transgressing a principle which we have accepted consciously or unconsciously.

First of all, let us examine the case of a religious person, because it can tell us quite a lot. His approach starts from this premise: 'I am following this religion (whichever it may be in this case), which obliges me to purify my qualities in order to be accepted by God, and since it happens that impure aspects still lodge within me, I feel guilty at not being able to comply with this standard.' These guilt complexes accumulate in the course of time because the undesirable qualities can be manifold, with the result that one reaches a psychopathic condition. From the guilt complex, from the transgression of some rule or principle, is born the opposite feeling of wishing to make amends, of repentance, and so one imposes upon oneself many repetitions, for example, of a specific prayer or *mantra*, or deprives oneself of food, sleep, or clothing; one may even go to the extreme of amputating a limb, and so on. After the act of making amends, 'penitence' or punishment, the consciousness calms down and resumes its equilibrium, because the 'offence' against God, the principle, and so on, has been atoned for.

Impurity or transgression will certainly show itself, because the opportunities to 'sin' are numerous, but particularly because one is making no attempt to remove the cause which determines the 'sin', the 'fall' being a mere effect. However, that punitive 'revenge' calms the feelings of the faithful. Confession is another means of making amends, because it favours two things. The latter consists in revealing, confessing the transgression in a way that is open and well-known; this involves a release of tension and responsibility. The former, consisting of atoning acts, of which we have already spoken, restores the consciousness to equilibrium. The transgression is actually *absolved* either implicitly by holding to certain rules or through the mediation of a confessor. Let us give a practical example in relation to a 'fall'. The religious person will say, 'My physical body (or my mental body) has made me sin; being guilty, I am punishing it because I must make amends for the transgression.' With these premises he may think up all the acceptable means for punishing the physical body, even to the point, as we said earlier, of cutting off a limb.

This conclusion is equivalent to the following one: 'Since my car has taken me off route or has involved me in an accident, I am going to hit it with a hammer or, if I want to exact my full revenge, I shall destroy it completely.'

In all of this we may note something false in the premise.

This restrictive, irrational, and repressive view is counter-balanced by another that is even more harmful with regard to ethics and the result of *sādhanā* (spiritual discipline). There are disciples who, after going through the phase of the guilt complex, give themselves up to acts that are immoral, sometimes even perverse, inventing coherent excuses to legitimise their licentiousness. They may even be cynics, or they invent philosophies which justify their qualities, which are far from being consonant with the initiatory way. And because there are also teachings of particular '*gurus*' which justify licentiousness and even encourage it, these disciples, like the previous ones, put their consciences to rest.

Unfortunately, we find ourselves facing extremist conceptions which, on the spiritual way, allow no progress and offer no solutions to the problems. What might be the right attitude when confronted by complexes of varying nature or by contents which seem to us in need of rectifying?

First of all, a correct approach is required to these undesirable qualities which represent, not an 'offence' to some God projected by our super-ego, but merely obstacles, hindrances, and diversions on the way of Liberation. If it is a question of offence, the offence is first of all against ourselves, against our own nature as thinking and spiritual beings, as well as against our fellows; it is against our own choice, our own coherence, our dignity as disciples.

Realisation/Liberation is synonymous with completeness, with *pax mentis*, with bliss and fullness. 'My peace I give unto you; not as the world giveth,'[1] says Jesus. Now will an individual who is haughty, envious, jealous, self-assertive, lacking in something at the psychological level, ever be at peace? If he tells us that he is, we are not obliged to believe him.

Liberation takes care of lack, deprivation, and the forces of *rajas*. It is not possible to be Liberated if there are expressions of lack and incompleteness: this is a contradiction in terms, for the two states are mutually exclusive.

We shall therefore have to agree that, to take *sādhanā* seriously, it is necessary to face the situation, but how is it to be faced? With guilt complexes and punishments? With continuous

---

[1] St John, 14:27.

justifications for our actions and our specific self-interested philosophy? Or by putting our heads in the sand, as is commonly said, thus avoiding the issue?

The Teaching offers us some methods for resolving, not the effect, but the cause of the 'fall'. First and foremost, one needs to have an idea of the psychosomatic and spiritual constitution in order to recognise which *state of consciousness* to assume and which attitude to adopt when faced with qualities which require rectifying or transcending. The being is formed of a coarse physical body, a mental/psychical body, and a spiritual body or mercurial consciousness. The various qualifications are principally the result of mental/psychical 'movement'; in the terms of *Vedānta*, the *guṇas*/qualities belong to *prakṛti*, to substance; they move and therefore express themselves, because the consciousness has abdicated its solar position as guide and director; it is the 'inner ordainer', according to the *Upaniṣad*; or it is the charioteer who holds the reins – or should do – but who has unfortunately fallen asleep, to use the beautiful image given by Plato.

Now, coming down heavily on the *guṇas* or the vehicles/bodies with an external and authoritarian act means producing inhibitions and making a solution impossible. To check a moving ball requires stopping its acceleration. It is impossible to stop and accelerate at the same time: the two actions contradict each other. So in order to solve the problem we shall have to put ourselves into that state of consciousness from which the impulse for movement of the qualifications, or the qualified rajasic energies, can be checked and resolved. It is an act of drawing back the consciousness until one is aware *directly* – and no longer through a mere psychological perception – of all movement whatsoever, both conscious and subconscious. If this solar mercury is gradually fixed in such a way that it is not upset by the movement of the contents, the work will proceed to good effect. Rather than placing the attention on the *guṇas*/vehicles, one should arouse the *charioteer*, because he is the one who holds the reins and the destinations of the 'horses' in his hands.

Another point is not to judge the various contents of which one is aware. There are many reasons for insisting on this. Whatever is *observed* – the spectacle (*dṛśya*) – is simply a mere *superimposition* on the mercurial consciousness. And in dealing with a superimposition (*adhyāsa/adhyāropa*), there is no need to create guilt complexes or make excuses for prolonging it: one just needs to be able to *integrate* it within the consciousness, to *release* it into the sea of awareness; 'mass' has to re-discover itself as pure energy. If there are undesirable things within us, we simply have to *transform* them, because we have the *power* to do so.

At the same time we could *evoke* qualities of a universal order: comprehension/love as a result of the recognition that life is one, noetic knowledge or psychological composure as the fruit of initiatory dignity. Furthermore, we could rectify and direct the energy of self-assertiveness in order to achieve spiritual self-realisation, and we could elevate egoic emotional feeling to universal Love, which necessarily embraces the closest people, too; and so on.

For the sake of synthesis, we may give a scheme of these final phases:

1. Separation of the mercurial consciousness from the qualitative superimpositions of energy.
2. Fixation of the mercurial consciousness so that it changes from 'lunar' to 'solar'. This involves drawing back the consciousness so as to be able to *observe*, directly, everything that moves in the realm of the psychosomatic spatiality.
3. No judgement, no condemnation when faced by the various psychological contents, and not even exaltation or gratification. Observation – or better, being aware – must take place impersonally and with 'divine detachment'.

4. Integrating the contents within the consciousness, solving the object/'mass' into the sea of pure awareness, that is, awareness which is not conditioned by the 'sense of ego' (*ahaṁkāra*). It will be noted that this operation is the opposite of the previous state, in which it was the mercurial consciousness that was to be integrated within the qualitative content/object, thus finding itself in a state of subjection, a state of 'fall'.
5. Evoking universal energies in such a way as to transfigure *citta*, the totality of a psychosomatic spatiality. The evocation presupposes that the universal qualities are already within us; we shall have to bring them from potentiality into act, and the evocation constitutes a very powerful means of doing so, although sometimes it is not embraced by the disciple.

If these five factors are put into action, the *sādhanā* will proceed in an appropriate way; but it needs to be emphasised that Realisation – or Liberation from conflict/pain – has to be *loved* more than any other thing of a contingent and phenomenal order.

CONSCIOUSNESS

Those who follow *yoga* or an Eastern realisative way have undoubtedly come across the word 'consciousness'. Indeed, most schools of *yoga* maintain that the being, in its most profound expression, is nothing but Consciousness.

In the West there may be disciples of initiatory schools who do not succeed in comprehending themselves as Consciousness, because they are subject to the particular cultural form in which they live. Western literature, then, considers man as an 'ego' who determines himself in a world of phenomena, but it never presents him as unchanging Consciousness or Awareness.

Leaving aside a great part of that profane culture according to which consciousness represents a mere epiphenomenon of the material, physical structure, the Western initiatory tradition has defined the being principally in terms of attributes such as those of will, intelligence, activity, power, and so on. Even in this last sphere no precise reference to Consciousness can be found. Consciousness always remains as a function of a *content* of varying nature, and without the content there is no consciousness. It is not acknowledged that the cause can still subsist independently of the effect or of an accidental attribute.

If we refer to the Eastern Tradition, and in particular to the Indian, Consciousness appears as an essential factor; indeed, *it is the beginning and the end of the enquiry.* All those qualifications (will, and so on) are nothing but superimpositions on Consciousness, which is *causa sui.* The *Upaniṣads* declare that the *ātman/Brahman* is pure Consciousness (*caitanya*); it is *caitanya/sākṣin*: the Self is the Consciousness/Witness of the superimposed conditions, including the vehicles/bodies of manifestation; it is, again, *caitanya/svarūpa*, the essence of pure Consciousness. The 'ego' itself (*ahaṁkāra*), in which Western culture – and frequently that which is esoteric – is particularly interested, is nothing but a superimposition (*adhyāsa*) on pure Consciousness.

That consciousness which we normally profess in the waking state and others turns out in fact to be a mere reflection, a ray, of the absolute Consciousness or the *ātman*. In their work on the *Māṇḍūkya Upaniṣad*, Gauḍapāda and Śaṅkara have developed this topic and have concluded that everything appears and disappears on the horizon of our Consciousness, apart from Consciousness itself. If we examine the three states of waking, dream, and dreamless sleep, we find that in the waking state we are *aware* of the objective physical world; in dream that gross world vanishes, but not so the Consciousness, for it is aware of the dream objects, and this is a proof; in the state of dreamless sleep the dream object vanishes, but not so the Consciousness: in fact, we are able to say that we were aware of not having dreamt or of not having had experiences of any kind. As can be noted, the object – in its various configurations and its degrees of appearance – can be there or not be there, and yet the Consciousness does not vanish, for it is conscious of both the presence and the absence of the object, just as it is aware of the presence or absence of an idea/concept, an emotion, and the empirical ego itself.

If we study the psychological mechanisms of perception, we can verify that, generally speaking, we do not discover ourselves as consciousness, but see ourselves by means of its attributions, which function as mirrors, and we are reflected in them. It is from this perspective that we declare 'I am strong-willed, I am emotional, I am mind-centred, I am self-assertive, I am weak, and so on.' *Yoga* would say that we know ourselves by means of the *guṇas* (the qualities of energy). From this is born, too, the projection of the qualified and determined (*saguṇa*) God-Person, an inevitable occurrence if we conceive ourselves to be qualified beings. Absolute Being (*nirguṇa*: without *guṇas*) is beyond all limitation/qualification. The *jīva*/soul and even *Īśvara* are not isolated realities to which one must submit and which one must worship: they are states of Consciousness to be realised and revealed. It is a tendency of the being to identify itself as 'I am this or that'. 'This' and 'that', as we have noted, are qualitative superimpositions upon Consciousness. And yet there is a state in which *one is what one is*, without any qualitative or quantitative adjunct: these come after the *what one is*, but, unfortunately, through identification we come to consider ourselves not longer as 'I am what I am' but as merely 'this', and thus we become alienated.

When the reflection of embodied Consciousness – that is, the awareness which causes us to acknowledge ourselves as beings with a name and a form, located in a well-defined time and space – is re-united with its source, it realises itself in what *Vedānta* calls *ātman*, whose nature is fullness (*pūrṇatā*). Since this state cannot be described in words, being completely outside the conceptual reference-frame of quantity and quality, it has to be realised directly: we would say that it is a fact of the *actuation of consciousness*.

We may conclude that the realisative process in the East – but also the metaphysical process in the West (Parmenides, Plato, Plotinus, and so on) – consists in putting oneself into the state of the *ātman* by transcending the world of names and forms or the world of *māyā*; or, rather, by integrating within the sea of pure Consciousness the duality or dichotomy of *saṁsāra*.

THE DEVELOPMENT OF QUALITIES

The entire manifestation has many planes of existence, many worlds or *lokas*, and on every plane certain qualities (*guṇas*) are expressed in a more determining way (and therefore not in absolute terms).

The being – the *puruṣa*, the *ātman*, the soul, and so on – possesses various vehicles, or bodies of expression, by means of which it is possible for it to dwell and live on each plane of manifestation. The individualised aspect, as we know, is expressed in the threefold world of the *sthūlaloka*, the *kāmaloka*, the *manavaloka* (gross plane and lower subtle plane). On this threefold plane, in a determining way, are revealed those qualities which we call egoic, the qualities of *ahaṁkāra* or the 'sense of I', because these qualities rotate around a centre which we have come to define as the psychological *I*, the I which is separate and is opposed to *you*.

On this plane – which is psychologically objective and subjective – is expressed a kind of consciousness that is separative, acquisitive, dependent, and centripetal, with all that these qualities may imply: self-assertiveness, acquisitive desires of various kinds, a strong distinctiveness which creates an insurmountable duality, a feeling of exasperation with certain qualities that is so strong that it becomes overpowering, violence, and cynicism when faced by *you*. Let us always bear in mind that we have two focal centres: one is constituted by *ahaṁkāra*, which is impermanent, and the other is constituted by the Self, or pure Spirit, which is permanent.

By contrast, the plane of *buddhiloka*, *hiraṇyaloka*, or the *universal intelligible*, expresses a *unitive*, all-embracing consciousness/quality of positive solar love (not lunar, psychical, or sensory). Here there is polarity but not separateness or absolute distinction; there is all-embracing love and not egoistic and acquisitive desire: there is intuitive/enlightening knowledge and not mental acquisition of phenomenal data: there is universal will, will for the good, not egoic, self-assertive, acquisitive will, precisely because *ahaṁkāra*, or the sense of *I* and *you*, has vanished, disappeared. On this plane the consciousness corresponds to an *inclusive vision* of life, and so there is Accord/Harmony/Love/Beauty. The Consciousness, being brought to peace through the absence of the conflictual ego, expresses peace, expresses the ability to make a just response. In order to enter this plane, there are two pre-requisites, one consequent upon the other: *awakening of the Consciousness* and the *development of the vehicle* appropriate to the plane, together with its receptive faculties.

On the plane of *Īśvara*/Being/causal body, or Plato's World of Ideas, the *consciousness* must be expanded to include within it the totality of Life; the *other* is not outside Consciousness, but within it. Here the *Unity* that pervades everything may reveal itself. One's own body of expression is the entire plane of existence; here the *multiple* becomes *unity*, and forms resolve into non-form. In truth, countless, distinct, and separate planes do not exist: there is *only one* plane, with differing degrees of vibration; there are not great numbers of *beings*, but there is Being, which expresses itself in indefinite aspects of consciousness, just as our mind, while being one, expresses itself through manifold thoughts. It is the World of Ideas, of Archetypes, of Being. In this apparent multiplicity of places and aspects of consciousness, every being is free to go where it chooses. It depends entirely on what it wishes.

We attract to ourselves those experiences and those planes for which we are prepared and for which we ask, consciously or unconsciously. Now, we could ask ourselves: What do we want? What is the purpose of our embodied life? What direction do we wish to impart to our thoughts, our emotions? These questions are essential and deeply determining. If we cannot answer them, we shall have to make better use of the sword of discrimination, that it may give us the possibility of understanding our movement in life.

For example, if we wish to awaken the consciousness which is universal, related to *buddhi*, intelligible, and so on, and which corresponds to the existential plane of *hiraṇyaloka*, because this is our *aspiration* and the purpose of our life – although one may dwell on an individualised plane where there is a specific expression of the sense of being distinct, an urge to appropriate objects and feelings, the desire of the ego, violence in its various forms, cynicism with regard to *you* – well, in spite of all this, *we shall have to grit our teeth* and wake up and manifest a consciousness which is *inclusive*, *universal*, or noetic.

Although we find ourselves in this world populated by self-seeking beings who are trying to harm the *you*, and although we may be overpowered and mocked, we shall have to learn how to resist because, if we succeed in doing so, one day – which will not be far off – we shall finally be able to blow the trumpet of triumph and victory and settle down in our true homeland, which is composed of *pax profunda*, Harmony, and Beauty.

The key is *being able to resist 'evil', disharmony, disaccord, violence itself.* If we can *resist* human stupidity – *avidyā* – we shall gain victory over the threefold individualised world.

We need to consider that for those few years of earthly existence (embodiment) which life offers us (and remember that we spend half of our existence asleep), we could jeopardise eternal Bliss and peace. And for those of us who have comprehended the vision and the teaching, to betray this recognition would be sheer folly.

If for a miserable handful of coins and a pitiful compensation of sensory enjoyments – enjoyments which come and go – we had to jeopardise the splendour of the Beautiful, the

Freedom of *nirvāṇa*, and the Completeness of the Self, this would truly be committing suicide.

Again, if on account of our petty, wretched, mean squabbles we were to lose sight of discovering our Gold – the Gold of the Hermetic Philosophers, that Gold which consoles us for everything and which, once found, dissolves away millions of our yesterdays lived in material, psychological, and spiritual poverty – that would truly be to act irresponsibly.

Of course, we would all like to find ourselves in a world of peace, joy, harmony, and beauty, but, we may ask, what are we doing now to express those *qualities* which would indeed allow us to be in such a condition, since like attracts like?

'One becomes what one thinks; this is the eternal mystery,' says the *Maitry Upaniṣad*. 'Where your treasure is, there will your heart be also', says Jesus.[1]

Therefore, if we can *resist* and not react to disharmony and psychological incompleteness with disharmony and incompleteness, we shall be able to say that finally, here on this earth and in this very life, we have attained the Eleusinian Ωsucàa: the Peace and the Silence of the Sage.

[1] St Matthew, 6:21.

MASTER/DISCIPLE

At this time there exist in the West spiritual and philosophical realisative Teachings which may seem foreign to our culture, and some seekers, conditioned by the form/image of the Western religious Tradition, find themselves somewhat disorientated and confused with regard to these Teachings and also with regard to possible relationships with *Swāmis*, *Gurus*, *Lamas*, and so on.

In this short note we can, however, examine some aspects of this question.

Apart from some schools of an initiatory order, the West has a completely religious and theistic spiritual typology, with an impress which is theological, dogmatic, creationist, with the creature subordinated to the Creator, and with the 'gratuitous Grace' of God, and so on; moreover, it has a rigidly pyramidal ecclesiastical hierarchy. Christianity then aims at the 'salvation of the soul', which, having rebelled against God through an act of pride, must now appease Him with rites and penances in order to atone for such a 'sin'.

It would be helpful for an aspirant approaching the Eastern Teaching to appreciate certain fundamental differences and certain theological statements, in order to prevent his approach from presenting values which pertain to his religious heritage.

The East, for its part, offers a variety of Teachings which, although aiming at the same goal, are presented with different methodologies and attitudes. For example, in Buddhism there are many interpretations of the Buddha's Teaching: there are the currents, or schools of thought, of the *Vaibhāṣikas*, the *Sautrāntikas*, the *Mādhyamikas*, and the *Yogācāras*, just to name the principal ones, in addition to many subdivisions which can be related to the various Patriarchs who in the course of time have proposed new interpretations of the Teaching.

In Hinduism we have six schools which start off from different presuppositions, even though they all aim at the liberation of individuals. They are called *darśanas* (different viewpoints, all derived from the *Vedas*). Some aspirants, for example, may not know that the *Vedānta darśana* itself is sub-divided into three authoritative schools: the *Advaita Vedānta* of Śaṅkara, which is purely metaphysical (non-duality); *Viśiṣṭādvaita*, or qualified non-dualism, of Rāmānuja, with a more mystical/religious emphasis; and *Dvaita Vedānta* (dualistic) of Madhva. These are three great interpreters of the *Vedas/Upaniṣads* who – especially the first two – have a strong following. Then there is *Yoga*, which – as a *darśana* – was codified by Patañjali; but we have a truly vast variety of *yoga*, enough, we would say, to suit every taste and predisposition: it ranges from the *Haṭhayoga* of a particularly physical/prāṇic order all the way to *Asparśavāda* of a purely philosophical/metaphysical order. We are obliged to give only these brief hints – because the subject would fill a whole book[1] – but they are sufficient to enable the Western aspirant to understand that it would be helpful to have at least a general knowledge before approaching a particular Teaching and therefore a particular Instructor.

Let us go back to the Master/disciple relationship. According to our particular approach, the word 'Master' can have various connotations. From a certain point of view we may say that we are all masters of someone; even mothers and fathers are masters with regard to their own children. A school teacher is always a master in front of his pupils, and so on. In specific initiatory schools there is the level of Master. A Christian priest, a Muslim imam, a rabbi, and so on, are always Masters in relation to the faithful who need to be instructed in the Teaching

[1] For a deeper understanding, see *Indian Philosophy* by S. Radhakrishnan and *Essence & Purpose of Yoga* by Raphael. Aurea Vidyā, New York..

of Christ, Mohammed, or Moses. In the Hindu context, as in the Buddhist, we find different levels of Master: some impart only the Teaching or a *darśana* and can be considered to be excellent scholars (*paṇḍits*); others transmit what they themselves have assimilated and realised.

Having made these simple premises, we are able to ask ourselves: What is a Master?

Unless we wish to be superficial, we shall have to acknowledge first of all that in the spiritual realm the word 'Master' is very weighty and pregnant with meaning.

An authentic Master is the *embodiment* of a divine universal *quality*: it may be Love or Knowledge. He may be the embodiment of right action or the divine Will. A Master may even have integrated and transcended the qualities (*guṇas*) or the divine attributes, so that, having to work on the manifest plane, he may express them as necessity requires. We would say that this kind of 'non-Master' Master may embody the full range of *sattva* and vibrate on various wave-lengths, while remaining a unity, which is what happens with the white ray of light which synthesises the whole range of the sun's spectrum.

He is able to give each his own, because he does not have a *specific* teaching to offer, nor is he identified with a specific traditional Branch. In effect, he is not Hindu, not Buddhist, not Taoist, not a *yogi*, not a Christian, and not any other. *He is what he is*, outside the context of the *guṇas*. We would say that he is *nirguṇa* (without qualities/*guṇas*). This state of consciousness is undoubtedly very high. A Master, however, is one who embodies, lives, and expresses – through thought, word, and action – a traditional Teaching. This implies that a Master is a universal *channel*.

It is said that Jesus is the embodiment of Love, and Śaṅkara the embodiment of metaphysical Knowledge/Wisdom. Many *bhaktas* in India are embodiments of Love. In any case, what we wish to emphasise is that a Master *is no longer* an individual, a being with a will of his own; he no longer has anything of his own with regard to an individualised and egocentric condition. A Master, in fact, is simply an Embodiment, a mere channel. We would add that a Master is the embodiment of a Principle, an Idea (in the Platonic sense).

In the Middle Ages there came into existence a spiritual current of great import known as Quietism, according to which there are three levels of union:

1. With Jesus Christ as man/God.
2. With Jesus Christ as an exclusively divine *person*.
3. With the divine Essence itself; with God beyond persons and attributes.

This implies that there could be three levels of corresponding Masters or divine Incarnations. This current had a purely traditional connotation.

Some are not Masters, but simply preceptors; others have merely assimilated a Teaching theoretically, so that they, too, are able to transmit it, but they are very far from embodying or *being* that Teaching or knowledge. One has to take account of this, in order to prevent an aspirant from falling, sooner or later, into delusion and frustration. However, from a particular perspective, every thing is in its rightful place.

We have referred only to the Master, but what shall we say of aspirants and disciples? Here the view is much more varied. There are many aspirants, with different and, at times, disparate motivations.

Setting aside false disciples and false *gurus* (these, too, exist in this world of *māyā*), we can put the aspirants into three categories: aspirants properly so called; active disciples; initiates at various levels. An aspirant is seeking something which he has not yet found; he may move with great ease from one Teaching to another; he likes just to speak of spiritual matters; he interprets the Teaching according to that meaning which is convenient to him; at times he wishes to act as the 'messiah' and he causes many troubles; he speaks too much and realises little. He is at the stage of making adjustments and finding his balance, including his psychological balance; he is still attracted by things of the world; however, he is on the search, and something within him is moved or is moving; on the other hand, he has to start sooner or later.

The disciple is now committed and cannot turn back; he has 'entered the current'; he speaks little and seeks to realise. We would say that he has already made a choice; he is more focused and is following a well-defined *sādhanā*. He has appreciated that the way involves actuation rather than words. *Acknowledging* that within him there are many elements which are far from acceptable, he becomes humble and ready to serve. There are certain things which cannot yet be said to the aspirant, who might react, being too identified with individualised qualities to be able to acknowledge them or to withstand the impact concerning the truth about his true state; he might vacillate or run away. The disciple is already qualified, and the truth about his state of consciousness and his psychological qualities does not offend him; he is prepared for everything, because he is ready to 'die while alive'.

One who is initiated begins to embody, to live, aspects of universal truth and, according to the depth of his awakening, may also begin to be useful to others. There are several levels in initiation, the last of which brings the being out of the context of quality and quantity, individual and universal, as was suggested a little while ago.

But let us go back to the aspirant and the disciple and ask ourselves: What is the right approach with regard to the Teaching and the Instructor? The question is vast, of a definite import and interest, even if at first sight it might seem simple and irrelevant.

We shall deal merely with one negative aspect of approaching the relationship, specifically the *psychological dependence* of the aspirant/disciple on the Instructor and the Teaching.

There are natures which reveal a certain 'psychological weakness'. This may be a passivity that is innate in them, a sense of insecurity, a failure of their psychical complex to integrate with the centre of consciousness; it may be inadequate education that is seen as an inferiority problem, or many other deficiencies which might encourage a feeling of *dependence*, to compensate precisely for the lack, the lacuna, in the aspirant/disciple. Unfortunately, it has to be said that there are also Instructors who encourage a wrong approach such as this.

On the other hand, let us set aside those aspirants who go too far in the other direction: they are essentially independent, self-willed, intolerant of every kind of discipline and dependence, and we are not speaking of psychological dependence, which could also be understood, but of the proper relationship with the Teaching itself. We should not put them in the same category as aspirants, because they are too individualistic, self-assertive, and arrogant. On the way of Realisation dependence arising from an absence of psychological harmony could act as a brake and be disadvantageous to spiritual growth.

An Instructor who is worthy of the name puts forward the Teaching, and his principal objective is to *awaken the consciousness* to the recognition of its essential nature. The Instructor cannot act as father, mother, psychologist, professor, or fulfil any other function; although he already has these qualifications within him, his task is to put forward the Teaching and *awaken* the consciousness of the neophyte through his *spiritual influence*.

No instructor – not even with all his good will – could impart immortality, intelligence, will, or knowledge itself to someone who does not have it by nature. Everything is within us in the state of potentiality. The Instructor has the task of bringing what we really are from potentiality to act. There are Instructors who declare that they can bestow bliss, paradise on earth, Knowledge, and more besides, as if it were a question of oranges or potatoes. Some give mass initiations in large theatres or hotels, even in stadiums; but in the *kali yuga* we can expect anything to happen.

Plato would say that we are in the realm of *pístis*, of mere beliefs based on blind faith. There are false Instructors, and there are false aspirants/disciples; needless to say, many of these are seeking 'compensations' of various kinds[1], appreciation and approval for things which have no value, or relationships of a purely personal nature, and so on.

The relationship of the Instructor is that of *spiritual influence* and maieutics, because the neophyte is already a soul and is in possession of his divine faculties. It is assumed that an Instructor has transcended the individualised state and has positioned himself in the universal state, from which he sends down the Influence which, in fact, is going to stimulate the consciousness of the pupil, awakening it to its own actualisation.

The relationship of the Instructor to aspirant/disciple can also be woven from *silences*. Or rather, if the neophyte embraces this kind of relationship, he will gradually come to the stillness of the *guṇas* and communicate directly, from consciousness to consciousness, so that the influence would act immediately. We would say that this represents the true way for the transmutation of the *guṇas*, 'communion', the merging of consciousness. Speech often satisfies only the empirical *manas*/mind.

The influence can also be transmitted by means of a rite, but the way of operation is of little importance; what is important is that it comes from dimensions which are sacred, universal, and supra-sensible. If the candidate does not present an uncluttered consciousness, it may come about that the Influence forcefully transmits itself through psychical channels and comes into contact with individualised energies and qualities, stimulating them to a point where psychological imbalances are created. Whatever the type of being, it is still a vibrating reality and a transmitter of influences; it depends on its state of

---

[1] See 'Realization and Psychological Comfort' in *Essence & Purpose of Yoga* by Raphael. Op. cit.

consciousness, its spiritual initiatory dignity, whether it vibrates in one way rather than in another.

A professor offers the student a number of notions relating to the phenomenal world, which the student memorises and understands through his sensible intuition. The Instructor offers no notions, nor does he give 'lessons' in knowledge relating to the nature of Being; in fact, he *is* Knowledge, and, being such, he has no mental notion to offer and have memorised. He is spiritual living Will, universal living Love; such is a true and authentic Instructor, the Elder Brother, and so on, leaving the name of Master solely to Śiva, Master of the Instructors. In fact, we should consider ourselves to be disciples of the Greatest Master, who is indeed the *Mahāyogin* Śiva. The authentic Instructor seeks a responsive, active, and solar *subject* upon whom to pour the Influence, not a mere passive object in need of treatment and attention, matters of a different order which, to be resolved, must be treated in their specific context.

MIND AND CONSCIOUSNESS

Consciousness is what we can experience as the illumination of any datum to make it visible. It is therefore a beacon, a reflector, which makes it possible to know something.

The mind conceptualises what the senses transmit; Consciousness illumines everything and, in fact, makes it possible to be aware of objects. The senses can be quiescent, imperfect, or simply missing; the mind can remain completely silent, without producing thoughts; but Consciousness cannot be extinguished; this is why we are able to verify that we are conscious of the absence of perception, thoughts, and so on. This implies that – contrary to what is maintained, which is that once the object has disappeared, the Consciousness disappears, too – Consciousness in fact perdures beyond the silence of the senses, thoughts, and will. When we say that a person is in a state of unconsciousness, this means that the Consciousness has moved to other planes of existence. In fact, on returning we say, 'I have been unconscious.' This, again, is why, when the physical body has fallen asleep, we are conscious of dreams. From other perspectives we may say that, at the level of experience, Consciousness consists of a *Presence*, a *Being*, which has within it the capacity for intelligibility. Some philosophers consider it to be Intelligence as a factor of knowledge, beyond the dualistic, conceptualising, and representative mind.

Vedānta considers *Īśvara*, Being, as *sat* (Being), *cit* (Consciousness/Knowledge), and *ānanda* (fullness). The *noûs* of ancient Greece is also considered as intelligence, conscious being.

This consciousness, at the physical/gross level, is a reflection of the Soul (universal consciousness), and it would be precisely this reflection that leaves the physical body and flies towards its divine counterpart, and not the body, which, having perished, frees the reflection.

The 'sense of I' abides in the mind, that of *being* abides in Consciousness. Mind (*manas*) understands; Consciousness reveals (comprehends). Thinking is the function of mind; *being* is the function of Consciousness.

The 'I' sees not, but thinks it knows and believes it is; Consciousness sees, knows, *is*.

The 'I' is born from a false perspective, which in turn is moved by a desire to appropriate. The 'I' is the 'offspring' of the mind, which has drawn subjectivity from Consciousness: 'I' and 'not I' are the same thing, object; it is only by means of reflection that the individual can declare, 'I am'. And this '*I* am', '*I* exist', creates a distance (a space) from what is not 'I' and allows the view of oneself as distinct from everything else: the individual, as the observing subject, on one side, and the world, as the observed object, on the other side. But this duality – which is irreducible for the 'I' – exists in reality only on account of the movement of that 'part' which has apparently been drawn from the all, on account of its ... going outside. This duality/movement becomes simultaneously the effect and the cause of the 'I', since it allows the 'I' to be perpetuated.

Leaving oneself (being) in order to *think* of being. Falsifying reality for the pleasure of ... dreaming. This is hallucination, but not for the 'I' which likes to think, dream, and be deceived.

The mind fears death because it knows not life. Its pseudo-life is made of memories and expectations, of movement/process/becoming, and therefore of death. We may say that it fears death because it has a presentiment of it. Life is constant presence, and thus immortality. Life is Consciousness.

The mind lives on 'non-existents': the past, which is no longer, and the future, which is not yet. Consciousness lives outside time: it lives on eternals, on realities, on being.

To have no history (past) and no evolution (future) means – for the 'I' – flattening, a uniformity, disappearance. But being born and dying are the inexorable destiny of all things ephemeral.

Of course, the mind *understands* all this, but does not *comprehend* it. We emphasise these words because they clearly indicate two different types of operation. The Italian word translated as 'understands' is 'intende', which comes from the Latin 'intendere' – 'to tend towards' – and indicates an exodus, a movement outwards. Thus one knows in a way that is mediated, superficial, and always at the level of the relationship (duality) of subject/object. The word 'comprehends', on the other hand, comes from the Latin 'comprehendere' – 'to embrace, include' – and indicates a precise movement of withdrawal, absorption, a movement towards the inner. In this second case one knows in a way that is direct, immediate, total.

The mind can understand a concept and can build on it other theories and concepts without producing any transformations in the individual, since its action, as we have said, affects only the outer. We could say that it is incapable of producing a 'third factor'. We had one concept, and now we have a hundred, but nothing has changed within us: what we were, we are.

Catharsis is made possible only by *comprehension*, by making that datum profoundly ours, to the point where duality disappears. Absorbed by Consciousness, the concept understood by the mind – or any other idea that is appreciated at the mental level only – comes to life and is expressed in the individual, through the individual. The original subject/object relationship is now resolved into a unity, since the idea has been made flesh.

The divergence between theory and practice, speaking and living, is all here: in understanding or in comprehending. Therefore, according to whether it is the mind or the Consciousness that is going to be expressed, we may possess the concept of a truth or we may live that truth.

Man acts as if totally absent, for he lives constantly on the projections of imagination. The mind superimposes itself on Consciousness, on a *presence* which is, so many 'photograms' at such close intervals that they give the *impression of movement*, innumerable 'flashes' which dazzle the sight and cloud the intellect, and the individual dreams and ... forgets.

But behind these dreams there perdures a continuity of being, an uninterrupted thread of existence, of which we are aware only for short moments. It would be sufficient not to break the contact, and then what fear would we still have of death?

To anchor oneself to being (*sat*) means to re-discover one's own centre, security, silence, peace. Suffering stops with the cessation of movement/desire, anxiety, fear.

To renew contact with Consciousness/Being and to stabilise it means to move from the circumference to the centre, from the aspect of form to the aspect of life.

In living impersonally – no longer in terms of name and form – the ego/mind restores to Consciousness the subjectivity which it had commandeered, and all distinction is inevitably obliterated. Since 'only Principle sees Principle, and similars merge only with similars', life then merges with life, and the being *lives* the unity of the whole.

THE INNER ORDAINER

To the concept of *ordainer* is linked that of intelligence; we speak, in fact, of an *ordaining intelligence*. This faculty is identified first with the rational/empirical mind, or practical reason, which gives order to sensations and emotions, then with the intuitive supra-sensible mind, or pure reason, which does not select, analyse, or distinguish, but synthesises, re-unites, includes.

It is this inclusive or higher mind which transcends the limits of the rational by giving order to it and, consequently, to the emotions and the instincts. It is this all-embracing movement which starts from the sacred heart of the Being and – precisely because it pertains to a plane of co-ordinates that is completely different from that sensory realm of individuality – may justifiably be considered divine.

On the Sephirotic Tree this Ordainer is represented, in *Tiphereth*, by the Intelligence Raphael, who presides over this *sephirah*. He lives at the heart of the Tree, at the central point of Being, in the shining tabernacle or niche, as the guardian of Love/Beauty, which gives order and heals.[1]

The first step on the way of comprehension/acceptance – that is, of the opening of the Heart – consists, for the disciple, in becoming aware of the disorder of the psychical energy within himself, by observing without judging.

Instinct, emotion, thought. And behind these movements there is the *mind*. But what is the mind? What is its rôle?

---

[1] See *The Pathway of Fire according to the Qabbālāh* by Raphael. Aurea Vidyā, New York.

The mind is a vehicle, an instrument, a *body*. Body is everything that occupies part of space – and the mind, in fact, occupies a space within Being, and at the coarse physical level it expresses itself by means of brain cells.

The mind is *matter*. In fact, all bodies, since they occupy a portion of space, consist of substance.

The mind is *plastic substance*. In effect, the substance or quality of the mind is plasticity.

If, therefore, the mind is a body and, as such, cannot move of itself [1], it follows that it will move only through the intervention of a force. This force, breaking the mind's state of stillness, will release energy that will go and strike the neighbouring emotional body, whose released energy will, in its turn, produce the same effect on the neighbouring physical body, or instinctive sphere, in a dangerous chain reaction. This is when the attention of the disciple moves from the mind/vehicle to the force which is activating this vehicle.

According to the Tradition of *Vedānta*, what moves the mind or *prakṛti* (individual and universal) are the *guṇas*: *tamas*, *rajas*, and *sattva*:

> '*Sattva*, *rajas*, and *tamas* are allotropic states of substance/ *prakṛti*. As long as arrhythmy, disharmony and the prevalence of one over another exist among them, there will also be activity, disorder, and movement as we understand it; when they are in perfect equilibrium, there will be stillness, rhythm and harmony.'[2]

From what we have said so far, it seems to us that two conclusions are clear:

1. One needs to act upon the *guṇas* if one wishes to resolve the cause of the disorder.

---

[1] 'The characteristic of bodies is inertia': this is the first principle of dynamics intuited by Leonardo da Vinci.

[2] Commentary by Raphael to *sūtra* 104 of Śaṅkara's *Vivekacūḍāmaṇi*. For the *guṇas*, see Chapter XIV of the *Bhagavadgītā*.

2. In particular, the mind will re-discover its state of quietness only when the dominant *guṇa* in the individual has been restored to equilibrium with the other two.

It is a question, depending on the case, of activating or de-activating: for example, more mercy (*sattva*) and less judgement (*rajas*); or more comprehension (*sattva*) and less dullness (*tamas*). As we can observe, it is always *sattva* which brings about the balance.

Moving to the practical aspect, we may say that to balance the *guṇas* requires a certain commitment, especially if one has not comprehended that it is not a matter of imposing a kind of behaviour upon oneself, but of modifying one's own vibratory state.

The opening of the Heart is therefore a condition *sine qua non* for moving away from the individualised, disordered, and conflictual sphere and embracing that Universal which represents the destiny of every soul enamoured of Beauty and Love.

The opening of the Heart is the way towards principial Unity, towards the primordial Ordainer, or the ontological Factor, the *Īśvara* of *Vedānta*, which the sixth verse of the *Māṇḍūkya Upaniṣad* defines thus:

> 'This is the Lord of All (*sarveśvaraḥ*), the Omniscient, the inner Ordainer, the Source of all; in it all things originate and dissolve.'

Īśvara, or *Kether* in *Qabbālāh*, or Plato's World of Ideas, represents the Alpha and the Omega, because in it all forms really have their beginning and their end; it represents the completion of the Great Work, the entrance to the Infinite, the Uncaused, the Absolute/Unmanifest, beyond all objects and all subjects, all effects and their causes, the eternal abode of authentic Fullness, birthless and non-dual.

KARMAN OR SACRIFICE

In every branch of the Tradition sacrificial action is taken into account. In the *Vedas* themselves an entire section, the *Brāhmaṇas*, is devoted exclusively to rite, or sacrifice.

The word 'sacrifice' comes from the Latin 'sacrum facere' ('to make sacred'), and this is its true meaning, even though this has been lost in the course of time.

Rite employs gesture and formula as means of connecting with the divine: they both serve to evoke in the officiant the right position of consciousness which is indispensable for the evocation. Rite, therefore, is a combination of *form* and *soul*. But even if one dispenses with form – which in effect constitutes a preliminary – soul, the consciousness aspect, cannot possibly be omitted. Thus rite is realised through the figure of the *Sacerdos*, who must necessarily make himself *available* to the Sacred and offer himself to the universal, from which the spiritual Influence comes down. He must possess priestly Dignity. Only then can he become Sacred, like the act itself, that is, he becomes someone *consecrated*.

In its turn, the *consecratio*, in its ritual aspect, represents the seal given to a state of consciousness which already exists in all its effects, like the *consecratio* of the knight at the moment of investiture. Thus it follows a consecration of oneself which the person has already contemplated and realised. This is the *surrender* envisaged by every Tradition.

There are levels of surrendering, or consecration, which are, of course, preliminary to full surrender, or consecration.

To consecrate oneself to the Universal means dying to the individualised. And a consecration, in truth, betokens a death and a birth, that is, an initiation.

We spoke just now of levels. There is no doubt that a consecration – at whatever level is being referred to – involves the whole being: body, soul, spirit, or, as Alchemy calls them, salt, mercury, sulphur.

The word 'sacrifice' contains the idea of the sacred and therefore gives us a clearer picture than the word 'rite'. But 'rite' also has a very precise etymological meaning.

'Rite'- *ritus* in Latin, *rythmos* in Greek – is derived from the Sanskrit *ṛta*, which signifies cosmic Order. Rite therefore has a function of connecting to the universals to whose rhythm it must, of course, be attuned.

We have used the words 'function', 'rhythm', and 'order', all of which are to do with acting. In fact, there is no action which does not have its own function, which does not follow its own rhythm, which does not move towards a balance (order).

The Vedic Tradition uses the word *karman* (action) as a synonym for 'rite/sacrifice'. Action, in truth, the only action worthy of the name, is that which is accomplished in a ritual way, a sacred way, in conformity with the cosmic Order. An individual's action is a reaction rather than an action, an impulse to do, which is determined, of course, not by his own will, but by his subconscious. Thus there is no freedom in his movements, but only necessity, subjection, and duality.

The subconscious (ego) makes the individual separate from the universal context. The result is that his action turns out to be essentially profane.

To transcend individuality means to be re-united with that All which represents the very meaning of the existence of every single aspect, apart from the fact that the individual, by re-instating himself in his true existential condition, restores to Existence a free space (channel), which he himself has taken from it.

Action presupposes an impersonal consciousness, like that of the priest during the performance of his office. In the absence of an agent (I), (profane) action is transcended and becomes non-action, becomes *ṛta*.

Every act can thus become a rite, a sacrificial act, the expression of the One in the multiple. It is sufficient to surrender, sufficient to 'die to oneself', to one's own desires, one's own claims, one's own expectations.

> 'The activity of an ordinary individual consists of *reactions* that are expressions of his particular individualised constitution. He is an 'ego' surrounded by pleasant and unpleasant, attractive and repellent objects/events, and his actions are in conformity with his desires, his fears, and his past. Thus all his reactions are false, partial, and inadequate, because they are based on the foundation of the ego, a foundation of separateness.
> The perfect Realised Man reaches the state where there is no 'I', no desire, where all the fires of reaction have been extinguished, and this gives rise to a type of action which is impersonal, spontaneous, innocent, and genuine.'[1]

[1] Raphael, *The Threefold Pathway of Fire*, II. I. 3.

DHARMA

> 'Better one's own *dharma*, however imperfectly performed, than the *dharma* of others, even if perfectly accomplished. It is better to die fulfilling one's own *dharma*, because that of another causes harm.'[1]

At first sight this *śloka* might seem disconcerting, because it is proposing a dismissal of others' needs in order to focus one's attention upon oneself. This might seem to be an incitement to egoism.

Let us try first of all to understand what is meant by the word *dharma*. In general terms, it indicates a 'way of being', a nature suitable for working in conformity with the state of consciousness. From other perspectives, *dharma* is that law which Divinity imposes upon itself. According to Plato, too, the Being-One manifests itself in the world as 'norm' and 'measure'. Unity in its relationship with the world is the supreme measure of being.

In our specific case, it is the duty/law which the individual has to fulfil in order to be in harmony with the purpose of his own embodiment and with the context in which his action has to be carried out.

We may bear in mind that the *jīva*/soul, before being embodied, has, under pressure from the *guṇas*, of course, already chosen the general lines to be followed. Thus the *śloka* recommends fulfilling one's own *dharma* in particular in order to avoid the non-accomplishment of the commitments undertaken at that time. But does this imply that we should take no interest

---

[1] *Bhagavadg¤tā*, III, 35, edited by Raphael, op. cit.

in others? Not really. The *śloka* is principally directed to those disciples who are extrovert and conditioned by activism and who are even in the habit of performing the actions of others.

Each embodied being has its own *karma* and its own *dharma*, which means that it has the duty of fulfilling its own *karma*, and no one should take the embodied being away from its responsibility because that would be stunting its growth. The help that can be given is that of encouraging the person's development; but if one does not work intelligently and in conformity with the proper relationship, one may even cause harm to the awakening of consciousness in others.

The *dharma* of a student, for example, is to study, to be diligent in attending school, and to develop the mind, the intuition, the will, and so on. Now, if we take over the student's development of his work, the results will be:

1. The abandonment of our *dharma*.
2. The lack of growth in the student.
3. A wrong relationship with society, because one day we shall offer it an individual who is unprepared.

It is one thing to help someone develop his own *dharma*, especially if he has a heavy *karma*, and it is another thing to take from him not only the responsibility, but even the very performance of action, for his own *karma/dharma*.

The resolution of this state of affairs inevitably presupposes two things:

1. Mastery of one's own energies which are qualified by *rajas* and tend to be over-powering.
2. Control of the emotions to prevent them from lapsing into sentimentality and therefore into weakness.

To help others is an imperative of our own *dharma*, but the *measure* that we must adopt in fulfilling the action must be evaluated and subordinated to the faculty of intelligence. To help others is very difficult, more difficult than one may think, and we often work superficially; we generally offer responses which have been concocted beforehand, so that, without wishing to, we impose our own convictions and our own way of working.

To comprehend Socratic maieutics and to be able to apply it would be excellent, but unfortunately we are always *impelled* to hand out advice even when it isn't asked for. The *śloka* is suggesting to us that action could cause harm even to ourselves, who have put ourselves into the state of wanting to forcibly carry out another person's *dharma*, instead of simply encouraging and easing it, being totally free from the game of attraction and repulsion.

Better therefore to fulfil our own *dharma*, even with some mistakes, than that of others, even in an exemplary fashion.

PLEASURE/PAIN

Without a *subject* and an *object*, pleasure/pain cannot exist: dualism is the basic prerequisite of any experience.

From the moment they appear, the two polar terms create time and space and therefore relationship, dependence. And from this dependence/bond are born all the reactions of consciousness on the plane of manifest duality, with form or without. We may say that the whole range of pleasure/pain, that is, the countless gradations of *feeling*, from Heaven to Hell, exists by reason of the dependence/identification of the subject with the object.

To identify oneself with a datum, it is necessary, before all else, to *believe* in it. Then, as a natural consequence, come movement and identification. This is a faculty of the psyche, which, according to the direction it takes, becomes limited or liberated, dives down or rises up, lives in ignorance or knowledge. But 'dream' and 'waking' are not two worlds that stand apart, distinct and in opposition: they reflect nothing more than degrees of clarity of consciousness.

Duality is time/space/causality. But is duality an absolute reality?

When the mind thinks, it seems to split itself into subject and object, thus creating an apparent duality, for thought is not separate from thinker. Thought is not outside thinker (space) and is not born before or after thinker (time), nor, much less, is it its own cause; thought lives *in* thinker, *with* thinker, *on account of* thinker. Then what do space and time represent, except a pure and simple imagination? What do hallucinations, dreams, and the ravings of the mind have to do with the underlying reality (consciousness)?

However, we are free to project whatever ideation we choose. But if the ideation becomes identification, then the actor will inevitably undergo events, which may even be dramatic.

To think without identification is to think without any dramatisation.

Thus the observer does not bring suffering upon himself as long as he remains conscious, but he does so when he abandons himself to the show, forgetting what he knows, forgetting himself. The 'dead man' is not dead, but if he believes that he is, the non-dead man is as if he were dead.

When I observe my reflected image, I cannot say that it is I myself (reality), since I can break the mirror and annihilate the image. But because I can see something, it is a question of understanding what it is that I see. This comprehension safeguards me from identification, allows me to remain in my state of an observing being, and prevents me from 'falling' into the image, from succumbing to it, as happens in the case of Narcissus, who, identifying himself with his reflected image, succumbs: this is the 'fall'.

Therefore, if I believe that image to be real/absolute, the mistaken evaluation will load the subject/object relationship with never-ending conflicts. The vicissitudes of the projection/reflection will make me so involved that I shall no longer find it very easy to re-discover my own reality of being, to discern the true from the false. Pleasure and pain will thus alternate endlessly, by accompanying the movement/rhythm of that image. I may experience moments of uplift (pleasure) or frustration (pain). I can also reject the image (repulsion), hate it, destroy it, or think of doing so. And all of this *feeling* begins from the moment I put myself in front of myself, objectify myself, thus creating an apparent and illusory duality, with which I identify myself.

But what is the purpose of the objectivisation? The ego makes use of it – without knowing – as a means of knowledge. The objectivisation allows the perception, albeit modified, of subjective, impersonal qualities which would otherwise remain unknown.

The love that the ego knows bears little resemblance to Love/Principle. Sensory love depends on a 'second', is acquainted with happiness and unhappiness, is born, changes, comes to an end. But to know that love exists is already quite a lot. To discover its true essence will constitute a second movement, this time to be accomplished by consciousness. Then the being will comprehend that everything objective is a mere reflection of itself: love, will, knowledge are its constituent elements. Previously it knew them as external to itself and desired them: now it no longer makes sense to desire them.

We have seen that objectivisation is used by the ego to know/feel. And this sensory knowledge, the link between knower and known, identifies itself with pleasure/pain. But for a pure (non-dual) consciousness, which has transcended desire, which sees the 'second' for what it is, which *knows* truly, and which is no longer moved by interests of any nature whatsoever, what reason is there to objectify?

Līlā, the divine play, is action/non-action. It is the innocent expression of life, the verse of the poet, the song of the lark, the opening of a corolla, the fragrance of freedom which is released by every 'sound' vibrating in attunement with the Beautiful, the True, the One.

It is innocence, freedom, and also humility. Humility which is not a feeling but an expression of the being which lives the Truth. And the Truth, say the Sages, is non-duality.

> 'Where one sees the other, hears the other, knows the other, there is finiteness.'[1]

And therefore error, limit, dependence, pleasure/pain.

---

[1] *Chāndogya Upaniṣad*, VII. XXIV. 1.

'Where one sees no other, hears no other, knows no other, there is the infinite (*bhūman*).'[1]

And therefore truth, freedom, immortality, silence.

---

[1] *Ibid.*

HEART AND LOVE

Heart and *love* are often spoken of: words that are not easy to comprehend, even though they might seem to be so. Moreover, they can arouse responses of an individualised and emotive order, and therefore subsequent psychological attitudes.

Now it needs to be said that when these words are referred to from an initiatory or realisative perspective, they have nothing in common with the meanings of a strongly profane order. It is good, therefore, to reflect, because proper comprehension will take us to the realisation of the Heart, and thus of Love.

Heart is the symbol of the centre, whether we are dealing with the microcosmic centre (individual being) or with the macrocosmic centre (universal Being).

Heart is the vital centre in which resides the *ātmā* (soul).

> 'This *ātman*, which resides in my heart, is smaller than a grain of rice, smaller than a grain of barley, smaller than a mustard-seed, smaller even than the kernel of a mustard-seed. This *ātman*, which is in my heart, is bigger than the earth, bigger than the intermediate sky, bigger than the sky, bigger than [all] these worlds ... In this citadel of *Brahman* there is a small receptacle in the shape of a lotus flower. Inside this there is a tiny space (*ākāśa*). You should find what is inside it; That, in truth, is what you must know.'[1]

> 'In that point I say truly that the spirit of life, which dwells in the most secret chamber of the heart ...'[2]

The centre (*cakra*) has as its geometric symbol two interlacing triangles in the shape of a hexagon. This represents the synthesis of total being; it is the abode of the *Puruṣa*,

---

[1] *Chāndogya Upaniṣad*, III. XIV. 3; VIII. I. 1.

[2] Dante, *Vita nova*, II. 4.

the *jīvātman*, as the 'Fire which shines unwaveringly in the windless abode'. It has twelve energy petals, another symbol of perfection and completeness.

> ' "O Yama, thou who knowest the Fire which leadeth to Heaven, do thou reveal it unto me, who am full of faith."
>
> ' "I shall teach thee that Fire, O Nachiketas, which will exalt thee to Heaven. Know thou that the Fire is the means for gaining infinite worlds; it is their very foundation and is hidden in a secret place [the centre of the heart]." Then he revealed unto him that Fire, wellspring of the world.'[1]

The heart is the Hermetic *athanor*, where the Great Work is accomplished. When the central vital Fire has consumed the peripheral individualised will-o'-the-wisps, it shines with the brilliance of a thousand suns.[2]

In the centre of the Heart is (initiatory) death, but in the same centre is the 'second birth', the awakening to what one really is. In the Heart, illusion/*avidyā* is extinguished, and wisdom/*Vidyā* is revealed, by whose means one flies towards the Infinite.

Knowledge of the Heart is divine Knowledge (*brahmavidyā*), and it pervades all the rays that form universal life.

Sensory knowledge is knowledge of phenomena, of forms which come and go, appear and disappear. This is why sensory empirical knowledge always has to be rectified, brought up to date: there isn't time to define a phenomenon, because it has already disappeared.

We need to distinguish between principial Knowledge, Knowledge of the heart or supreme Knowledge (*paravidyā*), and knowledge which is formal, representative or secondary (*aparavidyā*).

---

[1] *Kaṭha Upaniṣad*, I. I. 13-15.

[2] For further references to the Fires, see 'The Fire of Life' in *The Threefold Pathway of Fire* by Raphael, op. cit.

From the furthest circumference of quantity, multiplicity, or differentiation, the consciousness withdraws itself to the centre of the Personality/Quality, and finally to the centre of the principial Heart as the Essence of all.

The heart represents the point which, having no dimension ('smaller than a grain of rice' and so on), generates line, volume, space, forms, which can be 'bigger than the Earth' and so on.

The heart is the microcosmic spiritual sun, which in its turn conceals within itself the universal central Sun, and our *senses* cannot see it, touch it, or hear it.

The universal heart represents the great Unity, the great Peak, the great Sun, which is seen by the Sages at midnight, when its 'reflection', the daytime sun, is eclipsed.

> 'Ruling beyond the ether, the middle throne, and having as your face a dazzling circle, which is the Heart of the World, thou crownest all with a providence that is able to reveal intelligence.'[1]

Just as the physical heart spreads its warmth and life-blood to the whole of the cellular organism, so the heart of Heaven irradiates its life-giving warmth and its clarifying light to the entire manifestation, both the formal and the principial a-formal.

To be at the centre of the Heart means to have reached the end of the pilgrimage of *saṁsāra*. The central Fire is that Fire which diffuses Intelligence (*buddhi*) and Love/Bliss (*ānanda*). The sacred Heart is not the organic heart, although this may be understood to be so in an analogical sense, nor is it that heart which is commonly likened to emotion, which is of a psychological order.

The Fire that is found at the centre of the Heart is light and heat, that is, Intelligence and Love. But it is good to repeat that the love of the Heart is not emotion, or feeling. If Intelligence enlightens, love unifies and abolishes distance. Love is that magical factor which turns multiplicity into a 'synthesis'

[1] Proclus, *Hymn to the Sun*.

(unity) and nullifies distance, thus revealing the undivided point. 'God is Love' because Principle is Unity.

> 'Loving others means *reintegrating* them within one's own vibrating String. In this way, Love/Harmony is not an act of identification with the emotions of others and with their forms/ bodies, which are merely the *vessels* through which harmony has to reveal itself. It is not being involved in, or overwhelmed by, the physical movement of others. To express it differently, it is not a passive weakness but something more; it is resting in principial Identity, in the universal Note.
> It is not the condensed or individualised Fire that one should look at, but the very Essence of Fire.'[1]

The sensory mind splits, separates, and rejects; the *Intellect of Love*, or *Amor Dei intellectualis*, attracts, unifies, and fuses.

In the 'fall' Adam becomes a knower of good and evil, and this means that from that moment he sees the single Reality – corresponding to the indivisible Tree of Life – as dual. The point splits, and distances (subject and object) appear. Attraction/ repulsion keeps the duality alive: Love annuls it.

Feeling is the gratification of an emotional, egoic desire: Love is annulment of self as ego, the goal where every sense finds peace. Love 'comprehends' because it creates identity: analytical thought compares, discriminates, and divides.

Heart/Love is often compared to the sun, and mind/brain to the moon.

Moonlight is simply a reflection of sunlight; moonlight exists only on account of the sun.

Heart/Love is intuitive, comprehensive Intelligence: the brain, as the seat of the mind (*manas*), is discursive, rational intelligence. Discursive reason is a purely human and individual faculty; intuitive reason, or pure reason, is a supra-individual faculty. The first is mediate (moon): the second is immediate (sun).

---

[1] *The Threefold Pathway of Fire*, I. II. 27.

The knowledge of the heart is the direct perception of the intelligible Fire, the Fire irradiated by the spiritual Sun as the Heart of the world.

Emotion and Love have the same correlation as that between mediate knowledge and immediate knowledge. The Sun is the Love which lives by its own life, because it is that Point where all the elements (distances) have resolved into the single essential element: the moon is emotion which lives by reflection, relationships, haziness, and even blindness. Emotion/desire/passion distorts and blinds: Love bestows freedom and intuition.

We need to distinguish between sacred Love and profane love. The first is supra-individual and supra-sensory: the second operates in the realm of the individual and particular.

Two Souls which meet each other, and live Love, merge and become a single reality, having resolved space.

Harmony is the effect of re-establishing unity and synthesis.

Love manifests unity and harmony, and harmony is Beauty. Beauty is a unifying ecstasy. Love, Harmony, Beauty are consubstantial with the vital Principle and Unity, while repulsion and disharmony and every kind of ugliness are the legacy of the conflictual ego.

In the *Qabbālāh*, the *sephirah Tiphereth* signifies Beauty and constitutes the heart of the sephirotic Tree. It is the abode of the *jīvātman*, that is, of the Son of the Father (*Kether*) who dwells in Heaven. In the deep cave of the heart lives *Tiphereth*, who, at the plane of the manifest, represents the solar centre, while *Kether* represents the polar Centre not only of the formal manifest plane but also of the a-formal manifest plane, being the essential principial Point from which everything comes forth and on which everything depends. Around *Tiphereth* rotate all the manifest Powers/Intelligences, just as all the planets rotate around the sun in the solar system. Its Beauty irradiates the unifying Love of the *sephiroth*. The initiation of *Tiphereth* opens the eye of Harmony, because life is seen in terms of Harmony/Accord: the unilateralisms, the extremes, and the divisions of the individual *sephiroth* vanish, and microcosmic man merges with macrocosmic man in the Beauty of unity and synthesis. *Tiphereth* is Love in action, because it represents the cosmic Christ, the point of conjunction between the universal and the particular, the central point of the cross. Multiplicity, as seen by *Tiphereth*, is nothing other than the projection of countless vibrating rays which come from the single Centre of the heart. What unites the rays is Love; what the rays sound is Harmony; what they reveal is Beauty.

In its turn, emotion is the focal centre standing between instinct (physical) and rational mind (psychical); it unites the coarse/physical with the subtle/psychical. It operates in the intra-individual and the particular. To express itself the ego makes use of this centre, just as – on a higher turn of the spiral - the Self makes use of Love.

Emotion/feeling lives and perpetuates itself in the realm of *avidyā*, while Love lives and perpetuates itself in the realm of *vidyā*/wisdom/comprehension.

In the realm of emotion we have acquisition, attraction/ repulsion, aroused by the subconscious or by the instinct of animal nature. Emotion is expressed in time and space; it is a movement which is born, grows, and vanishes.

Feeling is a quality particular to the sentient ego, and its appearance depends on external stimulus.

Love, by contrast, is born independently of objective factors, being beyond time and space.

Love is immortal, because it is reality, while attraction/ repulsion is instability, because it is merely a movement in time.

The 'Knowledge of the Heart' (*hṛdayavidyā*) is knowledge of Love, knowledge of what is the deepest, most essential, innermost, and most noumenal within the being.

Love radiates *gnosis*: egoic emotion, by contrast, is mere desire. Love is centrifugal; it is warmth which spreads out without returning: desire/emotion is centripetal; it attracts the object to itself in order to be able to capture it.

Christ said, 'No man cometh unto the Father but by me', which is equivalent to saying that no one comes to the Father except through Love.

We have seen that *Tiphereth* is the Son of *Kether* on the plane of the manifest. To speak in terms of *Tiphereth*, of Christ, of the Son, of Love, is the same thing.

Love/Son unites individual man with universal man, creature with Creator, phenomenon with noumenon, substance with essence. Love is the *Logos*, the intermediary between the universal unmanifest pole and the manifest peripheral world.

Love is a quality of fullness. It fuses, resolves, and frees, while emotion is a conservative and acquisitive quality. The emotional ego has to acquire and obtain what it does not have by nature, so that it needs support, something to depend on.

The ego has put on a pedestal its own feelings, its own weakness, its own dependence, and its own insecurity. When we praise emotion exclusively, we are praising the ego, but the ego, simply to perpetuate itself, pays no heed to its own incompleteness. If the ego/emotion *feels*, it attracts the object to itself and is even capable of dying for it; if it does not *feel*, it remains completely indifferent to the world which surrounds it; if it then *feels* repulsed, it is capable even of insulting, mortifying, killing. As the psychologists say, the ego expresses itself with love/hatred. However, Love, as we understand it, does not belong to the ego. The ego makes use of some universal/principial qualifications, merely to degrade them, overturn them, in accordance with its method of *individualising* and particularising. If someone thinks – wrongly – that one should be insensitive, indifferent, and cold, it would be good to re-read what we have written on Love. An insensitive person neither *feels* emotionally nor loves. An indifferent person vegetates in no man's land; he is more isolated than all beings; he is the only one who doesn't make relationships, the only one who is incapable of seeing, feeling, or comprehending. Love is comprehension, and a heart that comprehends cannot be egoistic, or weak, or insensitive. As we have seen, comprehension is intelligence, and an intelligent heart cannot be cold, hard, or cynical.

Feeling is a disordered flow of emotions, impressions, sensations. The Heart fixes the flow, dissolves the impressions, renders the substance virginal. The Heart is *sulphur*, which burns mercurial time to ashes.

In thought/emotion there are doubts, uncertainties, excruciating expectations: in the Heart there are truth/certainty, the rhythm of eternity, and creative freedom.

If one is a 'Fedele d'Amore'[1], the eye of vision opens to the infinities of the heavens. Only then can one discover that every point of support no longer has any use.

Retracing the way of the Manes, one discovers earth, water, fire, and finally air; then the gates which conceal the Heart swing open and the pilgrim can take possession of the sparkling diamond.

If one lives in emotion and with emotion, the water will drown the careless experiencer; again, if one stays too long in the earthly or vulgar fire, the hallucinatory mental images will create mazes and webs that imprison and confuse.

The Way of the Heart is the way of the arrow which pierces the cloud of *avidyā* and bestows rainbows of uncreated light.

In emotion and with emotion, the acquisitive saṁsāric ego operates: in Love and with Love is expressed the Self, whose nature is fullness and bliss. The ego lives on weakness, even when it is violent: the Self reveals peace and harmony, composure and silence. 'My peace I give unto you. Not as the world giveth, give I unto you,' says Jesus.

Love pertains to the universal Being, emotion to the particular individual. The universal *Puruṣa* is the heart of life, where all particular possibilities find their solution. On the way of Return, the realisation of the Heart is an indisputable necessity.

[1] *Fedeli d'Amore*: (Followers of Love). A Confraternity in Medieval Italy, of which Dante himself was a member. They communicated to each other, in veiled rhyme and prose, their acknowledgement of the Science of Love.

One who has reached the centre of the Heart has reached not only his own centrality but also the centre of all things. He has realised identity with the central spiritual sun, which is the true Heart of all worlds; he has resolved all the dualities of *saṁsāra* and broken through the circling orbits. One who has reached the centre of the Heart takes nourishment from the fire of Love, that Love which 'moves the sun and the other stars'[1].

> 'Then it is necessary to look for that place [state] whence it is no longer possible to return [to manifestation] and seek refuge in the primordial *puruṣa*, from which came the original impulse [of manifestation].'
>
> 'Neither sun nor moon nor fire illuminates it [that place]: it is my supreme dwelling place from which those who reach it will never return [to manifestation].'[2]

If you seek the Heart you will find Love, and Love is supreme Knowledge, which offers rest and bliss to the weary traveller, and renewal and growth to the Soul sunk in *māyā/avidyā*.

---

[1] Dante, *The Divine Comedy*, *Paradise*, XXXIII, 145.

[2] *Bhagavadgītā*, XV. 4. 6.

EQUANIMITY

> 'The [true] sages are the ones who look with the same eye upon a *Brāhmaṇa* – crowned with wisdom and humility – a cow, an elephant, a dog, and a *śvapāka* [eater of dog meat].'[1]

This *śloka* from the *Gītā* is very important, because it indicates the optimal position of consciousness for an effective Realisation. It can also be interpreted from the psychological perspective and, even more significantly, from the perspective of consciousness and metaphysics.

First of all, let us acknowledge that human beings have the *instinctive* capacity to respond to the objective world, to *feel* emotionally things/events which are both within and outside themselves, and to have the *thinking* capacity to project opinions and interpretations concerning those things/events. Again, they may have over-developed the 'sense of I' (*ahaṁkāra*) or the individualised centre so as to be trapped by its own psycho-somatic movements, remaining indifferent – but in a negative, reductive sense – to things/events.

The *śloka* emphasises the fact that the Sage remains equanimous; this means having the same approach of consciousness towards things/events that are different and sometimes even opposite.

We may also express ourselves in the following way: equanimity is 'divine indifference' or divine impassiveness, imperturbability, neutrality, because all dualities are transcended and unified through it.

Two questions may arise from what has been said:

[1] *Bhagavadgītā*, V. 18, op. cit.

1. To which sphere of our being can we attribute equanimity/imperturbability?
2. What sort of obstacles can hinder the expression of equanimity?

We may find this line of thought useful: if our psyche moves towards the state of being perturbed, we shall have to ask ourselves: What is it that causes this disturbance, and in which sphere of consciousness shall we be able to find the lacuna?

Let us begin by saying that equanimity is the opposite of dual states such as attraction and repulsion. Therefore someone who is conditioned by the attraction/repulsion state of the psychological sphere cannot be equanimous, cannot remain impassive; and since impassiveness/equanimity pertains to the Sage it follows that that being under the dominion of attraction/repulsion can be anything except wise. But why, then, does imperturbability pertain to the Sage? Wisdom, being free from dualistic prejudices, can 'see' things as they really are (*viveka-khyāti*: right discrimination arising from the pure intellect).

Now someone who is determined or tossed about by psychological conditions of attraction/repulsion, in what sense can he use the judgement of truth? Unfortunately, he is conditioned or changed by that particular emotional moment. If perturbation masters our being, we shall necessarily be prey to 'opinions' which are subjective and not of universal validity, opinions which will hang a negative conditioning weight upon our view of life and upon our conduct.

Above all, the *śloka* shows us a *state of* consciousness. The Sage is one who is equanimous before everything, not just the events/things that come his way but also the 'opinions of the world of men'. Thus we can examine the *śloka* from this other angle.

If we acknowledge that the innumerable manifestations of life are resolved in the unity of Being, if we accept that all is One without a second, if we admit that 'All things arise and dissolve in it' (*Māṇḍūkya Upaniṣad*, VI), where is that datum, that thing, or that fact which can cause us disturbance, partiality, and excitation? Within our single, universal consciousness, can we ever find duality and differentiation? Are not the 'shadows' of the dog, the *śvapāka*, the *Brāhmaṇa*, and so on, silhouetted on the same screen of ours? Are not their movements the expression of that One which gives life to all? It is only identification with a particular 'shadow' that puts us on the plane of distinction and opinion, that is, of non-truth.

One who has a universal consciousness is equanimous because he is beyond dianoetic opinion; being a Sage, he is totally one with life; or rather, being totally one with life, he is a Sage, a *muni*, one who has placed himself within the all-pervasive Silence, precisely because he has left behind all polarity of every kind and degree.

Behind the world of names and forms, to whatever dimension they may belong, there exists that Reality single and all-comprehensive, that essence which is the metaphysical foundation of the intelligible world and the sensible world. And one who is privileged to *see* life in terms of unity/equanimity has realised *savikalpa samādhī*, or divine Consciousness.

RIGHT ACTION

> 'One who sees non-action (*akarma*) in action (*karma*) and action in non-action is the wisest among men; he is one who has realised *yoga*, who has fulfilled everything.'
>
> 'One who abandons all attachment to the fruits of action is always at peace, and thus he seeks refuge in nothing; he produces no action, although [in fact] he does act.'[1]

According to the *Sāṁkhya Teaching*, from which the *darśana Yoga* of Patañjali[2] developed, on the manifest plane there is no being which is not impelled by *prakṛti*/nature to move, act, do. One *śloka* of the *Gītā* teaches that no one can exempt himself from acting, which means that it is necessary to comprehend and distinguish right action from wrong action and also from non-action itself.

The *puruṣa* alone, which is in the state of *kaivalya*, isolation from *prakṛti*, remains in its perfect stillness, or divine Silence. Until this state is reached, to think of refusing to act – in a world of movement/change – is pure illusion; it would be like trying to believe one could be motionless on a planet which is moving through space at thousands of kilometres a second. Movement arises from the stimulus given to *prakṛti*/*śakti* by the *puruṣa*, which has imparted such an acceleration to *prakṛti* that even the *puruṣa* itself seems to be drawn into this vortex.

---

[1] *Bhagavadgītā*, IV. 18, 20, op. cit.

[2] See *The Regal Way to Realisation* (*Yogadarśana*) by Patañjali. Edited by Raphael.

Movement/doing/action are attributes of substance, while *sat* and *cit* (will and intelligence) are expressions of the *puruṣa*.

In the individual, movement unfurls through instinctive, emotional, and mental tendencies, under the appearance of *desires*. The individual's life is characterised, in the final analysis, by the urge of desire: desire to be this or that, desire to appropriate, desire for satisfaction through gratification of every kind. Since one cannot not act, it is useful to ask oneself: How can one produce right action, the right way of acting? Or, how can one move from normal action to acting without acting, as the *śloka* puts it, and ultimately to perfect Stillness?

Most people are not only constrained to act, not only bound to the fruits of action – thus entering the conflict of pleasure and pain – but are also conditioned by their lack of knowledge, because they think that action is performed by the *puruṣa*, the *ātman*, the *noûs*, rather than by *prakṛti*, the *guṇas*, or χώρα (to use Plato's word).

The first thing that has to be done by those who are beginning the spiritual discipline is the practice of detachment from the *fruits of action*.

Let us acknowledge that our action is always motivated by *reward*, material or psychological, and therefore by an *interest*. The reward may come from the approval of others or from our own satisfaction with acting, but when, for various reasons, it is missing, then we come to a standstill. We would say that one no longer experiences ... an interest in acting.

From what we have said, it is clear that the individual is constrained to produce movement/action, which, however, generates a cause; and every cause, in turn, determines effects. It certainly happens at times that the effect is disproportionate to the cause, as we have no doubt experienced. There, if action produces causes, and if we are aware of this, then we shall have to act in such a way as to ensure that the action is harmonious.

Most of our human brothers fall unconsciously and chaotically from one cause/effect to another, undergoing the dualistic cycle of the event.

Indeed, the initiatory philosophical Tradition seeks to tell those people who are beginning to awaken to be very careful about producing causes, in order to avoid negative consequences.

To think is already to provoke action, for every thought/imagination produces movement and therefore causes. Every thought/emotion attracts a related thought/emotion: hatred attracts hatred, war attracts war, violence attracts violence, and so on. These things are already well known. There is a fundamental law in the universe which we may define with the word 'concordance': one expressive quality corresponds to a concordant quality, one that is similar and attuned to it. There is no God who rewards or punishes: it is the beings who reward or punish themselves according to whether or not they know how to apply specific laws. We know and apply many laws of physics, but we do not know or comprehend those which govern the universal subtle realm.

The philosophical Tradition teaches us to be creative agents of harmonious events. When we repeatedly read spiritual texts, so that our qualities conform to them, then we attract related substance and are amazed by particular intuitions and possibilities. It is necessary to make the *aura* vibrate, and when a number of *auras* vibrate in unison with the right note/frequency, marvellous events are bound to occur. In this way an action (thought, emotion, and so on) may position itself in a subtle sphere of existence. How can we understand whether our action has touched or vibrated the sphere of the intelligible or the sphere of the sensible? It is important to examine this, in order to avoid falling into errors of evaluation.

There exist individualised spheres, universal spheres, principial spheres, with different degrees of vibration. The *śloka* which we have presented refers to a type of action which is not of the individualised order. In fact, the first re-education that one needs to apply to oneself is actually the release of the claim on the *fruits of action*, thereby making oneself free. But free from what? From *expectation*, material or psychological, because, as the *śloka* says, 'One who abandons all attachment to the fruits of action is always in peace.'

When two beings meet, they unfortunately create expectations which, sooner or later, will lead to conflict. An expectation/fruit of gratification for the psychological ego also conceals suffering within it, because pleasure and pain are always a unity, a coin with two sides. When the being tries to give up its claim upon the fruits of action, it may happen that it no longer moves, as was hinted at a little while ago. Why? Because the empirical ego moves only when stimulated by egoistic *interest*, and since the being has not yet resolved itself as universal Consciousness, it remains in a void, in sterility. Slowly a gap will have to open on the vertical line, towards the universal, in such a way that the consciousness, by transferring itself to another system of co-ordinates, is no longer enmeshed in those petty interests pertaining to the grasping ego.

At this point of consciousness, the being makes two precise acknowledgements:

1. That the *puruṣa* does not act, because acting is the function of *prakṛti*. The embodied *puruṣa* only gives direction to the action, just as the farmer, by closing or opening furrows, allows the water to flow to revive the earth.
2. That the *puruṣa*, being centred in itself as universal consciousness, is not subject to the appreciation or otherwise of the particular.

From this perspective, the embodied consciousness, though acting, does not act, because its action consists solely in directing *prakṛti* while remaining detached from all psychological polarities. This is non-action in action, this is the fulfilment of the first *śloka* we have presented.

It is said that any specific action can produce merit or demerit, that is, either favourable opportunities, or difficulties of every kind, both material and psychological; but they are conditions which, having a beginning and an end, operate in time and space. One who is Liberated transcends both, because his action is motivated by a consciousness which does not rely on any thing/event, being itself fullness. Everything that comes *after* the Consciousness/Witness represents a superimposition or a 'second'.

One who sees action in non-action is free from:

1. the energy of *rajas* which impels outwards;
2. an interested choice in the action itself;
3. the fruits, whatever their nature: material, psychological, spiritual.

This is the state of the *jīvanmukta*[1], one who is liberated while living, because he has transcended the polarities of every order and degree and is at peace with all that exists.

[1] For the state of the *jīvanmukta*, see *The Ocean of Bliss of One who is Liberated in Life* (*Jīvanmuktānandalaharī*) in *Short Works* by Śaṅkara, Vol. II, and *Vivekacūḍāmaṇi*, *śloka* 427 et seqq.

AVIDYĀ/MĀYĀ

The sensory apparatus, together with the mind (*manas*), knows non-being and knows not Being. Non-being is all that is perceived by the gross and subtle senses; Being represents the foundation of those perceptions. In the classic example given by Śaṅkara, non-being is the snake/appearance, while Being is the underlying rope/reality. According to Parmenides, Being *is* and non-being is merely *appearance.*

Non-being consists of all the possible indefinite superimpositions on Reality, the fruit of the imaginative mind. Thus, in place of the rope someone will see a snake, another a stick, a third a trickle of water, and so on; or, to express it better, we can say that the stimulation of an external event causes a subjective and imaginative response to flower. And this subconscious form/image, by externalising itself, then superimposes itself on the real datum, completely hiding it from the awareness of the observer.

At this point the obvious questions to ask oneself are: Without a mind in action (projector), without images to project (film), and without a space/time consciousness (light) to impart life and reality to an illusion, would not the rope (screen) remain a rope and nothing but a rope? Does *avidyā* therefore imply duality? And is this duality perhaps not caused by *movement*?

Avidyā diverts consciousness from the datum as it is, to the datum as it appears. This apparent datum (snake) has no absolute reality, because it *is born* when it is projected by the mind and it *dies* when the subject regains self-awareness. In brief, it is an imaginary dualism but it has an enormous effect on a subject that is not centred in its own being.

At first sight, this may seem to originate for reasons of a psychological nature and show itself subsequently as the result of a metaphysical not-knowing: becoming implies not acknowledging oneself to be complete, perfect, eternal. In fact, our objectivisations reflect urges for compensation and gratification, a feeling of physical and psychical insecurity. These are impressions of non-being, deeply rooted within us and ready to manifest themselves (*movement*) as soon as possible.

The externalising movement, which produces duality, covers the space and time which intervene between the content in the state of potentiality (*vāsanā*) and the materialisation (snake). The photograms exist, imprinted on the film of our subconsciousness. The consciousness has only to illumine them and the mind to project them, for the spectacle (object) to take life and for duality to be realised.

If we scrutinise the entire process, we may come to understand that the projection cannot be divorced from the existence of a fundamental element, the photogram (*vāsanā*). If we go even further back, we shall discover that at the bottom of everything there exists a state of ignorance (*avidyā*) which is born with the same individuality (*ahaṁkāra*) that finds expression at the various levels of manifestation by perpetuating itself until the knowledge (*vidyā*) resolves the causes and the effects and therefore duality, time, and space.

Māyā is a superimposition on Being, put there not by the mind of the individual but by *Mahat*, or cosmic mind, that mind which is the synthesis of all the minds that exist. Illusory phenomenon thus comes out from the microcosmic field to embrace the entire, universal, projective expression. And for the individual this movement, as we have seen, produces duality/multiplicity, which is only apparent because it is imagined by the mind within itself.

It is difficult for man to consider the universe as a mere image, an imaginative projection, the materialised form/thought of a Being/Mind which is dreaming. Perhaps it is the immeasurability of the time and space of the Being that makes it appear real and eternal to him.

For the Subject that is dreaming, as well as for the subject and object that are dreamt, *māyā* thus comes to assume totally different values: for the Subject *māyā* is movement (cause), and for the others it is form (effect).

As far as the individual is concerned, the forms – though they are *appearance* – assume reality and absoluteness, for his consciousness is identified with them. The 'sleeper' sees and believes in duality, and he takes to be real a mere projection, in which he himself moves, lives, and finds expression.

> 'The mind projects subject and object (ego and non-ego). Then the subject wishes to know the object, as if it were something distinct.
> In this chase to capture the object in movement, the subject fails to see that the object is nothing but the other facet of itself. This gives us the situation of the thief who dresses as a policeman in order to catch the thief who is himself all the time. Opposites are identical because their source is identical.'[1]

But the dream ego and the dream non-ego, being cloaked in *māyā/avidyā*, do not know that they are identical to each other and to the mind which has produced them. And so they fight each other, they 'love' each other, and they hate each other.

The *māyā*/individual relationship is, therefore, one that is based on the identification of the individual with the effects of *māyā*. As far as the Self is concerned, however, things are quite otherwise, for the very reason that its position of consciousness is different.

The empirical ego, being immersed in an infinitesimal portion of time and space, does not know the *whole*, and so it is a slave to events, to history, to the particular. The Self, on the contrary, is outside time/space/history; it embraces yesterday, today, and tomorrow in an eternal present which allows it to

---

[1] Raphael, *The Threefold Pathway of Fire*, II. IV. 21, op. cit.

be master of cause, space, and time. The Self therefore knows the laws of *māyā*, and, finding itself on the plane of manifestation, uses it in total freedom, playing with it (*līlā*) without being overcome by it. Moreover, being a mere Witness of *māyā*, it can intervene in its movement and resolve the *appearance*.

By contrast, the individual who *thinks* he is a mere being sundered from the universal sees only the outcome/effect of *māyā* and cannot, of course, do anything about its cause/movement, but he has the power to intervene in his own projective movement by causing the image of the 'snake' to disappear.

We can speak of *māyā*, beginning from the effects and going back, by analogical deduction, to the cause. But to define *māyā* is impossible, for it is *movement*, and movement cannot be encapsulated in a concept. In fact, it is sufficient to observe it to make it vanish. It is enough to observe a dream, from a perspective of greater awareness (the waking state) to see it disappear. It is enough to observe a form to note that it changes continually and is no longer what it was at first.

To define *māyā*, therefore, is impossible, but – as *Asparśa* observes – it is not important to have a mental image of *māyā*; what it is important it is to be aware of its working mechanism and transcend it.[1]

---

[1] See note 51 to Chapter 4 of the *Māṇḍūkya Upaniṣad with the kārikās of Gauḍapāda and the Commentary by Śaṅkara*, edited by Raphael.

INDIVIDUALITY AND PERSONALITY

It may happen that those aspiring to Realisation – Realisation of an Eastern or a Western inspiration – do not have clear ideas about words such as 'individuality', 'ego', 'personality' or about what needs to be rectified and then transcended.

It can be observed, moreover, that some aspirants, or those affiliated to some esoteric or initiatory schools, follow the Way by seeking to convince themselves that it is enough to be kind, affable, and well-mannered, or to study the history (and therefore the times) of initiatory Philosophy, to write about what the Tradition was, and things of this kind.

To resolve the 'rough stone' into a 'square' or a 'cube' is not a question of being erudite about the Tradition, or simply attending an élite group of intellectuals on matters initiatory or spiritual. To 'separate' and 'fix' the Mercury of the Philosophers is not a question of 'becoming erudite' about alchemical texts. To resolve the 'individualised condition' into the state of universal Personality does certainly not consist of ecological walks or 'brotherly *agape*' to promote the 'social animal' within us, although *agape* does have a profound esoteric value.

Now what do the words 'individuality' and 'personality' stand for?

The individualised condition (from which comes individuality) is that which is characterised by scissure from the universal caused by *ahaṁkāra* (sense of ego) – to use the word from *Vedānta* – and motivated by free will.

All the Traditions speak of a *primordial* unconditioned *state* in which the being first found itself before moving to the conditioned, contingent, and phenomenal state; or of an a-formal or incorporeal state before moving to one which is formal and corporeal. The same Tradition – Orphic, Mysteric, Platonic, etc. – speaks of a 'fall into generation'; or, again, of a degradation of the being, as unity/person, into the condition of individuality/duality (the Tree of Good and Evil), with all the consequences attendant upon this occurrence. The *person*, as such, is universal, or, rather, transcends manifestation itself, but one of its reflections, by *separating itself*, has found itself as a mere individual, with a name and a form, in opposition to other individuals who are also prisoners of 'I am this'.

Being, however, is not restricted to the individualised state by the mere fact of belonging to it.

The person is the wholeness/unity of what one is as the deepest nature. It is the soul, or the *jīva*, at its own plane. It is the Witness of the modifications of mind and body.

> 'There exists a single reality, an absolute being, which is the eternal substratum of the differentiated consciousness, the witness of the three states (*avasthātrayasākṣī*) and distinct from the five sheaths (*saṁpañcakośa*).'
>
> 'The one who knows all that happens in the states of waking, dreaming, and deep sleep, who is conscious of the presence or the absence of thought and its modifications, who is the support of even the sense of 'I' (*aham*) is the *ātman*.'[1]

In traditional terms, we speak of God as a person and not as an individual. Being, as the supreme Person, is not an individual, has nothing of the individual, no individual detail, nothing exclusive or distinctive. It is beyond the world of names and forms, although it constitutes their ontological foundation.

Individuality that is peculiarly human consists of: the 'sense of I', the factor of distinction; the mental and volitional faculty; the emotive/affective faculty; instinctiveness (the fundamental instincts of the species); and a coarse physical body

[1] Śaṅkara, *Vivekacūḍāmaṇi*, 125-126, op. cit.

with its related psychical and physical senses (*jñānendriya* and *karmendriya*).

Individuality extends beyond the coarse physical plane (the plane of *viśva*). It is inevitable that, being sundered from the Person/Witness as the universal state of consciousness, it will operate at the command of *egoism*, egotism, with all the consequences that we already know. The 'profane' being is really the one that lives exclusively as contingent and phenomenal individuality. The restoration of the *sacred* within us – and therefore in the world – can happen only when the universal Person integrates and resolves the individualised scissure.

In the profane condition the mental and emotional faculties are subordinated and directed by that 'sense of I' which, being something relative, will never be able to satisfy its innumerable and unforeseeable requirements. To be able to perpetuate the 'scissure', the 'fall', or its *avidyā* – to use the various terms that are given – it does all it can to procure means fit for the purpose. Yearning, thirst, the passion for the life of forms: these act to counterbalance a state of 'lack', of non-being. Not being the 'natural state' of the being, individuality obviously constitutes a 'second nature' that is artificial, fictitious, and superimposed on the first, real and original nature.

> 'And this is why man – in contrast to all the other beings that live on the earth – is twofold: mortal by reason of the body (individuality), immortal by reason of the substantial man. Although immortal and although he has full dominion over all things, he undergoes the condition of that which is mortal, because he is subject to destiny. While being above the harmonious complex of the spheres, he has become a slave to what is inside this complex. Although androgynous, being born from an androgynous Father, and although he is free from sleep, being born from a Father exempt from sleep, he is nevertheless a victim ...'[1]

[1] Hermes Trismegistus, *Poimander*, 25.

The initiatory Tradition in all geographical regions – for there is only one initiatory Tradition – constitutes a *corpus* of knowledge concerning the true nature of the microcosmic and macrocosmic being, apart from offering a practice for the realisation of that nature or that primordial state. Whereas Knowledge is always one, the means to actuate it are many and are adapted to the various vocations and aptitudes of the individual aspirants.

The identification of the reflection of consciousness of the Person/*noûs*/*ātman*, and so on, with mortal individuality means that most beings are alarmed when one speaks of 'initiatory death', solution of the 'individualised state', integration of individuality into the universal Person, transcendence of the 'sense of I' (*ahaṁkāra*), because they think of their own annihilation. Thus, for those who are identified with the coarse physical body (*annamayakośa*), or *sôma*, it is unthinkable that, if they were told to 'let go' or to separate themselves from the element of earth, they would be able to soar into the infinite spaces of Being. The element of earth, unfortunately, constricts and solidifies the consciousness. To return to the source, to the first-born Point, to Being, to the God-Person, and – for those who are ready – to resolve oneself into unqualified Being (*Nirguṇa* or *Ain Soph*; to proceed to an effective 'separation', 'fixing' and 'unification' of the Fires; to resolve the lower Kabbalistic quaternary (individuality) into *Tiphereth*, this state into *Kether*, and others still; to follow the same initiatory journey as Jesus: baptism, purification/rectification, transfiguration, death on the cross (individualised quaternary), resurrection or re-birth to the universal state, and ascension to the divine Source – all this constitutes an *opus* which only a qualified being, above all at a level of consciousness rather than a psychological level, can actuate in the secret of his *athanor*.

All this, then, has to be realised despite the various negative or positive vicissitudes of time and space which may arise and despite the interference of the 'opinions' of the individualised world.

One who is able to complete this *opus* has little or nothing that is 'human', apart from that bi-pedal physical body conditioned by the wear and tear of time.

In the *Māṇḍūkyakārikā* (III, 39) we read:

> 'The *yoga* called "without contact" (*asparśa-yoga*), is, in truth, difficult for many *yogis* [aspirants] to comprehend, because they feel fear where there is no fear, and are afraid of it.'

And, again, in *Poimander*, 28:

> 'Men born from the earth, why have you consigned yourselves to death when you have the ability to partake of immortality? Repent, you who have walked together in error and have found your companion in ignorance. Move far from the darkness, partake of immortality, abandon perdition once and for all.'

And the divine Plato gives his confirmation:

> 'And would it not perhaps be an adequate defence if we were to reply that one who truly loves knowledge should by his own nature move completely towards Being and without being content with the multiplicity of individual objects – in any case, they are only the contents of opinion – should forge straight ahead to his love without losing spirit and without fainting, having first grasped the nature of each and every thing in itself, together with that part of the Soul whose activity is directed precisely to gathering the essences – itself being of the same material –, and, with this part of the Soul, drawing nearer to, and uniting with, Being in itself, by procreating intellection and truth, should succeed in knowing, live a true life, have true nourishment, and thus, but not before, end the travails of childbirth?'[1]

---

[1] Plato, *Politéia*, 490b.

THE TRADITIONAL SOCIAL ORDERS

Life is one; from Unity arise the innumerable modes of existence. Beyond the One, there is only immutable Essence, the real substratum, complete in itself. The One is synthesis, harmony, Plato's 'World of Ideas'; in it rest the Seeds, the Ideas, the Archetypes, which, when that original harmony is broken, will manifest first of all as subtle or intelligible Ideations and then, on the plane of the physical sensible, as the geometry of compound forms. Thus, the single a-formal Body appears multiple, and every part – which participates wholly in the nature of the original seed as its integrating part – expresses, to a greater or lesser degree and in varying relationships, the allotropic qualities of the base/substance.

The *Hymn to the Puruṣa* (*Ṛg Veda*, X, 90) says of the *puruṣa*:

> 'What did his mouth and his arms become? What name did his thighs and his feet receive? His mouth became *Brāhmaṇa*; the Lawgiver/Warrior (*Kṣatriya*) was brought forth from his arms; his thighs were the Entrepreneur (*Vaiśya*); from his feet was born the manual Labourer (*Śūdra*).'

The principle of the institution of the traditional social classes rests on the recognition of the differentiation which exists on the plane of multiplicity: a difference which does not, of course, arise from the separative vision of pre-constituted classes but from the evident fact that there are different human temperaments and thus from the specific aptitude of each person to develop particular functions. It is based, then, on the recognition that on the plane of the 'different', according to Plato, there cannot be one thing equal to another, one movement identical to another ... There may be things or moments that are similar, but never identical; otherwise it would be equivalent to sanctioning the limitation of universal possibility. Only at the principial plane does differentiation vanish, yet we do not find equality among the parts, but Unity (for the parts have vanished).

In the same way, the existence of the social classes, with their co-ordination, disappears only where it is no longer man that exists, with his various component parts, but the 'Egg' from which man is born.

The institution of the social classes, which reflects the traditional way of living, keeps the vision of Unity steady; no independent, isolated, and hostile grouping could survive, just as in the microcosm legs could not exist separated from the head, or even a head detached from the body. Each part is perfectly co-ordinated with the others in the natural and obvious recognition that only comprehension of the proper rightful place and consequent action can cause the whole to live harmoniously.

Just as one leg could not think of moving in a way that is not co-ordinated with the other leg and could never think of making a decision on its own account and of imposing such a decision on the brain, but respects and performs whatever the brain works out in a unified manner for the organism in its entirety, in the same way each class, caste, or order – if it truly comprehends its own nature in time and space, and its position within the context – works according to its natural disposition with respect to its hierarchical niche in the organism as a whole. This happens on the plane of multiplicity, that is, where the One *appears* as many, because when the individual regains or, rather, gradually reveals his true nature, he re-acquires his original completeness. Such an individual thus embodies the original class (*haṁsa*), which transcends the four orders.

Keeping to the analogy of the *Ṛg Veda* that was quoted earlier, Manu expresses himself as follows:

> 'To the *Brāhmaṇas* [the mouth of the *puruṣa*] He gave as their heritage the study and teaching of the sacred books, the accomplishment of the sacrifice, the management of the sacrifices offered by others, the right to give and the right to receive.
>
> On the *Kṣatriyas* He imposed the duty of protecting the people, exercising charity, sacrificing, reading the sacred books, and not giving themselves up to the pleasures of the senses.
>
> Looking after livestock, almsgiving, sacrificing, studying the sacred books, trading, lending at interest, working the land: these are the functions decreed for the *Vaiśyas*.
>
> And the supreme Lord assigned a single duty to the *Śūdras*: that of serving all the other classes.'[1]

The first two orders, 'located' in the upper part of the body of the *puruṣa*, are considered sacred. To them, in fact, is devolved the exercising of spiritual authority and temporal power. To them belong those individuals who are consciously on the plane of Unity and universal principles, those, that is, who have completely transcended individualised action.

We find ourselves facing individuals who embody the Principle, who are pure channels of the Principle, because they are individuals in appearance only, while in the third and fourth orders we find ourselves facing a multitude characterised by a way of life that is decidedly individualised. The union of the first two orders takes place on the basis of a free and mature recognition of the naturally exercised function and the subordination of reason/reflection to direct/immediate visions; it is blind power putting itself at the service of enlightening wisdom; it is the Principle, complete in itself and rotating on its own axis, which uses the force (the second class) in order to be able to explain in silence its function as a 'bridge' between the unreal and the Real.

In this way, by submitting himself to the authority of the *Brāhmaṇa*, the *Kṣatriya* acquires centrality and is grafted into

---

[1] *Mānavadharmaśāstra*, I. 88-91.

the Principle, which transforms him from an individual who rules over other individuals to an impersonal *guardian* of the earthly Temple in which there has to be practised the alchemy of those consciousnesses which are trying to re-discover themselves. The force ceases to be the domineering energy of the subject and, in the sacrifice of oneself as individuality, is transformed into the instrument that is suitable for allowing the transmutation. The individual becomes a factor of devotion and dedication and by means of the 'arm' works on a horizontal line while aiming for a vertical movement.

The *Brāhmaṇa* is seen as the symbol of the 'unmoving Mover', while the *Kṣatriya* represents the symbol of movement. When the catharsis of the lawgiver/warrior has taken place and he has re-discovered himself as a true *Kṣatriya*, then the consciousness is fixed at the centre and only the vehicles radiate out towards the circumference. Thus the movement (*rajas*) of the *Kṣatriya* is only apparent, because his natural position is, in fact, stillness.

In this regard, R. Guénon states:

> 'The Symbol of the Sphinx – in one of its meanings – united the two attributes (*Brāhmaṇa* and *Kṣatriya*), seen according to their normal relationships. One may, in fact, consider the human head as a representation of wisdom, and the body of a lion to symbolise strength. The head is the spiritual authority which directs, and the body is the temporal power which acts.'[1]

If the subordination of the second social body to the first occurs through a free and mature recognition of the pre-eminence of the spiritual authority over the temporal power, of the pure intellect over reason, then the relationship between the second and the last two social bodies is based on the direction given with wisdom, inasmuch as the lower 'limbs' of the body of the *puruṣa* do not possess immediate knowledge.

---

[1] R. Guénon, *Autorité spirituelle et pouvoir temporel*. Guy Trédaniel Éditeur.

Manu says:

> 'The ordained law rules the whole of mankind, because a naturally virtuous man is difficult to find; it is from fear of sanction that the people follow only lawful actions.'
>
> 'All the classes would degenerate, all barriers would be broken, the universe would be nothing but chaos if sanction did not do its work.'[1]

By analogy we could think of the *Kṣatriya* as a mind which has been mastered, motionless, at peace, and which, as a consequence, holds steady the emotional and physical/gross sheaths (the third and fourth orders), thereby allowing the intellect (*Brāhmaṇa*) to operate directly. The mastered mind makes possible the perfect alignment of all the vehicles, or bodies, the perfect measure in relation to the Principle.

---

[1] *Mānavadharmaśāstra*, VI. 22. 24.

IS DEATH THE END?

Everything is born, grows, and dies, whether it be a star, a human being, or any other form of life.

We become attached to objects, of any nature, under the illusion that we shall be able to keep them, but how can we keep something that vanishes? Life is movement, so how could we stop it, crystallise it? It would cease to be life.

The embodied reflection of consciousness becomes identified with the physical body, but since it knows the transitory nature of form, it fears death: it is afraid of perishing along with its own body. The mere thought of death terrifies it, and it does its utmost to ignore it. It considers death to be an extraordinary event, while all around it, within itself (consider the cells of the body) this process goes on without a moment's respite (movement appears continuous, even though it is not). Nothing escapes this natural law, which, as we shall see later, is important for life itself.

Every form expresses quality: beauty or ugliness, for example. We see a flower, and desire, which is acquisitive, impels us to take possession of it. We possess it, and then we are afraid of losing it, of suffering. In spite of this, the flower will wither and die, which is what happens to everything.

What has become of the flower? Where has it finally gone? A baby is born. It goes through adolescence, youth, old age, and then dies. Where has it gone?

Undifferentiated electronic energy has condensed to produce a form. Once a certain cycle has been completed, it disintegrates, and we see it no longer. Has it been destroyed?

'Nothing is created and nothing is destroyed, but everything is transformed', science declares. Energy, for example, is transformed into heat, which in turn is converted back into energy, and no quantity is lost in the transformation.

It is a process where three kinds of force which are in perfect balance with each other operate. They are symbolised in the Indian *Trimūrti* by the figures of *Śiva*, *Viṣṇu*, and *Brahmā*. *Śiva* represents the energy of the first aspect, the energy which transforms and disperses the forms. *Viṣṇu* represents the energy of the second aspect, the energy which preserves, conserves. Lastly, *Brahmā* represents the energy of the third aspect which creates forms that are new and ever more perfect. *Śiva* apparently operates in opposition to *Viṣṇu* and *Brahmā*, although, in fact, none of the three could manage without the other two. Death, which is thus a change of state, is, as we have said, important for life itself, which would cease to be life without the propitious intervention of death.

When we speak of manifest life, we are referring to the modification of *prakṛti*/substance which is always taking place, to the phenomenon which appears to our eyes and enters the sphere of our perception/senses, and to that which lies outside the coarse physical plane, that is, it concerns subtler planes of existence, such as the plane of the emotions and the mind.

We have said that life is movement: therefore a form of any nature is certainly unable to crystallise itself, to be permanent. To claim the contrary is to provoke a clash of forces, and thus a conflict. Can we stop the sun? No, it is impossible. At sunset it will inevitably 'die', only to be 're-born' the following morning.

At this point we may wonder: is death the end?

The human being is a universe. Its reality, according to the Tradition, embraces three spheres of existence: physical/coarse, subtle, and causal. Let us consider the last two.

Man lives projected towards the past: his thought, which is based principally on what he remembers, sends him back to old patterns, often at odds with the present. This is how he lives out his psychological drama, torn between two powerful forces: the force of yesterday, which holds him back, and the force of today, which impels him to go forward, to re-create himself.

> 'Life is always something new, always a genuine and immediate experience of extraordinary vitality which has to be lived and synthesised.'[1]

Rather than live, we *are lived*, but, like the sun, in order to live we should die every day to ourselves.

It is this continuous refusal to 'loosen the grip' which leads man to conflict, and therefore to suffering; it is the fear of losing himself. But what is it in him that is afraid? Precisely that part which does not wish to know about dying: his past, his crystallisations.

We are the product of our thought. This means that the mind is the cause of our individualisation. If the individualised being represents the effect, if it depends on a cause, it is obvious that it will try with all its resources to prevent this cause from being resolved.

It is natural that as long as the individual allows himself to be lived by his subconscious contents, by his *vāsanās*, following the line of least resistance, he will agree to the perpetuation of a typical inertial movement, without any possibility of glimpsing a way out.

When he raises his eyes from his blind alley and discerns the light, he will seek resolutely to escape from the darkness, confronting both conflicts and neuroses, but preferring them to that condition of torpor.

This sudden change of course calls for courage, resolution, perseverance. It is necessary to really turn one's back on the past and walk on with a firm step without ever turning back.

Mythology and ancient scripture offer us, in this respect, allegories that are rich with meaning. We recall the myth of Proserpina and the biblical account of Lot.

---

[1] *Autoconoscenza*. Associazione Ecoculturale Parmenides, Roma 2011.

What frightens the ego is the fear of losing itself, the concept of death understood as an absolute end. But is there an end in the absolute sense? The beginning and the end (birth and death) are merely relative. There cannot be two absolutes. On the other hand, if one of the two were absolute, that is, real, it would exist at all times and in all places, which is not the case.

They are phases, movements in time and space, which come and go, one following the other.

The seed germinates and the plant is born, from which come new seeds. Then the plant dies, but the seeds go on to germinate, producing new plants. 'Nothing is created and nothing is destroyed, but everything is transformed.' What is the purpose of this ebb and flow, this incessant coming and going, this continuous experiencing? It is to make the being ever more aware of its own immortality.

How, then, can we speak of an end?

It is simply a question of breaking a circumference and gaining a greater awareness of what one is. And every time we 'loosen a grip', it does not mean that we are losing something, but rather that we are finding something in a wider context: as we go higher, the horizon extends.

The Realised Man is total *comprehension*, because he has embraced the whole. He is the synthesis, the vertex of the triangle born from the fusion of the two poles.

'Dying to oneself', therefore, does not mean destroying something – which would be completely unscientific – but comprehending in order to synthesise.

The One, the Archetype, contains within it all the possible potentialities which unfold in time and space before returning to the One.

The dreamer projects an unlimited variety of forms which go back into his mind when he wakes up. But for this to happen, he must wake up; it is necessary for everything that has been projected in the dream to be re-absorbed into the waking state.

Every time an integration, an act of consciousness, an effective comprehension, happens, a wonderful event occurs in that being: a resolute step towards the *source*, the birth of something – in short, an *initiation*.

UNIVERSAL ORDER (*ṚTA*)

The Decline of Customs

'When the *Tao* was disregarded,
there was [only] man and [his] justice;
when guile and mistrust appeared,
then there was hypocrisy;
when discord took birth among relatives,
then there was [only] commiseration and affection;
when the kingdom fell into anarchy,
then the indulgent minister emerged.'[1]

When the 'Will of the Heaven' is disregarded, man, having lost the point of reference and being alone with his tiny ego, legislates unjustly; from this are born, as consequences, all those qualifications which pertain to an egoic consciousness: guile, mistrust, domineering, hypocrisy, sentimentality, and so on.

When the just accord with the celestial Norm is lost, then there arise among relatives discord and false relationships directed by mere individual feelings.

When the Vision fades, the government falls into anarchy and there emerges the 'prince' who, to perpetuate his rule, seeks to be indulgent and accommodating towards his subjects.

The being, forgetting the *Tao* as the metaphysical foundation, gradually sinks down from one level of consciousness to another, eventually becoming mere disorder (mere quantity), and society itself, rather than being an expression of people governed by the Sacred, represents a formless mass of individuals that is guided by utilitarian emotions which often turn

---

[1] Lao-Tze: *Tao Tê Ching*, XVIII.

into physical and psychical violence. This is the stage of all against all (*bellum omnium contra omnes*). It is the stage at which universal, sacred, and hierarchical Values are sidestepped and often attacked.

In the dark Age there is the triumph of the philosophy of becoming, material form (quantity) at the expense of quality; the triumph of nihilism and therefore of anti-traditional forces; the assertion of merely emotional social relationships which pays service exclusively to the body/mind, a service whose value and ideal religions themselves, trapped through decadence in the contingent process alone, exalt.

When the transcendent Principle – towards which the being should be moving in order to regain that universal Consciousness which it has lost – is avoided, then every institutional expression – religious, political, socio-economic – is darkened. Religion becomes doctrine, particularly moral and sentimental doctrine (sphere of the ego); politics becomes a utilitarian doctrine of power, demagogy and self-assertiveness; the economy becomes a gigantic machine for exploiting the environment, and not only the environment.

In the dark Age, Truth is transformed into opinion, which varies with the situation, and the usefulness of the being and of the beings elected to govern human dichotomies. There is nothing stable, nothing permanent, nothing higher than the empirical ego; what is real is nothing more than what the eye sees and touch touches. A truth of the moment is contradicted by another truth of the following moment, a law of one day is contradicted by a law of the following day; a judiciary sentence is contradicted by another sentence later; the individual of today is contradicted by the individual of the next day.

In this kind of society there are no *values* to act as guides, no values to refer to or in which to find valid motivations for one's own regeneration or that of others. It is a society that is levelled out, darkened, at the service of those few who know how to raise themselves aloft and become demagogues.

In such a society there is no *Sacerdos* capable of ferrying the fallen individual towards the Universal; there are no *Kṣatriyas*, endowed with *virile ingenium*, who before taking action have been able to impose Order upon themselves or have found that solar *Dignitas* which comes from a higher Stature; there are no *Vaiśyas* to produce what is *needed* and not what is demanded by the insatiable desires of contingent man (consumerism).

In this society, the social Orders are overturned, ruining the traditional structure and causing customs to decay.

All revolutions based on a socio-political transformism have failed, because they are not upheld by the 'Will of Heaven'. But a revolution ordained from on High requires *Sacerdotes*, repositories of the Sacred Science, and genuine warriors (*Bellatores probi*), defenders of that Science, who can with one hand stretch out towards the Principle and with the other hand wield the sacred Sword which re-establishes the values of the universal Tradition, of *Ṛta* (universal Order). In an exclusively 'profane' society – with profane culture, institutions and emotions –, a society which has reached the limit of the degenerative abyss, and in which the *sacrum facere* is extinguished, there is a need for elements (rather than men of 'goodwill' driven by *kāma/manas*) who are capable of transcendent Will and of gathering together heroic Souls (and not a mob of empirical egos) that can awaken in the heart of the being that Eros – the thirst for the divine and the sacred – which alone can have the strength to resurrect the 'living dead' in enlightened consciousnesses.

In a phase of *extrema tempora,* there is a need for highly motivated consciousnesses to stem the rising tide of levelling and petrifying darkness. And if these consciousnesses were to come into the open, the result would undoubtedly be positive.

To re-establish the *Tao* there is, therefore, a need for beings that are noetic and aristocratic in the traditional sense, not for those that are guided by dianoetic and nihilistic thought and devoid of all spiritual legitimacy. Consciousnesses are needed that can express themselves with irrefutable metaphysical superiority derived from a state of being (and a lifestyle) which can control the lower nature (the spirited and appetitive parts of the soul, to use Plato's words) and from an ethical norm which comes directly from 'Heaven' and therefore from the original Tradition.

The *Kṣatriya* consciousness is not subject to the will of the world of men, but is first and foremost at the service of the original *single* Tradition. This implies that the *Kṣatriya* is not at the beck and call of the specific particularisations of sectors of the human species: the religious (as a single traditional Branch among many), the party political, the economic, and so on, everything that pertains to time and space. The *Kṣatriyas* are the Ascetics of the heroic life whose discipline is forged by the inner *Virtus*; they are a *celestial Militia*, an *élite* of qualified consciousnesses, whose Sword is exclusively at the service of re-establishing the universal *Ṛta*, which has been overturned and darkened (but not shattered) by the deceptive *avidyā* of the world of men, or, to put it better, by the individualities which are sundered from the universal context.

In truth, the *dharma* of the pure *Kṣatriya*, which – it is important to emphasise once more – is at the service, not of fallen man, but of the Divine, can be actualised in an authentically traditional society.

The *Kṣatriya* is outside the ideologies proposed by individualities, outside the different speculative currents of thought, outside all the contingent interests which oppress the mass of beings. The *Kṣatriya*, comprehending the universal Order, because it is presented by the metaphysical *Sacerdos*, and having seen it, with the spiritual eye, asserts his authority only when that Order is disregarded. When 'what is below' no longer corresponds to 'what is Above', the *Kṣatriya* comes forth, with his *Dignitas* and with his *Potestas*, to bring the social *avidyā* back under the aegis of the Right, or – to express it in terms of the *guṇas* – when *tamas* and *rajas* are triumphant, the *Kṣatriya* intervenes to eliminate, or at least restrain, the disorder, so that the *Sacerdos* can represent that Teaching which is able to ferry people towards the realisation of the state of consciousness of *sattva*/harmony.

When – as expounded in the *Bhagavadgītā* – the Order is disregarded, Arjuna, under the direction of Kṛṣṇa (who represents universal Consciousness) takes the sacred Bow and fights to restore the Equilibrium, which has been undermined.

The Tradition is represented by a *corpus* of Knowledges which is expressed at different levels and sections of human activity: Knowledges which do not arise from dualistic, individualised thought, but come down from 'Heaven' through qualified consciousnesses in order that the being may be reintegrated within the universal Order (and go even further), the first and final goal of fallen Adam. All this is Rhythm, as life itself is Rite.

In time and space this knowledge becomes adapted to the various peoples, thus manifesting in what we may call the traditional Branches of the sole primordial Knowledge. If this knowledge represents the trunk, the Centre, the single metaphysical and supra-historical foundation, then the various Branches are its ramifications. Where a single political party or a mere traditional Branch, among the many, tries to appropriate the single supra-historical trunk by making it particular and exclusive to its own ends, we have a reversal of values: the Universal now depends on the particular, and not vice versa. Now it may also happen that this 'particular', in the name of the Universal, cunningly and violently imposes its own 'theological idealism' or 'political idealism', superimposing it on the metaphysical Principle. However, it has to be remembered that everything which comes from an exclusive and time-bound mentality belongs particularly to that historical period which is called *kali yuga* or Age of Iron.

The Universal expresses itself through laws and constitutions. Plato's *Politéia* (rather than *Republic*) is understood as a Constitution based on Order, *Ṛta*, universal *Dharma*, and is neither a political party nor a theological party. Thus the *Vedas*, the *Upaniṣads*, the *Dharmaśāstra*, and others, do not represent a political, theological, or any other party of a contingent order, but they put forward, instead, the Legislation of the great universal Lawgiver, given that the entire universe, including the various beings which dwell in it, is governed by Laws, by perfect concordances, by number, and by lines. Here is the divine Cosmos, and here is human legislation, which should be commensurate with this Harmony.

If in a particular historical period, through the power of the collective desecrating unconscious which numbs even the best, it becomes difficult to find supra-individual Consciousnesses, it is sufficient to prepare those few who are predisposed to support future events.

On the other hand, if the true Revolution (*metánoia*) cannot be actuated for most people, then let the cycle turn inexorably towards sunset, because from a 'catastrophe' ordained by 'Heaven' there cannot but be reborn a purified and enlightened age. After sunset there is always dawn, and this is not the first time humanity has undergone this alternation of darkness and Light.

One who is *fixed* in the Principle *which is* and does not become has nothing to fear. Beyond all bourgeois sentimentality there are cosmic *necessities* which are able to heal the blindness of beings that have preferred darkness to Light, death to Immortality, and non-being to Being.

SPACE

According to Newton, space is real and must be considered as the 'sensorium' in which God has immediate perception of the material universe. According to his follower Samuel Clarke, space is an immediate and necessary consequence of the existence of God, the property of an incorporeal substance, the place not only of bodies but also of ideas.

'We have ideas, such as those of eternity and immensity,' says Clarke, 'ideas which it is absolutely impossible for us to destroy or banish from our spirit and which must therefore be the attributes of a necessary, actually existent being ... Space is a property of the *substance* which is self-existent and not a property of any other substance. All other substances are in space, and space penetrates them, but the self-existent substance is not in space and is not penetrated by space. It is, if I may express myself in this way, the 'substratum' of space, the foundation of the existence of space and of duration itself.'

According to the 'nativistic' doctrine (which admits of the innate and congenital character of a function, an organ, a quality), space is an absolutely 'a priori' datum which we find within our spirit and which we apply to things; its essential properties, which are homogeneity, or the perfect identity of its parts, vastness, and limitless divisibility – properties which by their very nature cannot be grouped by experience – prove that it is a natural datum which is *a priori* to thought.

Thus, according to Kant, space is the multiple *a priori* as the form of the external sense; every representation of an 'outside' presupposes, in fact, the notion of space as the basis. The original representation of space is necessary because, however much objects may be abstracted from space, one can never abstract space itself, and it is the representation of an infinite quantity, which, as a concept, embraces an infinite number of other representations: it is therefore a 'synthetic *a priori* vision' which conjoins within itself empirical reality and transcendental idealism.

According to Hegel, space is pure 'form'; it is the way in which the idea becomes other than itself, estranges itself in nature.

> 'The first immediate determination of nature is the abstracted *universality* of its *externality*, whose indifference, devoid of mediation, is space. Space is the *rightful position* of the ideal whole, because it is the being which is outside itself and merely *continuous*, because this externality is still completely abstracted and has within it no determined difference.'[1]

According to S. Alexander and C. L. Morgan, 'space-time is the matrix of the world from which have emerged matter, life, consciousness, and divinity. The world, as we know it, has evolved from the original space-time.'[2]

Albert Einstein and Leopold Infeld, in their book *The Evolution of Physics* write:

'Let us remember that the velocity of light *in space*, otherwise called ether, is about 300,000 kilometres per second, and that light is an electro-magnetic wave spreading out through the ether ... Let us consider another experiment, based on a very simple idea. Let us imagine a wheel which is turning very quickly. According to our supposition, the ether is drawn along by the movement and participates in it. A light-wave passing near the wheel would therefore have to have a different velocity, according to whether the wheel is in motion or at rest.

---

[1] G. F. Hegel, *Enciclopedia delle scienze filosofiche in compendio*, 254. Laterza, Bari.

[2] Dagobert D. Runes, *Dizionario di Filosofia*. Mondadori, Milano.

The velocity of light in the ether at rest must be different from that in the ether which is drawn along quickly by the movement of the wheel, precisely as the velocity of a sound-wave differs according to whether the air is still or moving in the wind. But no such difference has ever been observed. From whatever angle we approach this question, and whatever the preconceived crux of the experience, the verdict always goes against the supposition that the ether is drawn along by movement. Therefore, the result of our considerations, confirmed by numerous arguments of a technical nature, is:

'The velocity of light does not depend on the motion of the source of emission. It must not be supposed that a moving body draws along the surrounding ether.

'We must therefore abandon the analogy between sound-waves and light-waves and contemplate a second possibility: that all matter moves through the ether without the ether taking any part in the movement. This means admitting the existence of an ocean of ether in which all the systems of co-ordinates are immersed, whether they be at rest or in movement relative to the ether.'[1]

Although this is Einstein's intuitive conjecture, it is very enlightening and significant.

The traditional Teaching maintains that prior to the formation of universes – whatever their size and level of substantiality – there exists a primordial matrix which *Vedānta* calls *mūlaprakṛti* (the root of *prakṛti*) and from which each and every thing, including the various polarities, has come forth. This is Plato's χώρα.

We may say that prior to any objective or subjective manifestation – gross, subtle, or causal – there exists metaphysical Space, or abstract Space, represented in every traditional Teaching by the circle, not as an enclosed limit but as infinitude.

[1] Albert Einstein and Leopold Infeld: *The Evolution of Physics*.

This space, however, is not the Absolute as such and is not *Nirguṇa*, which is devoid of all qualification, but is the pre-causal determination from which there originates the entire unlimited manifestation. In other words, Space is the *determination* of the Absolute, which, to be such, does not exhaust itself in Space but transcends it – while at the same time being immanent within it.

Understood in this way, space is pure power, and from the simple fact of being potential, featureless, undifferentiated, and also unqualified, it is the only principle that can be called unintelligible – not because it cannot be known but because there is nothing in it in the form of a distinct object which can be known.

The matter studied by the physicists cannot be considered to be the essential space of the Teaching, because the physicists suppose space to be endowed with certain properties, properties which represent *actual qualities*. The matter studied by the physicists may be considered to be a *materia seconda*, while that of the Teaching is a *materia prima*, the supra-sensible χώρα of Plato. The space of which we are speaking is therefore not the measurable space of science because it has no extension and occupies no 'place' correlated to any other place or spatial point. Number and geometrical points emerge from metaphysical space but are not metaphysical space. Our space may be considered to be unmeasured, because it has no possibility of being measured. It is *amātra* (without measure), to use the word in the *Māṇḍūkya Upaniṣad*.

The unmeasured is the unlimited, the origin of the finite/measured and of non-finite without measure. This metaphysical space is the original Darkness from which, by means of *Fiat lux*, there emerges the manifested and the principial unmanifested, or *avyakta*, to use the word in *Vedānta*.

From the metaphysical 'spatial zero' there emerges the Point or the seed of that which will be a manifestation: the golden Egg.

In the initiatory symbolism it is, in fact, represented by the point within the circle. In its turn, the point doubles, thus realising the primordial polarity; the positive and the negative emerge from primordial Night and begin to react with each other, creating a taut field. This stage of development is represented by a horizontal line inscribed in the circle. The inter-relationship of the poles (*Puruṣa* and *Prakṛti*; *Chokmah* and *Binah*; Father and Mother) causes the emergence of a third factor, which represents the Word, the Logos, the Idea, in which all the potentialities of manifestation are included.

In this way, metaphysical space is the receptacle for an essential triad which represents the archetype on which all things are modelled.

We may therefore picture to ourselves, following the various branches of the Tradition, a symbolical series of triads which constitute the principial archetype.

There is no aspect of the manifestation which does not demonstrate these three factors: the one Point, by dividing itself, determines the dyad, and then the triad – the son of Father/Mother. In the microcosm/man, too, the triad *ātman/ānanda/buddhi* (essential triad) manifests the material, tangible, and spatial quaternary.

From the metaphysical space, within which dwells the fundamental or principial triad, there descends to the intermediate space – a projection of the preceding triad – a space which represents the subtle universal plane, *Hiraṇyagarbha*, or the cosmic Egg, the egg which, on opening, manifests the physical space (*Virāṭ*) in which all electrical phenomena develop.

Science is currently interested in this kind of space, whose extensiveness can be measured, an exclusively physical/coarse triad consisting of the proton, the neutron, and the electron, with its innumerable transformations, interrelationships, and potentialities. However, it is worth noting that man, in his present state of development, has become aware of the primary triadic archetype of physical space, or 'mass'.

But, as we have been able to note, this material triad of *Virāṭ* is the reflection of a reflection of the first triad. In our age we shall have to acknowledge that one has gone beyond this gross triad, but not so far as to discover the intermediate triad, which constitutes the 'universal psyche' and which is of another order and another dimension.

We, as empirical beings, are obliged to stop at this kind of physical triad, a shadow of the shadow of the Real, because to go further would necessitate a change of methodology and investigation. We call it an atomic triad because we wish to point out only the three essential and fundamental aspects of the atom, as the first building-block of the material edifice or fabric, without going into 'field theory'.

At this point we might wonder: What holds the three factors of the triad together, as well as the triads themselves? For example, when hydrogen and oxygen bond to form the compound of water, what is it that binds these atomic triads together?

Science has discovered that the interrelationship among the various triads happens on account of certain forces which, according to their functional level, are called gravitational forces, weak forces, nuclear forces, strong forces, or electromagnetic forces. The nuclear force, the most powerful, acts inside the atomic nucleus, binding protons and neutrons. It seems that mesons play a relevant part in this game. The electromagnetic force, a hundred times weaker, guarantees the cohesion of the atom by binding the electronic complex to the nucleus. The weak force acts in the disintegration of particles and is responsible for radioactive phenomena. The gravitational force, the weakest, is negligible at the atomic level, but it becomes more important as the mass increases and it guarantees the cohesion of our solar system.

It may be noted that – in different ways – the same law operates: the law of *attraction* and *repulsion*. The sun attracts, but also repels, the planets, keeping them at the right distance. Empedocles had already pondered this problem. Birth and death, according to the philosopher of Agrigentum, are nothing but a blending and a separating of the four fundamental elements (of course, not those of the dense physical plane). But what is it that drives the elements to unite with each other and to separate from each other? Empedocles answers: Love and Hate as cosmic forces, not as moral qualities.

We speak of this law, considering it capable of 'responding' or 'not responding'. It is an effect of the fundamental polarity of life; it is a unifying and constant law which we find at all planes of existence. The human being itself (a triadic compound) powerfully attracts and is attracted, repels and is repelled; in other words, it is subject to the polar law of attraction/repulsion. We should make a deep study of what is commonly defined as 'desire' or, better, as the 'force of desire'. We note that some human atomic unities rush towards others to form a dyad. Have we observed that there are beings which are powerfully *attracted* by the individualised world, rotate around the individualised gravitational centre, experience revolutions (rebirths) around the powerful electromagnetic centre which is *viśva* (coarse plane) or *taijasa* (subtle plane)?

Let us return to 'desire'. In the human field, then, it is a *force* which impels, pushes, stimulates, which means that it *determines*. This word conceals one of nature's ways of working, just as the words 'electricity' and 'polarity' do in another context.

We should 'observe' this psychical movement and seek its source, its potential emergence, and its later maturity. It has its laws and its rhythms. If we do not comprehend the polar mechanism at work within us, we shall not be able to solve our problems of growth. A *mystic* is an experimenter.

In the universal order, is the force of attraction/repulsion a cause or an effect? Again, does it determine or is it determined? Science suggests that gravitational force, for example, is governed by mass, but it is also a movement, so that movement determines attraction/repulsion. Even the electrical positive/negative charge attracts and repels, but the electron itself is also movement. If movement is the cause of many phenomena, is it also its own cause? In other words, is movement the ultimate cause of cosmic becoming?

We can say, No. Movement is an effect, because it, too, is determined. The manifestation is movement, 'movement towards' something, but this movement is not its own cause. It is in polarity with 'stillness'. Then what is its cause? The Teaching tells us that the cause of movement, at whatever level and magnitude it may occur, is 'Breath', 'Fire'. Science would call it heat. But we need to say straight away that heat is a particular manifestation of Fire/Breath at a specific level of existence. At other levels this may express itself in quite different ways, which is actually what happens. There may be a Fire which does not heat or burn, because we are not referring to the fire that we commonly know. Physical fire, we repeat, is only one of universal Fire's possible ways of expression.

We must bear in mind that a law is not the same for all existential co-ordinates. For example, the law of gravitation applying to bodies (mass) is not valid for the infinitesimally small. Some laws of classical mechanics have no correspondence in the sub-atomic field.

Therefore Breath/Fire is the cause of movement, which, in its turn, determines laws and behaviour.

From what we have expounded we now have this threefold expression:

1. Breath/Fire.
2. Movement.
3. Interacting forces (those that we have spoken of and those yet to be discovered).

However, these are none other than three aspects of a single Reality: a tri-unity, which only the empirical mind can separate.

In Alchemy, too, it is said that fire animates, matter sustains, form fixes. From the union of Sulphur and Mercury is born the fruit which takes the name of Salt.

We have spoken of 'metaphysical Space', which represents the limitless circumference within which the *fire is kindled*, the *movement is started* and the *interacting forces are activated.* The whole determines objectivisation, manifestation, form. If space is the first determination of Being, and if Breath/Fire is the producer of Movement/Form, then we can also have the following triad:

1. Being,
2. Space,
3. Breath/Fire,

which calls forth the fourth event: *māyā*.

> 'In the beginning there was, in truth, nothing but this darkness (*tamas*). It was in the Supreme (*Brahmā*).'[1]

Agni is the solar god that produces the manifestation. Agni is the mystic name of the primordial Fire, or divine Breath, which, hovering over the primordial waters of Space, infuses movement/life.

Being is the principial essence which contains all the potentialities of the manifestation. It is *Īśvara* prior to his awaking; space is *mūlaprakṛti*, the root of substance; Breath/Fire is the power which electrifies, activates, and vitalises substance.

At the level of *Virāṭ* we speak of electromagnetism, but, as we have noted, this is the final effect. This triad, with its product, can be taken back to the point, to the triangle, and to the square, and the whole is manifested by the movement of the swastika (the lengthened square, or rectangle, is the rough stone or the as yet unperfected substance, while the square represents the cubic or perfect stone).

---

[1] *Maitry Upaniṣad*, V. 2.

Thus we have:

the point •

the dyad • •

which denotes the birth of polarity, which means that the point is polarised into active/passive, positive/negative (thus constituting the triad): and finally the square:

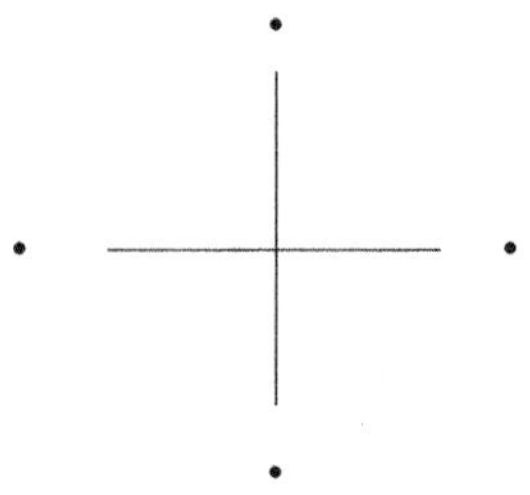

which represents generation, and when it is in movement it creates forms, becoming, formal life, whose symbol is the swastika.

We can apply this symbolism to the microcosm as well (as above, so below), which gives us: individuality (square), *jīvātman*/soul (triad), *ātman*/pure spirit (point).

Now we might wonder: How can the square resolve into a triad, and the triad into the point? How can we resolve Salt into Mercury, and Mercury into Sulphur?

How can we dissolve a molecular compound into atoms, and atoms into undifferentiated energy? This undertaking is very important for Realisation or Liberation.

There are two methods we could use:

1. *Acceleration* of the movement of the compound in order to obtain the electromagnetic disequilibrium and the destabilisa-

tion of the element, so that the atomic compound is resolved into energy.

2. *Neutralisation* of the electrical charges, that is, a deceleration of the movement, so that the atom dies to itself and becomes:

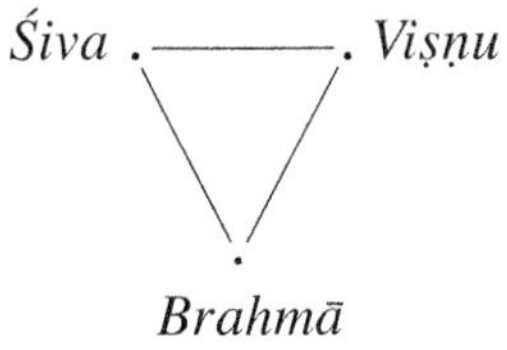

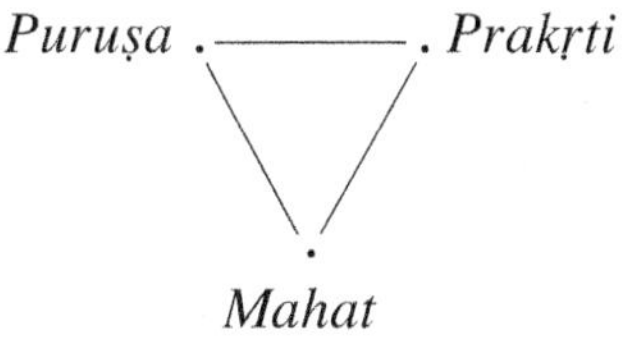

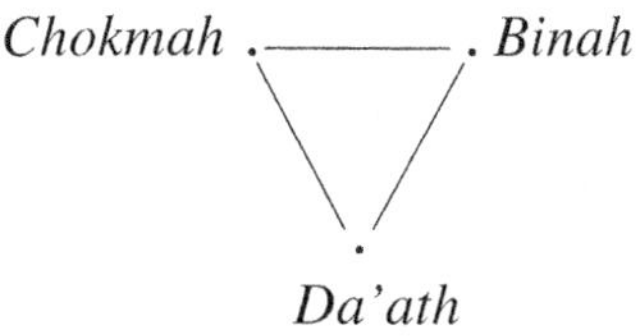

And, at the level of coarse physical space:

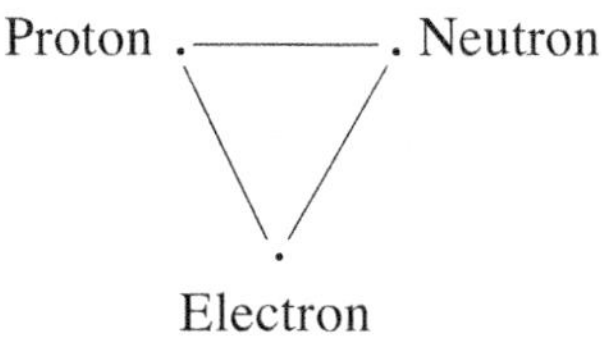

something else; it is like deflating a balloon. In this way we can make an effect on □-△ or upon 卍.

If we move to the individual, we see that, in order to resolve the □ (saṁsāric individuality) into △ (*jīvātman*/soul), we have two means: make a violent impact upon *kuṇḍalinī* by unbalancing the prāṇic/physical polarities and freeing the accumulated energy, or slow down the extrovert, formal movement of the 卍; in other words, produce an effect on 'desire', that force which is indeed movement. The first method works on mass/substance; the second, on fire/heat. The first produces disintegration of the mass and fixating of the released energy at the top of the head; the second generates the extinction of movement through the removal of fire/heat.

The natural end of a *manvantara*/universe or of a star happens as a result of the gradual slowing down of Fire to the point when *Hiraṇyagarbha* (universal Soul) is removed from *Virāṭ* (universal physical body).

We know from science that stars die through the extinction of electrons (white dwarfs), the extinction of electrons and protons (supernovae), and through the consumption of their own fuel (the most common case). In every case, it happens because the Fire of *Īśvara* contracts, thus annulling the compound.

In the three 'deaths' mentioned above, the force of gravitation, as a result of the contraction of mass, becomes enormously enhanced, sufficiently to exert an influence on neighbouring stars. But, as the fire of the soul diminishes, even the physical body increases in mass and hence in gravitational force. In fact, the individualised being, on the death of the physical element, undergoes a powerful *attraction* from the coarse body, so that in most cases the separation is delayed. This is an irrational force which often the being itself does not control, unless the being, while still alive, has begun to activate the complementary law of 'repulsion'.

Again, we can see the condition of the individual from another perspective.

Triads of the microcosm

The manifest human being is formed from the basic, elementary, or archetypal triad:

Principial triad

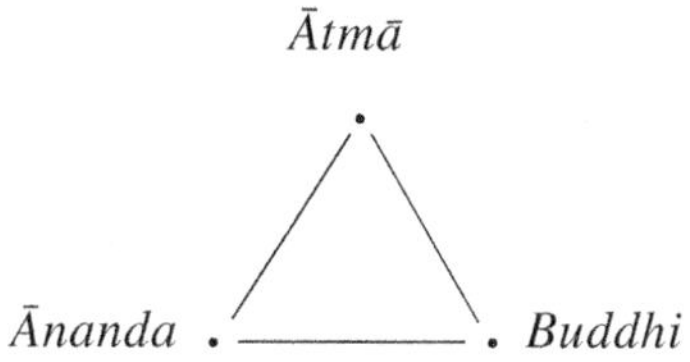

And from the individualised and composite triad:

Peripheral individualised triad

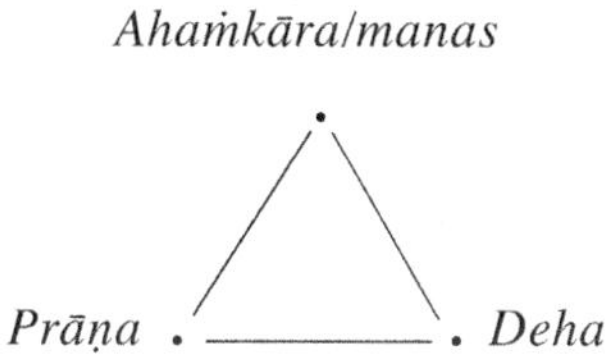

The *ātman* as such is beyond the principial triad.

When the *prāṇa/deha*/physical element disappears, *ahaṁkāra/manas* becomes unstable, and two things can happen at this point: either *ahaṁkāra/manas* takes up again (through transmigration) the densest two elements, thus regaining stability (always relative), or it lets itself 'die' and then the centre of consciousness is once again in the triad *ātmā/ānanda/buddhi*, which is the principial triad; in this case the compound known as the human individualised being no longer exists, because the *ātmā* operates at other frequencies and at different intensities of consciousness.

We know that hydrogen has an atomic weight of 1 (1.008), and so it has only one proton and only one electron. If its electron were to disappear, there would be two possibilities: either it would attract another electron and would become stable again, or it would disappear as the element hydrogen and would become an ion.

We have spoken of Being/space/breath/movement/formal life: this is a synthetic sequence. In fact, there are other elements, but there is no need for us to go into details: what we need is a unitary, or archetypal, view.

Let us go back to space; in this connotation it represents the unlimited – abstract space which has not yet been made 'mass' as we understand this word. Although science may say that space is represented by mass/body, the Teaching maintains, instead, that unlimited, 'abstract' Space exists, which can be devoid of mass/bodies. Or rather, mass is determined within this ideal primordial space, which can neither be measured nor be an object of touch. Measure is related to mass, because mass is quantity. Divine Space, when populated by triads and compounds (this is the birth of 'mass'), presents different levels or vibrational states of substance which form the varied systems of co-ordinates. In fact, in the field of atomic physics, too, for example, F. Capra maintains that 'The quantum field is seen as the fundamental physical entity: a continuous medium present everywhere in space. Particles are merely local *condensations* of the field, concentrations of energy which come and go and consequently lose their *individual* character and dissolve into the field underlying them ... The conception of things and of physical phenomena as *ephemeral manifestation* of a fundamental, underlying entity ...'[1]

And Einstein himself says, 'In this new kind of physics there is no place where field and matter can be put together, for field is the only reality.'

---

[1] F. Capra, *The Tao of Physics*. The italics are ours.

We were speaking a little while ago of levels of existence which, when simplified, are – to use the words of *Vedānta* – *Virāṭ*, *Hiraṇyagarbha*, and *Īśvara*; or, if we wish to be more particular, the plane of the physical/*prāṇa*, the plane of *manas*, the plane of *buddhi*, and so on. As we can note, there are unlimited vibrational planes within which are manifested *life*, *quality*, and *form/appearance* (quantity). The further we go down into the compound, into mass or sensible χώρα, the more the *light*, the lightness, the *freedom*, the power of the faculties or operative possibilities diminish. The closer we approach the source of Being, the more enhanced become the freedom and the power of the faculties. Likewise, the further we descend from the chemical/mineral compound to the centre of matter, represented by the atom and the atomic nucleus, the greater the light, power, lightness, radiance, and so on. The atom shines with its own light on its own plane, in contrast to the compound/mass of iron, which is heavy and dark.

From what we have said, we can appreciate why the subtle or hyper-physical beings of existence are lighter (so that they can move through the mere power of thought), brighter, and more resplendent.

As a matter of fact, we are unable to see the subtler bodies, because the retina of our eye is correlated only to a very low frequency of vibration. On the other hand, we cannot see a moving electron, although it belongs to the physical dimension. We also need to note that it is not distance which obstructs our visual perception, but *movement*. The subtler planes are also within our ... rooms: we don't have to take an aeroplane to find them.

All this we can understand in scientific terms: matter is 'empty'; between the atomic nucleus and the electrons there is a gulf, and if we were able to place the electrons next to the nucleus, the earth would become as small as a billiard ball; this is what happens when a star becomes a dwarf. This means, strangely, that matter is formed of 'void', but this void is not absolute, for within it there lives and operates another system of co-ordinates which we call the subtler or hyper-physical plane. The manifestation takes the form of Chinese boxes. The closer we get to the source, we repeat, the greater the simplicity, splendour, lightness, identity, freedom; the further we descend into the complex and the compounded, the greater the darkness, the multiplicity, differentiation, heaviness, resistance, and the reduced faculties.

What remains to be emphasised is that the manifestation does not develop gradually or in time and space (these data are mere subjective references), but in the eternal Present. Space, for example, is of several dimensions, as is the individual, and these dimensions are not successions in time, but are simultaneous. A solid, a square, are already formed, but a being with faculties of two dimensions (bi-dimensional) does not see or perceive in three dimensions at the same time, but has to change position, *move*, thus creating distance and time, and although he may get glimpses of three-dimensionality, he will never have the synthesis and unity: he will always have to superimpose one dimension on another. The individual, as such, will never be able to grasp the vital, poly-dimensional totality, but will be able only to superimpose one space/time on another, without catching hold of the present Eternal.

Śūnyatā means vacuity, void, and is a very good explanation of the state of *māyā*, but also of the latest scientific findings, which give us to understand that the manifestation is nothing but a phenomenon; Gauḍapāda, Śaṅkara, and Parmenides would call it an 'appearance' which, as a phenomenon, appears and disappears, providing always that it has as its metaphysical foundation absolute and supreme Being, the One-without-a-second.

Fire of Awakening

Unity in Change

REALISATIVE METAPHYSICS

In this age, when contingent values are desecrated, there is also the systematic desecration of values which, far from being contingent, are related to subjects which we would call absolute and inalienable.

The word 'metaphysics' – debarred from the scientific world for the obvious reason that empirical science deals with 'physics' – with its multi-faceted connotations, is used by some to bolster their lines of reasoning or, worse still, is employed by many who follow disciplines which are definitely not metaphysical.

So, we might wonder, why ever are these people using a specific term, which has its precise meaning, in a way that is inappropriate and wrong?

Let us leave aside, of course, those who have the habit of embellishing their talk with words that will make an 'effect'; fundamentally they are innocent.

Professor Giovanni Reale writes: '*Metaphysics* is the best-known philosophical word, and at the same time it is the most misunderstood. One could even say – to use the terminology of Descartes – that most people have "dark and confused" ideas about metaphysics, and only a few speak of it with ideas that are "clear and distinct".'

From many meetings with people who are interested in teachings which are occult, spiritualist, and so on, we have become convinced that what they call metaphysical is something that is 'hyper-physical', something that is not strictly material in the usual sense of the word. Thus a psychologist who is interested in the psyche (something intangible) may call himself a metaphysician. In the same way, an occultist who operates at the level of hyper-physical energies may call himself a metaphysician.

In other words, all the *branches of knowledge* which treat of the invisible (to the sensory eye) are misunderstood as metaphysical.

Now this kind of interpretation can only distort the true meaning of the word 'metaphysical' and mislead all those who approach *science, with its gross and subtle* (hyper-physical) *realms*, as well as those who would be interested in a pure metaphysical enquiry.

'Originally the term *metaphysics* meant a series of texts which, on the basis of the order given to the works of Aristotle, came after the texts called *Physics*. The subject treated by Aristotle in that series of writings was called *Philosophia Prima*.

'In time the term took on the meaning of "beyond" matters belonging to the physical sphere, to become the "science of the real in itself, seen as *beyond* immediate tangible appearance".

'From this point of view, metaphysics holds a higher position than the other fields of knowledge. Above all the various sciences of the *finite*, which deal with the partial, phenomenal and incomplete relations of being, there is the science of Reality in itself.

'Metaphysics is the science of *aseity* (the property of a being which has in itself the cause and the end of its own existence), while physics is the science of *abaliety* (the property of a being which finds the cause of its existence in something other than itself).

'We may add that physics deals with the relative or contingent, which depends on something other than itself, while metaphysics deals with what *is* or the Absolute, for it rests on itself, with itself, and by means of itself.'[1]

---

[1] See 'Metaphysical Realisation' in *The Pathway of Non-Duality*, by Raphael. Aurea Vidyā, New York.

The word *absolute* means etymologically that which is *free from relationships.*

Metaphysical *Advaita* speaks of *a-sparśa* (without relationships).

To give a correct view of what is physics and what is metaphysics, we offer a diagram (see page 266) which shows how manifestation unfolds according to some traditional teachings (*Vedānta*, *Qabbālāh*, Platonism, Buddhism, and Taoism).[1]

The unconditioned is the realm of pure Metaphysics.

The causal level is the ontological and teleological realm, the primordial or principial source of cosmic Motion.

The subtle level is the realm of 'occult or magic Science', the world of subtle energies.

The gross level is the realm of academic science, the world of forces and crystallised masses.

In the diagram we can note three states of a single Reality, that is, the totality of Being. These three states represent three modes of energy: the gross material (formal) mode, the subtle formal mode, and the formless causal or principial mode. The Unconditioned transcends every consideration; it is the Absolute in its undetermined condition.

These states are none other than states of substance at different frequencies of vibration, which originate in, and dissolve back into, the formless and principial. When we say 'formless' it is because both the gross physical and the subtle obviously have form.

Even the individual's psychical state is material, although it is hyper-physical, and this is why its state of vibration is different from that which is strictly physical/gross; and this subtle condition is always formal and *tangible* to those who have developed a particular *touch*.

---

[1] For a deeper understanding of the correspondences between *Vedānta*, *Platonism*, and *Qabbālāh*, see *Initiation into the Philosophy of Plato* and *The Pathway of Fire according to the Qabbālāh by* Raphael. Aurea Vidyā, New York.

States or Levels

Teachings	*Unconditioned*	*Causal*	*Subtle*	*Gross*
Vedānta	*Nirguṇa Brahman* (*Turīya*)	*Saguṇa Brahman* (*Īśvara*)	*Hiraṇyagarbha*	*Virāṭ*
Platonism	One-One (One-Good)	World of Ideas	Universal Soul	Sensible World
Qabbālāh	Aziluth	Briah (First Triad)	Yezirah (Second Triad)	Assiah (Third Triad)
Taoism	*Wou-ki* (Metaphysical Unity)	*Tai-ki* (Great Unity)	*Tien* (Heaven)	*Ti* (Earth)
Buddhism	*Svābhāvikakāya*	*Dharmakāya*	*Saṁbhogakāya*	*Nirmāṇakāya*

There is, in addition, something else that is very important to take into consideration, and it is this: the three states form what we call 'Nature' or the natural; in fact, they constitute the nature of the principial Being. It is therefore another mistake to speak of the supernatural with reference merely to the level of the subtle and the level of the causal/principial itself.

If these three states refer to the nature of Being, then everything that is determined within the ambit of this triple sphere assumes a natural character: all the apparently extraordinary, unusual phenomena that an individual may realise, throughout the various spheres, are not supernatural, but *natural*, events or actions.[1]

For the East all this is obvious, but not so for the West, where even a sensitive person's telepathic possibility is considered supernatural.

Academic science is interested in what is natural, but the so-called occult sciences are also interested in the natural, although at a different vibrational dimension.

In fact, Sacred Science (which is included in the 'Lesser Mysteries' or *aparavidyā*, knowledge that is secondary rather than supreme), in its most authentic meaning, comprises cosmogony, sacred magic, esoteric astrology, and so on. But although these branches of the true Knowledge relate to the *natural*, they are unfortunately derided these days, simply because the enquiry of many occultists has nothing to do with the authentic traditional Knowledge.

If many of today's practitioners of the occult (with some exceptions, of course) have nothing to do with true esoteric Knowledge, so that they desecrate something truly noble, even more do they profane metaphysics – when they refer to it – for metaphysics transcends not only the gross physical and the subtle but also the principial formless, and thus the threefold

[1] See Gauḍapāda, *Māṇḍūkyakārikā*, edited by Raphael, where the three states of Being are considered, together with the Fourth/*Turīya* or the Unconditioned. Aurea Vidyā, New York.

natural, since its precise focus is the Unconditioned, which is the realm of the Absolute as such, the Infinite, the Unqualified, the Constant, the authentic Supernatural, the A-formal, and the Permanent (and so it is included in the 'Greater Mysteries' or *paravidyā*, first or supreme Knowledge).

Many philosophers have sought to give a theoretical, rational proof of this supreme Cause, this Absolute; or rather, like many materialists, they have maintained that everything which is not subject to rational proof is unknowable. We may say that if the supreme Reality could express itself in a duality – losing its identity of Unity, of course – then this dual reality could also be proved rationally.

Operating in terms of subject and object, the mind would thus have the possibility of knowing something distinct from itself: a second, or the object of knowing. But since reality is one and one alone, all these philosophers, although they might have been able to discourse upon the ultimate Subject, have not been able to know it or prove it with the empirical mind.

If we accept Being as absolute Unity, we shall have to agree that it cannot be known or proved on the basis of a dualistic mind or on the basis of relationship. But if Being cannot be proved and yet is considered as undivided Unity, then it can only be *realised*. Non-realisation of the being within unity would involve admitting duality (I/Being), and this would invalidate our previous assertion.

On the other hand, everything that shows itself as manifest, being a second, or something other than Being, can be an object of proof; and if truths of a 'subtle' or hyper-sensible order have not yet been proved, this is because human beings, in their present state, have not opened the 'windows' of perception which they potentially possess.

An intelligible world is perceived, comprehended, and expressed through means of a hyper-sensible order: so much is obvious. Only the world or sphere of the material or physical sensible can be perceived and known through physical, material means and the five ordinary senses.

Of ultimate Truth, therefore, we can speak in terms of conscious Realisation: to know is to be; and this declaration of identity through knowledge is the very principle of Metaphysics, which is and remains exclusively 'Knowledge of Identity'.

It should be noted that there are different levels or aspects of realisation.[1] The word 'realisation' connotes 'activating, effecting'. So we can speak of psychological realisation, which involves *actualising* the harmony of the mind/psyche/body unity of the sensible being; we can speak of realising the intelligible, which involves *actualising* or *effecting* the unity with the intelligible or supra-sensible; we can speak of ontological realisation, which involves *effecting* the principial One or Being as the first expression of the One-without-a-second; and lastly we can speak of *metaphysical realisation*, which brings into actuality, as such, Non-Being, the Absolute, the One-without-a-second, or the Infinite, beyond the physical and concrete sensible and beyond the formless intelligible.

> 'I have found the long, narrow, ancient way and I have travelled along it. By it the wise knowers of *Brahman* go from this world (*loka*) and reach the celestial world when they are liberated.'[2]

To what we have already said we should add this concluding note: those – and there are indeed many of them – who speak of 'metaphysical experiences' (the metaphysical cannot actually be experienced in the usual sense of the word) do not experience anything other than individual and collective subconscious contents. In other words, they experience illusory aspects of the psychical condition. Therefore when they speak of metaphysics, which in its true meaning is the Knowledge of the first principles or final principles (according to how

---

[1] For more on this theme, see *Essence & Purpose of Yoga* by Raphael. Element Books Limited, Shaftesbury, Dorset.

[2] *Bṛhadāraṇyaka Upaniṣad*, IV, IV, 8.

things are seen), they should be speaking of pure illusions or subconscious projections. And between the ultimate Truth of data and the illusory 'truth' of things another word intervenes: *avidyā*, which really means metaphysical ignorance. Now one feature of *avidyā* is actually to mistake something for something else, a rope for a snake, the reflected light of the moon for the light of the sun, the truth of things in themselves for their mental representation.[1]

---

[1] For Realisation according to traditional Metaphysics, see the third Chapter of *The Threefold Pathway of Fire* and *Tat tvam asi* (You are That), by Raphael. Aurea Vidyā, New York.

SILENCE

If we consult any dictionary, we shall find the following definition for 'silence': 'complete absence of sounds, noises, voices, etc.; cessation of speaking; being silent.' We may also find 'religious or monastic rule imposing silence and abstention from any noise'.

If we analyse these definitions, we can ascertain that the word 'silence' is 'absence of sound' of any kind and degree, which means that the idea suggested by silence is opposite to that given by noise/sound.

Now noise/sound is the result of a vibration which, in turn, is the result of a movement. So we have the sequence of movement, vibration, sound (although they are all one). All this is expressed in terms which are rational and, at least, scientific. For us this is extremely important, because it allows us to understand where we shall have to intervene in order to realise silence or bring our vocal and mental sounds to silence. Speech is represented by sound, which, as we have said, is the result of vibration; in this case, vibration specifically of the vocal cords.

In order to become manifest, the vibration itself must have an impulse behind it; to make two strings of a piano vibrate, a movement must be imparted to the corresponding keys.

Our speech, therefore, is the result of a vibratory condition and an original movement or impulse. In philosophical terms we may speak of an efficient cause, an instrumental cause (in our case, the vocal cords), and a final cause (sound). In order to be able to neutralise the sound, we shall have to go back to the efficient or motivating cause; otherwise we shall make an error in the operation and have merely a forced inhibition. So to continually inhibit the sound (the final phase of the motivating cause), without intervening at the source of the process, indicates a failure to solve the problem.

In order to be silent we certainly need to stop movement (*vṛtti*), for unless this happens the vibrations will continue to produce sounds/noises. We have said that we shall have to stop movement: this implies that behind it there must be 'someone' who has the power to *stop* or to *activate* this movement, movement not being *causa sui*.

Now we know that the human being is composed of consciousness, psyche, and body/ *sôma* .

The consciousness is *sat-cit-ānanda*, and it therefore has within it the possibility of *being*/willing, knowing, and acting. The psyche has the possibility of 'feeling', perceiving, moving certain qualities, while the physical body is able to outwardly transmit the qualitative movement of the psychical.

At this point we may summarise what we have said in this diagram:

consciousness = deliberating Being; it is *causa sui*

psyche = qualified movement

physical = vibration/sound

Movement is *rajas*; *tamas* is sound; and sound/vibration, as we know, is nothing other than movement which is solidified, materialised, and fixed. In the realm of the psychical, movement can be equated with desire, which is a movement that activates the physical. The word 'emotion' actually suggests the idea of movement.

Silence is therefore the result of stopping movement, stopping the psychical; otherwise we would always have sound/ noise. But who can stop movement? Certainly not movement itself; so we shall have to go behind movement, where we shall find the deliberating consciousness or *puruṣa*. If consciousness deliberates, declares, and determines, then it can stop movement and thus make the sounding instrument silent.

Now we are broaching another important question and giving our attention to other aspects of the problem.

So far we have had technical data which are inherent in the proper understanding of how sound/noise develops; we have analysed them into their causal components and we have reached certain conclusions. But it is clearly not sufficient to know the working technical mechanisms of sound in order to make sound disappear. Within us there must be *deliberation*; in other words, we must be *conscious*, aware of the choice to operate and of the reason for making a decision. So we shall have to put *cit* into operation, and this will give us deliberating *knowledge*, the knowledge of why, the *sat* to affirm/be that knowledge, the action (*kriyā*) to set the *cit* and the *sat* into practical activity. Therefore: I know, I affirm, and I am (what I know and affirm).

Let us return to silence. We have said that it is the result of the cessation of movement/vibration/sound/noise. We have elucidated the working mechanism of these elements, so that it merely remains for us to establish the *why* of silence.

The *Upaniṣads* tell us that *Brahman* is Silence. The realised one/*muni* is also Silence. It is also said that *Brahman* is pure Consciousness, the state in which consciousness rests in itself, through itself, and with itself, without any superimposition of movement/vibration/sound.

> 'One who has realised the bliss of the *Brahman*, from which words turn back, together with thought, being unable to grasp it.'[1]
>
> 'Having transcended the characteristic peculiar to each one [sound, all these sounds], they go to merge in the supreme, unmanifest, soundless *Brahman*. There they lose their own properties and become indistinguishable ... .'[2]

---

[1] *Taittirīya Upaniṣad*, II. IV. 1.

[2] *Maitry Upaniṣad*, VI. 22.

Now if a disciple is seeking the ultimate foundation from which there originates the phenomenal world of sound, he must, as a consequence, practise a *sādhanā* (spiritual discipline) which will lead to this result. Therefore, for the serious disciple, metaphysical Silence, or pure Consciousness, is the beginning, the way, and the end of his realisative journey. Why Silence? Because it is the metaphysical foundation of the entire manifest word, the source from which we started our journey and to which we must return; because, having resonated the manifold vital sounds in time and space, we have finally decided to return to the origin of Being, which is and does not become (movement/sound).

If we adopt a purely esoteric standpoint, we shall note that the manifest realm is an electro-magnetic game of sounds which attracts to itself all that lives: an idea, a person, or a planet constitute a *Centre*, a *Point/Vortex* of sound which attracts or repulses other weaker centres of sound. When someone states ideas, these are nothing other than a vibrating electrical potential, with all its possible consequences. Human passions are vortices of forces, produced by vital centres, which can commingle, embrace, or repel. From all this we can understand the importance of *metaphysical Silence*, which alone is withdrawn from the gravitational force of countless imprisoning sounds. Liberation is obtained when there is no longer any *reaction* or electrification or response to the various sounds of the beings which work in *saṁsāra*. Those who have attained Silence have put themselves into a condition where there is no magnetic interrelationship at any level.

'Silence is your praise'.[1]

[1] *Psalms*, 65: 1.

BEING, FREEWILL, LIBERATION

We have been told that *Īśvara* (Being/Person) represents *one* of the *countless* determinations of the *Nirguṇa* Absolute, and that one *manvantara* (cosmic cycle), in the compass of Being/*Īśvara*, constitutes the totality of the unresolved seeds of a previous *manvantara*. We may say, with Plato, that the world of Ideas/Being is one of the *countless* possibilities of the One-One or the One-Good, which is higher in 'dignity' than the Being/World of Ideas.[1]

We stress the word 'determination' and then the concept of 'seed'. Determination is the exact specification or limitation of an expressive condition in the realm of operative and ideational possibilities; it is something definite, fixed, and established by a Reality which is all-transcendent. This means that such a Reality, in its essence, is undetermined but has the potential to determine. This limitation always constitutes something 'less' in comparison with absolute Reality, just as the successive lower generations are always 'less' than principial Being. Let us say that a compound is always less than the essence or the uncompounded.

A determination is therefore a restriction, an impoverishing restraint.

According to Plato, too, Being manifests itself in the world as 'norm' and 'measure', that is, with precise determinations. If the atom (to give an analogy, and it should be understood as such), as an archetype of molecular substance, were not what

[1] See 'The sphere of Being or of Ideas' in *Initiation into the Philosophy of Plato*, by Raphael. Aurea Vidyā, New York.

it is, we would have, unceasingly, transformations which would be unthinkable, chaotic, confused, and unpredictable, so that science itself, in all its branches, would be compromised. We can conceive of privation only if we compare it with the metaphysical Infinite, with *Nirguṇa Brahman*, or Plato's One-One.

On the other hand, if the *nature* of the being were determined absolutely, we would not even be able to posit the problem. Anyway, who could do so? There are no issues apart from those inherent in the nature of the being, which means that no simple material form – the last developmental step of an Idea – is either better or worse than another; it is, and it corresponds precisely to its *dharma*, its end, and its function. Determination represents nothing other than the predicate of something, the lowering of the object to which precise reference is being made. We are, in fact, obliged to ask ourselves: What determines itself? Who is determined? Let us answer: Being is determined. What determines itself? Its function, its state of Being, its potential for life, determines itself.

But can this Being be expressed in a better way, so as to distinguish the subject from its predicate?

We may give this diagram as an answer:

Being/Essence ⟶ *Prakṛti*/Substance
Consciousness ⟶ Principial Seed

Īśvara or *Saguṇa Brahman* is nothing other than a Reflection of consciousness of *Nirguṇa Brahman* or, in Plato's scheme,

Being/World of Ideas ⟶ Intelligible χώρα

Being, as the first determination of the metaphysical One, contains a seed, a qualified nucleus, a Point, an archetype, in which are enclosed all the *unlimited* developmental potentialities of manifestation. This is the world of archetypal Ideas. Determination is related to this Seed/Point, to Idea, inasmuch as it contains one specific possibility and not others.

Being/*Īśvara* is such because it is such and cannot be different from what it is, for if it were different it would not be Being. In the same way, the seed of a flower contains all the potentialities and future developments: the seed *is already* the flower. The Seed/*Īśvara* is beyond time and space, but not beyond cause; in fact, it is considered to be the universal causal Plane. Space-time, being relative to different subjects, is a limit with regard to manifest beings. *Hiraṇyagarbha* (intelligible plane) and *Virāṭ* (sensible plane) are nothing but developments, substantial elementary combinations of *Īśvara*. Essence and substance are not in opposition and do not constitute an absolute duality, just as the intelligible plane and the sensible plane in Plato's Teaching do not constitute an absolute duality. The sensible and the intelligible are developments of the principial seed, which represents the metaphysical foundation for all that exists. The dichotomy of Spirit and matter is meaningless, because these two factors arise from the polarisation of the Point, which contains them and at the same time transcends them.

We can now ask ourselves: if Being already contains determined potentialities and not others, if it is already defined, to what extent can we speak of freewill or the freedom of Beings? If universal life is the effect, the precipitate, the externalisation, the projection, etc. of seeds which are already established and qualified, how can we free ourselves from the bondage of becoming? This is the crucial aspect we have to consider. If someone declares, 'The being is free and it lives of and in its freedom', we shall be able to object, 'Is this freedom relative or absolute? And to what does it refer?' There is, in fact, a freedom of custom, a freedom of morals or social ethics, and a psychological freedom; and there is a freedom relating to the ontological state of the being. On the other hand, it is quite true that since Being is determined and limited, it must have its own development: quantitative and qualitative, limited and relative.

Since this is how things are, we shall have to conclude that beings are completely under the thrall of the law of *necessity*. If everything is necessitated, then the beings involved in the process must be so, too. But is it possible to support such a hypothesis?

To make a proper scrutiny we shall have to consider two aspects of the question. The first is this: when we speak of determination/limitation, we are not viewing it as a single, unilateral line moving in one direction only. Being is not the seed of the flower or the physical atom. Determination, or qualification, provides for a multiplicity of lines which fan out in countless different directions and on various parabolas. As Plato declares, Being is One-many; in Being there are innumerable expressive possibilities. Beings are free to move throughout the range of possibilities, while remaining within the sufficiently vast compass of the determination of Being. Although the seed/atom is determined within its own specific compass, it is nevertheless capable of fashioning countless molecular structures. If we had deeper intuitions, we would be able to create other molecules in addition to those which science has already discovered.

However, if the game had to stop here, we should have to admit that freedom is only a half-freedom from which we could never escape. As a result, a relativistic and reductive philosophy would be envisaged, so that it would be impossible to advance the hypothesis of a development or an awakening of consciousness, or propose its emancipation. Someone could even maintain that if everything is determined in the realm of Being, then beings are subject to the law of fatalism. Even here we should have to understand what is the *free choice* of the being in its ontological state and what is the causal determination at the level of phenomenon and *prakṛti*/χώρα. With an exclusively materialistic view of life everything becomes mechanical, fatalistic, and nihilistic, but the initiatory Teaching is not so reductive and unilateral.

We shall have to draw a distinction between the two poles of reality: consciousness/essence and substance, *puruṣa* and *prakṛti*, *noûs* and *sôma*, and so on. As we have already remarked, we are dealing with aspects that are polar and not absolutely dual. *Puruṣa*, both macrocosmic and microcosmic, is pure consciousness which reveals itself through substance/*prakṛti*; or, for a better understanding, the Spirit reveals itself through 'matter', which in its becoming follows laws that do not pertain to Spirit/*puruṣa*, *noûs*; and so we must make a certain distinction. The world of matter is the world of necessity; the world of the Spirit, in the context of determination of Being, is the world of liberty.

When we promote a cause at the level of *prakṛti*, we enter a determined mechanism which operates by means of a rigid concatenation, although even here we are not speaking in absolute terms, for we can transcend a causal law only with another law, which is what has happened with the force of terrestrial gravitation, which has been superseded. This is an ever-present possibility when dealing with the development of the qualities of Being. In the realm of secondary causes (the first cause concerns being only) there is no freedom; however, as was mentioned earlier, beyond time and space, cause and effect, there is the *puruṣa*, the *noûs*, the *ātman*, which is free in its choices and also free not to make choices. We need to bear in mind three phases of the process: the free decision to choose or not to choose, the free decision to opt for the object or content of the choice, and the final fulfilment of the decision. Once we move to the fulfilment of the choice, we are subject to the necessity of causal generation, because the fulfilment of the pre-selected object can take place only within the compass of substance/*prakṛti*. It is from this perspective that Plato maintains that, since sensible χώρα is much more resistant, heavier, and less responsive to the will of the Soul/Demiurge, the prototypes which emerge never correspond perfectly to the Idea. Thus there is a freedom *ante* and a necessity *post*.

We may say, incidentally, that the being has perfect freedom to ascend and descend the various levels of existence; it is constrained only by the limits which it imposes upon itself.

When *karma* is spoken of, it always refers to cause/effect or the production of a specific cause/action which contains the effect within itself. Even here the being is free to produce a particular action, just as it is free to neutralise the effect by putting into operation an equal and opposite cause. It is in this way that *karma* is transcended; in brief, *karma* is the result of not knowing established laws.

Ontological fatalism is when beings have neither freedom of choice nor freedom to influence the effects, so that they are nothing more than impersonal mechanisms of fate.

On the other hand, no traditional Teaching gives consideration to a fatalistic and mechanistic theory. We would also say that the unfolding of the manifestation has already been written in that causal principial Seed and that we are simply glancing through the pages and interpreting them.

No one will ever be able to change the original Archetype or the world of Ideas. All we can do is embody and reveal them. The freedom of beings consists in the fact that they can interpret or embody any written page they wish. The 'parts' of Being are innumerable, its states are manifold, and all beings can choose the parts that please them most, the existential states which they like most; no one can prevent them from being this or that with the range of the unlimited possibilities of Being.

According to Plotinus, life is a great stage on which each individual is reciting one of the manifold, unlimited parts offered by the text, but he is so identified with the 'part' that he forgets to recognise himself for what he really is.

> 'Just as on the stage of a theatre, so people like to gaze upon killings and all kinds of death and the conquests and sackings of cities: everything is like a change of scenery and costume; even tears and lamentations are feigned! For even down here, in the individual events of life, it is not the innermost human soul, but the outer soul, the reflection, which sobs and laments

and creates all its parts, while men create their own fictions everywhere, on that stage which is the whole earth.'[1]

The traditional Philosopher, the Sage, aware of this truth, has freed himself from all alienating identifications, including that which the world of sleeping men might consider the most important, elevating, and precious.

Hence the *pax profunda* of one who is realised, the fruit not only of having understood intellectually but especially of having *consciously comprehended*. We may also say with the *Muṇḍaka Upaniṣad*:

> 'The *Brāhmaṇa*, having acknowledged that the various worlds are [the results] of [unresolved] *karma* (*karma-citāh*), detaches himself from them, [recognising that] through that which is transient one cannot attain that which is eternal (*akṛta*, not generated).'[2]

There is freedom, therefore, both in the realm of the determinations/qualifications of Being and in the realm of the potentialities of the archetype of a particular *species* of life. But can we escape from the actual determinations of Being?

There is now the question of the second aspect to which we alluded earlier. We need only to remind ourselves of the first proposition expounded at the beginning of these notes in order to appreciate our problem.

We said that qualified Being is not the Absolute, not the metaphysical Infinite, but simply the *first* determination of the *Nirguṇa Brahman* of *Vedānta*, of Plato's One-One, or of the *Ain soph* of *Qabbālāh*.[3] *Nir-guṇa* means 'having no *guṇa*, quality, determination', while Being, as such, is *Sa-guṇa*, that is, 'with qualities, attributes, and so on'. The *Saguṇa* finds its

---

[1] Plotinus, *Enneads*, III. 2. 15.

[2] *Muṇḍaka Upaniṣad*, I. II. 12.

[3] See *Pathway of Fire according to the Qabbālāh* by Raphael. Aurea Vidyā, New York.

raison d'être in the *Nirguṇa*, and therefore the authentic root of the being rests in the metaphysical Infinite.

Besides, to speak of the full Liberation of beings and of the life of Being without the presupposed *Nirguṇa*, or a metaphysical foundation, would be fanciful.

The being also has the freedom, which is granted to it by its transcendent source, to rise above the *limit* (and the non-limit, as Plato would add) of the principial seed, to re-discover itself as perfect metaphysical unity without a second.

Traditional Philosophers, both past and present, who faced the problem of complete Realisation were beset by such questions as:

1. Can one escape from the human individuated determination? (Space/time or the world of generation and corruption).
2. Can one escape from the universal determination of life? (World of the subtle or intelligible).
3. Can one transcend the actual determination of principial Being? (First cause).
4. (If the answer is positive). How can one escape from it and with what means?

These have always been the initiatory issues throughout the ages, and Initiation or the acceptance of a qualified disciple was dependent on a genuine conscious grasping of these fundamental urges of consciousness.

As we have seen, if the being is free in its decisions, then it can direct itself towards the Way of Return, the Way of *re-integration* with its own metaphysical Essence. When each of us, as disciples on the Way, is asked if he has taken advantage of ... this sort of acknowledgement, he *will have* to put this question to himself in the secret of his own heart, if he is a true disciple, remembering that either he determines himself or he is determined by *prakṛti*/χώρα. In this case, however, there is no need to reprove or condemn any 'anthropomorphic God' projected by our anxious compensatory mind.

> 'Now these are the impediments (to the uncovering) of knowledge: in truth, the origin of the net of bewilderment is that one who is destined for heaven has connections with those who are not ready for heaven. This is the origin. Even if a vast tree with wide-spreading branches were pointed out to such people, they would go and take shelter under a low shrub.'[1]

We can summarise everything as follows:

Absolute freedom	=	the metaphysical One, Plato's One-One, *Nirguṇa Brahman*, absolute Consciousness
Determined freedom (but within unlimited expressive possibility)	=	World of qualified and determined Being (*Saguṇa*), World of Ideas
World of necessity	=	Manifestation, World of generation and formal becoming

[1] *Maitry Upaniṣad*, VII. 8.

BROTHERHOOD

It frequently happens that most 'spiritual organisations' promote and peremptorily urge their members to express *tout court* what is known as 'brotherhood'. There are also religions whose objective is precisely to promote universal brotherhood by means of what we might call emotional activism.

There is no need to substantiate these statements, because their reverberations undoubtedly constitute adequate proof for those who observe.

The question of brotherhood is not restricted to our day, for it is lost in the mists of time. As part of certain esoteric teachings, brotherhood was spoken of even in the distant days of Atlantis. The words may change, but the essence remains the same.

Now all this complies with truth, and there is certainly no desire to refute it. Those who accept the 'one truth without a second' cannot but affirm the unity of life, unitary love, and its corollary at the human level, brotherhood.

The question, therefore, does not concern the affirmation as such, but is related to another aspect of no small importance: the desire, no less, to present this question merely theoretically, in words that are totally simplistic, with an emotional emphasis and, as we said earlier, with an activism strong enough to condition even the freedom of others.

In other words, the individual is told, 'Do good, consider others as your brothers, do them no harm', and so on.

These words have been handed out generously and continuously, day after day, for thousands of years. Unfortunately, in spite of all the broadcasting, individuals today are no better in their 'hearts' than they were in the days of Christ, the Pharaohs, and so on. This fact is even more evident than the one that was enunciated at the start. Something is certainly going wrong, either in those who are uttering such words or in those who are listening to them, or in both. And this can only be another proof. Some might even come to the conclusion that the idea of brotherhood is not feasible. And yet it exists, but this is not the place for philosophical and doctrinal proofs.

Why, then, is brotherhood not translated into reality, in spite of being proclaimed, 'published', and shouted out to the four corners of the earth for millennia?

Why is this truth – which, in brief, constitutes the reflection of a universal principle – not embodied in the world of the particular and individual?

Here are some possible reasons:

1. Because it is an empty word in those who declare it.
2. Because the minds of the listeners are often unreceptive or insufficiently prepared.
3. Because as long as there is the individualised state (*Vedānta* speaks of the *ahaṁkāra*, the 'sense of ego' in opposition to another ego), there is no possibility of being able to express truths which pertain to a different order and to different dimensions of being.
4. Because the 'dark forces' are doing their utmost to ensure that this truth is propagated exclusively as nothing more than a trite, emotional propaganda slogan.

There may be other reasons, but for the time being let us consider just these four points, which are, of course, interrelated.

First of all, we should repeat that, at the human level, the urge for brotherhood is the effect of a cause which is of an order that is principial/universal. The name of this cause is Love. A corollary of Love is actually to consider the other as part of oneself, because Love reveals and makes known the *unity* of life. We are drops of the same ocean, children of the same universal Father/Mother. Life is undivided unity, but 'fallen man' has sundered himself from the undivided whole and has set himself up as an autonomous, independent being, forcing himself into loneliness and conflict (the myth of Narcissus).[1]

Love, then, rests on another universal principle, which is Knowledge/Wisdom. Love, if not directed by Knowledge/Wisdom, is a blind and irrational force: hence the different human passions which are forms of degenerate love. But Knowledge itself that is not infused by Love becomes unproductive, devoid of fire and soul, and inoperative. We may say that these two principles are like the two sides of a coin, so that there is Knowledge of Love (Intellect of Love) and Love of Knowledge (*Amor intellectualis*).[2]

In the human realm, brotherhood is therefore the result of an act of awareness regarding the universal Truth. Where this is absent, there cannot be an effective expression of Love or, therefore, of brotherhood.

The lover follows two movements. The one that has special priority is directed to the 'desire of Love divine ... by seeking to show that the force of Love is none other than that which leads the soul from the earth to the lofty peaks of heaven and that one cannot reach supreme bliss except through the prompting of the yearning of love'[3], which involves *going into oneself*, a dive into one's own Presence as a substantial image of the Divine. Love can become genuinely active in those who are permeated by the celestial image.

The other movement turns outwards; because the person who loves *possesses* Love, he reaches out beyond himself and turns towards the other to understand and comprehend him, enveloping him in his own fire of Love.

---

[1] See 'The fall of the Soul' in *The Pathway of Non-Duality*, by Raphael. Aurea Vidyā, New York.

[2] On this subject, see *The Science of Love* by Raphael, especially 'Platonic Eros'. Aurea Vidyā, New York.

[3] Plato, *Symposium*.

But true Love, with a capital letter, is a yearning for the good of the Soul, because it is intelligible Love which works within immanence, and the good that we can offer to the Soul which is fallen and in conflict, the Soul with its wings clipped, to use Plato's expression, is to show it the way of salvation and its own transcendence, and to restore its wings that it may fly towards the splendour of the divine Beauty.

The *Upaniṣad* says:

> 'In truth, it is not for love of the husband, my dear, that the husband is dear, but it is for the love of the *ātman* that the husband is dear. In truth, it is not for the love of the wife, my dear, that the wife is dear, but it is for love of the *ātman* that the wife is dear. In truth, it is not for love of everything, my dear, that everything is dear, but it is for love of the *ātman* that everything is dear. My beloved, it is the *ātman*, in truth, which must be realised, heard about, reflected upon, and deeply meditated upon. In truth, my dear Maitreyī, when the *ātman* is known through hearing, reflection, and deep meditation, then all this becomes known.'[1]

It is clear that some things, which pertain to the level of Principles, cannot be 'publicised' or repeated like commercial slogans or imposed, for the simple fact that a Principle is not a 'concept', a notion, or a mental representation, to be given as if it were a vegetable or a coin.

A Principle, and love is a Principle, can only be *comprehended, integrated, lived.* And all this requires the death of egotism, egoism, and the 'concept' of mental duality. This, in turn, involves perfect Realisation; in other words, it requires 'initiatory death'. But dying to individualisation is not for all, because 'many are called, but few are chosen', which means that in the course of time what has been given to individuals hungry for themselves and their own separateness has been, in fact, the hazy 'mental concept' of brotherhood. But concepts

[1] *Bṛhadāraṇyaka Upaniṣad*, II. IV. 5.

are not reality: they are merely mental images, appearances which produce nothing; in short, they are *words* which do not *vibrate*, because the word which comes forth solely from the empirical mind is a dead word.

Conceptualisations are useful at the level of quantity but not at the level of quality. Quality cannot be conceptualised, but it can be *realised* and *lived*.

Initiatory Knowledge cannot be conceptualised because it is Knowledge of identity and therefore assumes a symbolic character. The Will of the Good cannot be conceptualised; it can only be evoked and actuated. And when we seek to discourse on universal truths, we generally do so in terms of 'not this, not this', that is, by 'solving' what is not. Certain things of the intelligible order can be transmitted only through the use of *influence*, and not by means of conceptualisation, least of all if the conceptualisation is emotional and emphatic.

We know from evidence that the neophyte, even if advanced in the mental realm (rather, it is this type of neophyte) enlarges his psychical sensibility so that – since the ego is still present and is necessarily present – he can have very strong reactions. He may even become fanatical about his ideas/concepts, his path, his teaching. And when speaking to him one has to be very attentive because he is easily offended and may even become violent. A great Master said that there is no worse egoist than the disciple, not because he is inactive but because he wants to give himself to others in order to satisfy his 'concept' of truth, to gratify his own passion, his unseemly emotions, his absolutism; and this kind of behaviour can be fuelled even more by pseudo-instructors, to the extent of driving the poor fellow to a state of estrangement. There are religious organisations which have forcibly imposed the message of Love/Brotherhood by banishing, isolating, and even killing. In truth, there are many 'speakers' but few 'doers', to use the words of Saint Paul, and it is because of this that, in the absence of true labourers, the harvests rot.

There are two reasons why the mind of the hearer, and then his consciousness, often fail to receive the message:

1. The message, being couched in terms of mere mental representation, does not come from the *heart*, which alone is able to comprehend, able to bestow itself intelligently, able to vibrate harmoniously; and therefore the message cannot penetrate into the depths of the consciousness.
2. The neophyte, not being totally ready, must be prepared in some way. And this is where the work of the Teaching comes in; whether it shows itself using this method or that method is of little importance, provided that it relates to the *awakening* of the *heart* of the neophyte.

We have seen that the flowering of the principle of Love involves the death of the separatist empirical ego; now we must repeat that this act is not for everyone. Not all are qualified (although all are potentially qualified) or disposed to comprehend and to *transcend* the empirical ego in order to rediscover themselves in the ontological I. We say again that not all wish and are prepared to love truly.

Many disciples, directed by their emotional sentimentality, proclaim to all indiscriminately, by word and pen, the principle of brotherhood, and they merely succeed in stimulating the sentimental, emotional, and therefore *subjective* egoistic element in the aspirants and in all those who approach (even out of curiosity, for profit, or for psychological compensation) the spiritual Teaching. What is therefore obtained is the development of a wholly subjective feeling which operates in the psychological realm and is characterised by the duality of attraction and repulsion. Hence the fanaticism and unilateral passionateness of the neophyte, a passionateness which often spills over into the realm of sexuality.

But, as we have seen, Love – and therefore brotherhood, its effect – is neither a concept nor a subjective feeling: it is a Principle, an Idea, an ontological Reality which excludes all subjective duality and all dianoetic conceptualisation.

If people are violated or killed, as we have already mentioned, in the name of Knowledge and Love, it is because these realities are not being *expressed* in their purity or at the right level that is appropriate to them, but show only the 'emotional' side of knowledge and love, and this is a quite different matter.

The inference from all this is that where there is the wish to maintain the 'individualised state', the offer of universal truths means an ever greater empowerment of this state, because the 'sense of ego' (*ahaṁkāra*), or the 'spirited soul', is a prism which fragments the unity of the Light (Being), and then there is identification with a particular colour, making it absolute (individuality/becoming).

And in the world of politics, do we not find the Blacks, the Reds, the Whites, the Greens, and so on, which contend with each other for the truth and the expression of pure brotherhood? And do not different religions contend – not always in strictly verbal terms – for the very God of Love and Knowledge?

And does it not happen, in some esoteric groups, even in initiatory groups, that the Teaching is individualised and made fanatical to the point of opposition with other groups? It may come about – and this is not unusual – that a 'spiritual group', esoteric or even initiatory, will establish a group ego of extraordinary power which may be capable of doing anything.

Although the most sacred and the most beautiful things may be offered to individuality, it fashions them into a mere 'concept' and then deceives itself into believing that it is living a reality which is, in fact, behind the concept.

> 'Give not that which is holy unto the dogs, neither cast ye your pearls before swine, lest they trample them under their feet, and turn again and rend you.'[1]

---

[1] St Matthew, 7:6.

Since the individualised state pertains to the order of becoming, it expresses only 'having' and not Being, and so it clings to all those things which can be quantitatively possessed and which – since they represent mere objects (concepts, feelings, urges, and so on) – are not and can never be.

There is something more, because certain 'dark forces' – whether they are conscious or unconscious is of little importance; the conscious forces generally make use of the unconscious – work precisely in the realm of the psychical/emotional, exactly where there is talk of 'brotherhood', 'of passionary knowledge', of subjective egoic love, of doing 'good'; in short, of wishing to redeem all humanity; or, if sufficiently stimulated, these people are capable of undertaking verbal crusades, in writing and in actuality, even to the point of violating the freewill of every soul. This is what gives rise to the struggles, oppositions, and acts of violence among various spiritual groups and even within the same confraternity.

The 'enemy' never attacks head on (if he did, it would be clear that he is only a low-grade sorcerer), but he uses the language of his adversary, at times even the same Teaching. It may be said, however, that he imbues it with passion and fanaticism, intensifying it so as to create obscurity, unilateralness, and delusion in the consciousness and mind of the neophyte. Once this is done, the rest comes by itself. On occasions, the 'enemy' avails himself of the expressive content of a true Initiate, but he twists it to his own ends; or rather, it may happen that he associates his own name with that of the Initiate in order to enhance his own worth and credibility.

It is often assumed that the real 'enemy' of spirituality (using this word in its widest meaning) is produced by materialism; but this is not always true, for the genuine and unsuspected 'enemy' is actually within the realm of the spiritual. Materialism, as such, has no masks: it is clear, obvious to all; it has always existed and it will always exist in the realm of the individualised empirical. One may even recognise its function:

after all, it can be seen as part of a polarity. By contrast, in the spiritual/initiatory context the 'enemy' is no longer a mere polarity but an element which disharmonises, alienates, destabilises, and is anomalous. It is believed that behind every kind of religious/spiritual fanaticism of an intellectual or emotional order there are 'dark forces' which are working discreetly but powerfully and effectively.

When we speak of 'intellectual fanaticism', we mean that the empirical mind of these people is moved principally by passionateness, and therefore by the realm of *feeling*. Now if an emotionally passionate person is capable of folly, and not just of a frivolous nature, then a mentally passionate person is even more dangerous, more insidious, more destructive. Indeed, the 'dark forces' which are more authentic and at a higher level make use of these 'manasic' *powerful individualities* to exaggerate, to oppose, and to actually contaminate the aspect of traditional or initiatory 'culture', which is the most significant feature of an initiatory organisation. (Culture is not erudition; it is something more. Its degeneration is culturalism).

It is obvious that this empirical intellectualism and this emotionalism always operate in the realm of the individualised, which is the only area where these 'dark forces' can act.

The Intellect of Love, or the Intellect of the Heart, is the key which unlocks the mystery of the Kingdom of Heaven.

Brotherhood is only an outcome of the principle of Love; but we need to understand that if this Principle is not grasped first of all, in other words, if the vertical line is not followed, then the horizontal line cannot be effected. Where there is no realisation, there cannot be the expression, the actualisation of anything. And yet – we repeat – so many spiritualistic organisations and groups do nothing but incite their own neophytes to 'do good', to offer themselves – in a disinterested way, as they say, (meaning to other empirical egos) – not to isolate themselves, but to live in the world of the collective unconscious, because to look out for oneself, they tell them, is egoism.

This is the reversal of initiatory truth. This is how the 'dark force' works: by coercing or persuading the true neophytes not to be self-interested, so that they cannot practise self-introspection, cannot know themselves, cannot enrich themselves spiritually, by putting them into a condition where they cannot offer themselves truly and usefully.

But, it might be objected, how could they give themselves, offer themselves, unless they have first filled their own knapsacks? How can they practise brotherhood unless they have first discovered, through the *realisation* and the actualisation of their own potentialities, what Love and brotherhood are? How can they offer the (initiatory) Art unless they first go to school to learn it?

And who would dare to tell a student – engaged for at least a third of his life in dealing with himself and his studies – that he is an egoist? And how could Realisation of the Self/*ātman*/*noûs*, which clearly and necessarily involves the implementation of universal Consciousness, mean a closing-in and egoism? And isn't the opposite perhaps true: that by involving the neophyte more and more in the activism and dynamics of the collective unconscious (so as to be a mere 'intriguer' in profane set-ups, and he couldn't be other than this, since he is ignorant and in the company of acquisitive egos) one will lead him into a real and true alienation?

Wherever there is ignorance there is also a potential channel for the 'dark forces'.

It should also be said that nowadays the 'social trend' is towards gatherings, the herd spirit, crowds, group conditioning, social activism, objectivisation (and this for reasons that are purely political, reasons which are not to be tackled here because they are outside the scope of this note), with the result that individuals feel already in conflict if they manage to spend half a day at home collecting details and becoming aware of their own weaknesses and faults, or of their own imperishable Self.

The authentic Traditions, however, maintain that the end of man is *contemplation* (*theoria*).

Activism is a wholly profane phenomenon, mainly of recent times, as a result of which even spiritual organisations, unfortunately, suffer from this impulse of the collective unconscious.

In short, the fundamental question is not 'What to do?' but 'What to be?' The question is not one of wishing to create 'activity' in the profane world, which is totally depleting, but of filling oneself, through *theoria/contemplation*, with Wisdom and with Love of the Soul.

Spiritual enquiry is not a 'way of having or obtaining' something (the gratification from, and of, doing), but a *way of being* in Simplicity and Silence; and the highest *theoria/contemplation* is precisely that which leads to metaphysical Silence, which reveals itself as an authentic *living creation*[1]. Acting is concerned with individuality and the world of individualities, the realm of interpersonal relationships, in which conflictual duality finds its place.

> 'Action, therefore, subsists by virtue of contemplation and vision. This is so true that, even for those who act, the aim is contemplation, as if, being unable to attain something directly, they seek to acquire it in a roundabout way.'[2]

Action that is true and right in the world of the individual must be in accord with universal *Dharma*, universal Order, and universal Harmony (*ṛta*). But if we lack the universal Vision, the fruit of realisation, how shall we be able to act justly?

Today's culture has completely sunk to the level of *doing* and *producing* (the rule of quantity), reducing man to a mere technical/metallic/reductive element. This constitutes the victory of the 'praxis of materialism' over the quality of the Soul and the intelligible, although here and there some compensatory

---

[1] See Plotinus, *Enneads*, III. 8. IV; Plato, *Phaedrus*.

[2] Plotinus, *Enneads*, III. 8. VI.

signs can be noticed. But in our present condition we are not *persons*: we are merely 'consumers'.

Now those who aspire to pure Knowledge would have to take care not to get caught up in this quantic activism and this exclusively emotional 'doing' which governs the collective unconscious and leads inexorably to the realm of appearances and to an ever greater forgetfulness of the Self, the Self towards which, by contrast, the first and last *dharma*/duty of our existence must be directed.

Love is a universal principle which does not touch the world of forms and compounds, but the world of Souls; it stands behind appearances, being the fruit of spiritual discipline and realisation. Love involves union and is also the burning thirst for the Divine within us:

> 'Radiant Love requires completeness and unity of consciousness. It is the magical agent which allows you to saturate the phases of the *Opus*. Remember that Love moves and unifies the substances of the *Opus*, while Will provides concentrated, definite force, and Intelligence gives wise direction.'[1]

And union cannot be found at the individual level of form. Where there can be pairing and emotional sympathy, there can be solidarity and emotional participation (all things in time and space), but not perfect unity, which pertains to a supra-individual dimension and is beyond time and space. Only those who have *unified* themselves can comprehend all the others (within themselves); but to unify oneself it is necessary to actually come out from that collective unconscious composed of passional individualities, just as it is also necessary to detach oneself from the very plane of the sensible. It is only when one has regained unity, and therefore universal, immortal Knowledge and Love, that one can 'sacrifice' and bestow in the world of men and the collective unconscious.

---

[1] Raphael, *The Threefold Pathway of Fire*, II. IV. 3.

The individualised existential problem is twofold and pertains to the realm of becoming and impermanence, and so it cannot be resolved. When one problem is eliminated, two others rise up; and when these two are resolved, yet others appear. This is self-evident. The conclusion may be drawn that the problem arising from individuality cannot be resolved but can be merely transcended; and to transcend it, it is necessary to reach that self-unification which we have mentioned earlier. In the world of Principles there are no problems, because there are only truths to be revealed, just as a flower naturally reveals its fragrance.

Problems arise in the world of psychological duality, movement/*māyā*, becoming, the desire and restlessness of *saṁsāra*, and not in the world of Being.

In order to actualise and reveal unifying Love, and consequently brotherhood in the human realm, a precise realisative path has to be followed, and preliminary qualifications are necessary, without which there will certainly be failure. If a simple neophyte who is starting on the way of *premavāda*, the Pathway of Love, is told 'Love and serve others', the journey on the Way has been reversed: he has been offered the Omega but not the Alpha of the ascent.[1]

It would therefore be good not to have premature and over-ambitious calls for a desire to redeem the whole of humanity or to promote 'emotional and affective chains' to help individualities which still have need of the sensible level and its experiences, individualities for which there are already social situations that are able to satisfy their contingent needs.

> 'If they ask you to speak, reply
>   "Give me the Fire of knowledge."
> If they ask you to love, reply
>   "Give me the Fire of love."
> If they ask you to relieve someone of a burden, reply
>   "Give me the Fire of power."

[1] See *'Bhakti Yoga'* in *Essence & Purpose of Yoga* by Raphael. Element Books Limited, Shaftesbury, Dorset.

The "Way of Fire" is for those who wish, before all, to fill their own knapsacks.
You cannot give what you do not have.
The many hope to give what they do not have. The many hope to give without possessing. The empirical ego lives and perpetuates itself in delusion.'

'Seek not to "transform" others. Transform yourself. Your fulfilment alone fulfils the circumambient space of life. The "Way of Fire" is to resolve oneself in order to resolve.'

'We are at war with each other, because we are at war with ourselves. We shall never be able to establish Order, Accord, and Harmony - attributes of the Gold of the Philosophers - until Harmony is acquired by the consciousness of the individuals. Anyone who claims that Order can be established without being first realised within each being is far from comprehending the cause that determines human conflict.'[1]

[1] See *The Threefold Pathway of Fire*, I. I. 26-27; II. IV. 25, by Raphael. Aurea Vidyā, New York.

BEING/THE CONSTANT

We have seen elsewhere that time/space/movement is nothing other than what *Vedānta* calls *māyā* and what Plato calls the world of the sensible or the world of generation/corruption.[1]

As we have already noted, time/space is not a cause but an effect, because it expresses an event, a process, which has a beginning and an end, and therefore a discontinuous reality. If we now wished to look for the Reality which is absolute or supreme, that is, the Constant, where could we look? It seems obvious to us that the Constant must exist; those spatial and temporal states can subsist precisely because they stand out against the background of a Constant; otherwise we might have the continuity ... of discontinuity.

Photons, being waves/particles, must of necessity possess a *continuum* which presents them in succession. In the same way, none of our various actions could be known and proved unless we had a continuous consciousness – in the background or as a substratum – which made them clear.

If, therefore, space/time is merely an instant/moment or 'point of occurrence', it cannot be the Constant; nor could we find the Constant in it. To think of putting Being and becoming on the same level is pure fancy. Being is, becoming appears and becomes. Becoming can only participate in the reality of Being, but it is not Being, to use Plato's words.

---

[1] See '*Māyā*: apparent movement' in *Tat tvam asi*, and 'Time/space and knowledge' and 'Space' in this book; see also Śaṅkara, *Vivekacūḍāmaṇi – The Crest Jewel of Discernment*, translation from Sanskrit and commentary by Raphael. Aurea Vidyā, New York.

Being exists independently of becoming, while becoming cannot exist without Being. Being is the metaphysical foundation of becoming or of time/space. Time/becoming is 'the moving image of eternity'.[1]

So where should we seek the Constant? At this point we need to be very careful, because the word 'seek' is misleading. Seeking involves going in search of something that we don't have. We can seek an event in our past because it is no longer in the present; we can seek a future event because it doesn't yet exist and therefore is not in our present. In other words, we can seek that which becomes, that which appears and disappears.

We have mentioned elsewhere that in order to come out of space/time we would have to no longer *become* but to 'fix ourselves', be still/stop. From this we infer that the Constant, being the metaphysical foundation on which are superimposed the vicissitudes of space and time, has to be found in that which we really are at certain levels of existence. The Constant, therefore, is what we are, as pure Consciousness without superimpositions. The Silence of the movement of the *guṇas* represents the realisation of the transcendent or *nirguṇa ātman*.

If the *ātman/noûs* is what we are, we cannot say, 'I have to look for my ātmic consciousness', but we can say, 'I am eliminating from the single undivided Consciousness the superimpositions of every kind and degree, for they are mere projections whose quality is that of 'appearance'.

A form, an individualised being, and 'I': these are a moment/instant, a discontinuum, space/time/movement. And this phenomenon, which appears and disappears, only to re-appear in a different form, needs to be stopped in the case of those who thirst for the Constant.

Being reveals itself when the sequence of becoming is halted, because becoming can be and not be; in fact, it is said that *māyā* is and is not; this is because phenomenon is not a

---

[1] Plato, *Timaeus*, 37d.

nothingness like the horns of a hare or the son of a barren woman; it is not, because *māyā*/phenomenon, in comparison with Being, appears and disappears like a mirage in the desert. Being /the Constant is evident when *māyā* has been silenced; once movement has ceased, Being can shine forth innocently.

In music it is the rest which puts the note into relief. A continuous sound is impossible (just as a continuous universe is unthinkable), but such is the speed of the sound that we miss the rests; we miss the reality that has no sound. Our mind, our emotions, and our instincts stand for the sounds, but they are necessarily subtended by 'pause', that is, by silence. Let us prolong the 'pauses/silence' until we are masters of the sounds and, if there is a thirst for transcendence, let us resolve the sounds themselves.

What needs to be noted is that Being, or the Constant, is not in some distant paradise, in heaven, or elsewhere; nor is it to be realised only after the death of the physical body or other bodies. Parmenides states that Being is 'always a complete whole now', so that it can be revealed at every moment precisely because, as we have already suggested, it does not depend on time, space, or causality.

The sensible, though participating in Being, is not Being/the Constant, and so to think of making absolute *that which is not* (since it lacks sufficient reason) means to find oneself in a dichotomy, in the irrational, in conflict, and in the realm of the perishable, with no solution. This condition is typical of the *kali yuga* or Iron Age, in which we invest not only social values but even Reality, which, as Plato says, represents the 'standard and the measure' of all things.

Referring to Being/the Constant, here is how the *Māṇḍūkya Upaniṣad* expresses itself with regard both to Being (as the causal body, *Īśvara*) and to Non-Being (as pure, supreme Being); in this short note we have chosen to consider Being from this latter perspective, according to the pointers given by Parmenides.[1]

> 'This is the Lord of All (*sarveśvara*), the Omniscient, the inner Ordainer, the Source of all; in it all things originate and dissolve.'
>
> 'It is not knower/conscious of the internal [world], or of the external, or of both together. It is not a homogeneous unity of knowledge/consciousness. It is neither conscious nor unconscious. It is invisible, non-acting, ungraspable [by the senses], indefinable, unthinkable, indescribable. It is the single essence of consciousness as the *ātman*, without any trace of manifestation. It is peaceful, auspicious, and non-dual. [The Sages] consider this to be the Fourth. That is the *ātman* and as such must be known.'[2]

Still with reference to this supreme Being, here is what Plotinus says:

> ' ... since the One has no abode.'
>
> 'If one sees oneself transfigured in the One ... *the end of the journey has finally been reached* ...'
>
> 'This is the life of the gods and of divine and blessed men: detachment from the remaining things down here, a life that is no longer satisfied by earthly things, a flight by oneself alone to oneself alone.'
>
> 'This [the One] is therefore not Spirit, but is prior to Spirit! For Spirit is already "something" which is included among beings. The One, by contrast, is not "something", but is prior to every thing and is not even being, since being possesses form, as it were – the form of being – but the One has no form, that is, it does not even have spiritual form.
>
> 'To explain: precisely because the essence of the One is the support of all things, it (essence) is none of these things; so

---

[1] See 'Parmenides and his vision' in *The Pathway of Non-Duality*, by Raphael. Aurea Vidyā, New York.

[2] *Māṇḍūkya Upaniṣad*, *sūtras* VI and VII.

it is not "something", not quality, not quantity [that is, it is *nirguṇa*], not Spirit, not Soul; it is not in movement or, on the other hand, in stillness; it is not in any space or time; instead, it is the sole Ideal, totally self-enclosed ...'

'Strictly speaking, neither "this" nor "that" should be applied to the One [*neti neti* of *Vedānta*].

'... But as for the One, let us never try to find "how" It was born, because truly and properly It was not born [*ajāti*, non-birth, or *asparśa*, in *Vedānta*].

'But what will one be that does not even enter existence? Silence, and we retreat from it. Caught in a blind alley through our way of reasoning [merely discursive], we no longer seek anything!'

'And you, while seeking, seek nothing outside the One; but even while plumbing the innermost depths of the One, seek only the things that come after the One ... [This is not an object of experience, but a state of consciousness to be realised].'[1]

And Plato pursues the same theme:

'He will suddenly be aware of a Beauty astounding in its nature, Socrates, for which all the previous travails had been experienced, that Beauty which is eternal before all else, which does not become and does not perish, does not increase and does not diminish.'[2]

'This [*ātman*] is the eternal splendour of the knower of the *Brahman*, which is neither increased nor diminished by any action.'[3]

And in fragment 8 Parmenides states:

'What origin (γέννα), in truth, will you seek for It? How and from what would it have grown'

---

[1] Plotinus, *Enneads*, V. V. 8; VI. IX, 11; VI. IX. 3; VI. VIII. 10, 11, 18. (Italics and square brackets are ours.)

[2] Plato, *Symposium*, 210e.

[3] *Bṛhadāraṇyaka Upaniṣad*, IV. 4. 22.

In the *Corpus Hermeticum*, X, we read: 'When you are able to say nothing of Him, then alone will you see him, for knowledge of God is divine silence and the end of all our sensations.'

Again, in part three of the *Atharvaśira Upaniṣad*, we read:

> 'The subtle *puruṣa* was prior to sun and moon.'[1]

Finally, this is what Parmenides writes:

> [From this it follows that] there remains only one discourse of the Way (ὁδός) that is. On this way there are revelatory signs in great numbers: that Being is unborn, incorruptible;
> indeed, it is whole in its entirety, motionless, and endless.
> It never was and will never be,
> because it is now all together one and continuous.
> 'What kind of birth for it will you actually be seeking? How and in what way would it have grown?'
> Of non-being I will not allow you to speak or think,
> for that which is not cannot be spoken or thought of.
> What kind of necessity would ever have constrained it to be born,
> earlier or later, if it originates from no one?
> Thus it is necessary for it to exist in its entirety, or not to exist at all.
> Nor from Being will strong certainty allow anything
> to be born that is close to Being,
> and consequently the goddess Δίκη granted
> neither birth nor death to Being.
> Thus birth has vanished, and death has died.
> Nor is Being divisible ...
> For it, all of those things that the mortals decided,
> convinced that they were true [that is absolute], will be names.[2]

---

[1] See *Five Upaniṣads*, translation from Sanskrit and commentary by Raphael. Aurea Vidyā, New York.

[2] See Parmenides, *On the Order of Nature*, fragment 8, by Raphael. Aurea Vidyā, New York.

YOU ARE THAT

> 'The *Śruti* proclaims the identity of the *ātman* with the *Brahman* in the statement "*tat tvam asi*" (You are That) given in the *Upaniṣads*. Only the actual comprehension and realisation of the non-dual Self constitutes the right understanding of the words of the *Śruti*, beyond the formal (that is, literal) meaning, which seems to contradict (lower) knowledge and common experience.'[1]

The consciousness which has now matured to proper universal comprehension is effectively free from all possible involvement in the 'modification' that is inherent in common experience and knowledge.

Empirical knowledge and experience concern the individual realm and are related to the sensory (lower) mind (that is, the *manas*) and to the faculties proper to it: analysis, reflection, and so on. As a result, common experience and knowledge are closely related to the 'formal representation' and, in their being, cannot really be detached and distanced from the aspect of form.

However, since the teaching of the *Upaniṣads* has an initiatory character, as such it seeks and establishes an inner 'experience' based on the real transformation of consciousness. For this reason, it is totally outside the common mental representation and, in its symbolic expression, which is proper to every 'teaching' and is directed to the attainment of the universal, with the transcendence and dissolution of the individual, it may sometimes find itself at odds with the purely literal and discursive interpretation.

---

[1] Śaṅkara, *Sarvavedāntasiddhāntasārasaṅgraha*, 699.

'To know of is not Knowing; to Know is not knowing of.'[1] Gnosis is Knowledge, Consciousness, Realisation, Identity, Being. 'Knowing of' is mere rational philosophising, and so it is confined to the mental realm, which is formal, finite, and limited, and thus incapable of embracing the Real.

Besides, the mind itself (and all that co-exists with it) and the individual in general must be transcended in order to be 'comprehended' and to draw the real Knowledge, which is in the realm of the universal.

So on the one side we have the literal interpretation of the statements made by the *Śruti*, and on the other we have the 'meditation on the symbol', in which these statements are expressed, as a means of spiritual practice and realisative 'support'.

Hence the literal expression in general, although 'substantiated' by the highest truths, is fundamentally no more than a formal expression whose 'representativeness' or 'symbol' has to be identified and distinguished by the pure intellect (*buddhi*) on the necessary and irreplaceable basis of adequate maturity of consciousness, by which we mean the state that is attained through the right and indispensable 'evolutionary' development of the being's consciousness. This means that, at a given 'moment' (of consciousness), for the being itself 'the vision of things is transformed into a vision of symbols', and its very life is then transformed and renewed by this 'second birth', which is spiritual, inner, and, from this perspective, the only one that can be called *true*.

'Intelligence' is therefore not an aptitude or capability (in the 'volumetric' sense of capacity) for acquiring erudition, even if it is on the basis of logical acumen, because all these are part of the mental, analytical, and rational realm.

'Intelligence' is intellectual freedom from the conditioning caused by the presence of objectifying contents and formal representations in general; and it is therefore the capacity to

---

[1] Lao Tze, *Tao-Tê-Ching*, 81.

intelligere, which is directly related to the intuitive penetration to the heart of the symbolism revealed in this new universal 'vision' and particularly in the precepts of the Teaching.

Symbol is the expression of synthesising Knowledge and, being such, it is to be penetrated, actuated, and lived.

In this respect, therefore, it differs from the analytical/rational 'concept' (merely a formal representation) for which there is nothing to do except acquire and absorb it, thus making it part and parcel of one's own 'mental and behavioural model'.

Thus analytical knowledge, like discursive philosophy, is theory, conceptualisation, fixation, and mental crystallisation, whereas the Teaching is de-coagulation, solution of every mental crystallisation: Life.

If the 'mentality', however learned, knowledgeable, and expansive, is merely this fixation/crystallisation of mental substance, the Teaching – the practical Teaching of the Tradition – involves rising above it, and this cannot happen except through detachment, solution, and the transcendence of this mentality.

For this reason, if the formal expression of the Teaching appears to contrast with common experience (direct evidence) and with analytical knowledge, this is because this symbolic expression constitutes the synthesis of a Teaching and therefore does not regard the individual (even in his collective or general aspect), but regards the universal, the realm of first Principles, the essence.

> 'In the same way, my dear son, know this: when a being is deserted by the vital principle, the living soul (*jīva*), it can live no longer and so dies. But when man – like every being – dies, speech [sound, the symbol of the vital expression of being] is re-absorbed into mind, mind into *prāṇa* [vital energy in general], *prāṇa* into *tejas* [principial Fire, impulse of energy itself], and *tejas* into the subtle primordial Essence. In truth, all that exists is animated by this Essence; all this exists through It [the cause and means]; with regard to this Essence, it can be said that It is the substratum of every being and is the soul of all things; It is the only truth (*satya*); It is Being itself, which, although

impossible to grasp [and understand], is omnipresent; therefore It is the only Reality, the *ātman*, and You are That, Śvetaketu.'[1]

The proper approach to the Teaching of the *Upaniṣads* requires sufficient stability of consciousness at the intuitive/synthesising level and total transcendence of the analytical/rational realm, of individual mind, of separate and empirical consciousness (sense of ego), with whose ways of working it can appear to be in sharp contrast and opposition.

Synthesis is comprehension, while analysis implies the exclusion and separation of that which, in itself, is unitary, indivisible, and non-dual.

This is why the realisation of Essence requires the transcendence of substance and the Comprehension of form.

[1] *Chāndogya Upaniṣad*, VI. XI. 16.

MAHĀPURUṢA, PURUṢA, AND PRAKṚTI IN ADVAITA VEDĀNTA

'This whole universe, which ignorance projects in myriad forms, is none other than Brahman, free from conditioning thought.'[1]

According to the metaphysics of *Vedānta*, the gross (including the physical bodies of the various beings/*jīvas* that are involved), subtle, and causal/germinal (with the *guṇas* connected thereto) manifestation originates from *prakṛti/māyā* or *pradhāna* (that which precedes every thing), which is initially found in the pure unmanifest state: Plato's intelligible χώρα.

This is primordial Mother Nature, and it represents only a projection or *polarisation* of the universal *Puruṣa* (Eve, as we know, is born from Adam's rib), and the universal *Puruṣa*, or *Īśvara*, is a reflection of the consciousness of the *Brahman* or *Turīya*. The supreme *Brahman* or *Mahāpuruṣa* is beyond movement and hence beyond time/space/causality; it is the metaphysical substratum of ontological unity and apparent multiplicity. It is Plato's One-One or One-Good.

Now it is necessary to eliminate a series of perceptual, perspective, and cognitive errors which lead people to mistake that which is the Constant, the universally valid, the invariable, for the merely evanescent phenomenon which appears and disappears.

The first is the error of considering the 'world of names and forms' to be real, when it is not, for it is a mere movement of *prakṛti* which materialises into points, lines, and volumes that

[1] Śaṅkara, *Vivekacūḍāmaṇi*, 227.

appear on the vista of perception and then disappear. This world is not a 'nothingness' like the horns of a hare or the son of a barren woman, to use the examples given by Śaṅkara; and so it has its own degree of truth, but it is not the Constant, not the absolute Reality; it is a mere phenomenon, an appearance, like a mirage. It is Plato's world of 'shadows' or Parmenides' world of 'appearances'.

The second error is to consider the Substance with which these volumes are made to be the sole reality, all that exists, the absolute (materialism, hylozoism, absolutistic śaktism, and so on), while it (*Natura naturans*) is nothing but a *polarisation* (universal Eve) of the principial *Puruṣa-Īśvara*. Substance/*prakṛti*/*māyā* is a *polarity* of the principial Essence, which, being moved by the *guṇas*, determines the appearance of forms through which the qualities can be expressed. According to Plato, the Dyad (limit/limitlessness) or the intelligible χώρα is a polarity of Being or the World of Ideas.

This is how, at the individualised level, a qualified desire (*guṇa*) prompts the mental substance (manas) to create the form/image of the object of desire to which the consciousness adheres, taking it then to fulfilment: in this way, the desire/*guṇa* has broken an individualised equilibrium.

Similarly, on the universal scale, the unresolved *vāsanās*/*saṁskāras* of a previous *manvantara* break the still equilibrium of *pralaya* by prompting Substance/Mother/*prakṛti* to produce – through the fivefold interactions of the subtle elements – forms, volumes, and objects, by means of which these *vāsanās*/qualities can be expressed.

The third error is to consider the universal *Puruṣa*/*Īśvara*, or Being, as the absolute God or the sole universal Constant, when it is nothing other than the first determination, or a reflection of consciousness, of the supreme *Brahman*, just as the various manifest *jīvātmans* are, in turn, reflections of the universal principial *Puruṣa* or *Saguṇa Brahman*. This is how, according to Plato, Being finds its root and foundation in the

One-Good, which, in dignity and power, is higher than the divine World.

These errors are the fruit of *avidyā*, that 'ignorance' which concerns the real nature of things or, rather, the nature of Being inasmuch as It *is* and does not become. Thus *pradhāna/māyā* makes things appear which, in fact, are not; by adapting itself through the *game* of movement, it determines *appearances*, and the individual mistakes these appearances (including his own coarse physical instrument) for things that are real and absolute.

Vedānta employs two powerful working techniques to resolve these errors: discernment, or noetic discrimination (*viveka*), which distinguishes the noumenon from the phenomenon, the constant from the movement/*māyā*, by putting everything in its rightful place; and *vairāgya*, which consists in detaching oneself from what is considered to be inconstant, not universally valid and unchanging, and thus withdrawing until absolute Being is found and revealed as what *is* and does not become, and in creating identity with It, because every *jīva* is, as we have already mentioned, but a moment of consciousness of the universal *Puruṣa* (*saguṇa*), which, in its turn, is a moment of consciousness of the absolute Being, which *is* and does not become (*nirguṇa*).

For greater clarity, see the diagram on the next page.

Māyā is therefore a movement in substance which creates forms, volumes, in a continuous process of birth and death, appearance and disappearance; and the various *jīvas*, dazzled by these forms, forget themselves and force themselves into a never-ending wandering and transmigration in an attempt to grasp those forms (events/things) which no sooner are they held than they slip from their hands.

This is the myth of Narcissus: falling in love with his own form/body, which he sees reflected in the water (*prakṛti/māyā*), he hurls himself into the world of forms and generation, forgetting his own immortal Being/Essence.

Turīya/Nirguṇa Brahman

↓

Īśvara/Saguṇa Brahman

↓

Īśvara/Śiva(Viṣṇu/Brahmā) → *Prakṛti/Māyā*
Essence → *Pradhāna*
Substance

↓ ↓

Jīvātman World of names and forms

THE DISCIPLE'S ABOULIA

> 'When a person is no longer bound to the objects of the senses or to actions and has renounced all his ideations, he is said to be a yogi.'
>
> 'One who has mastered the individual ego realises himself as the *ātman*, and remains the same in cold and heat, in pleasure and pain, in honour and dishonour.'
>
> 'When the mind is silent, free of sensory desires, stable in the *ātman*, it is said to have reached yogic harmony.'[1]

Why is one bound to sensory objects? Why is one attached to egoic ideas? Why is one driven by the polarities of attraction/ repulsion, pleasure /pain, and so on? Why does the mind not remain silent, being a vehicle/body of the reflection of the Self?

These are questions which an aspirant/*sādhaka* must ask himself if he wishes to practise his *sādhanā* seriously and profitably.

If we reflect upon the psychological mechanisms that are at work, we can establish that the embodied consciousness identifies itself with the impulse to go outwards, with the driving energy itself, and with the result of the action, until it feels like an object itself, thus losing sight of – or rather, forgetting – the Subject, the witness of the whole process.

When the mind turns its attention to the particular, it makes itself particular, ' ... Rather, it becomes the object itself

[1] *Bhagavadgītā*, VI, 4, 7, 18.

… and allows itself to be shaped by the object that is being contemplated.'[1]

A sincere and faithful disciple, recognising that he is in this state, will have to confront and resolve the problem of identification or assimilation to the object. So what will he have to do? First of all he must have the right knowledge of his nature as a being. But to what does this knowledge lead? It leads to the recognition that we are neither the action nor the result of the action, neither our own vehicles/bodies of expression nor the individualised empirical ego. And to what will this recognition lead? It will lead to the discovery that we are the all-pervading *ātman/noûs*, the fount of bliss and fullness.

> 'There exists a reality, an absolute entity, which is the eternal substratum of the differentiated consciousness, the witness of the three states and distinct from the five sheaths.'[2]

We are therefore the Witness/Consciousness of the whole process/becoming within us; that is to say, we are the Witnesses of the whole phenomenal 'second'. To regain our deepest nature we shall have to resolve the *stimulus* or urge to turn outwards which makes us leave our state of being. It is clear that these things are *experiential* and not theoretical.

Desire is a movement towards … which, in turn, is characterised by the movement of attraction/repulsion. This being the case, we may have the following sequence: the original urge, the movement which tends towards (desire), action properly so called, the result of action, which, according to the outcome, may bring us pleasure or pain.

These movements of extroversion are often resolved by flight. There are people who flee because they reject things and events; or they flee from the attraction itself or from the pleasure, for fear of possible negative consequences. We know that some have never loved (desired) on account of fear; they

---

[1] Plotinus, *Enneads*, IV. IV. 2. 5.

[2] Śaṅkara, *Vivekacūḍāmaṇi*, 125. Aurea Vidyā, New York.

have fled through fear of finding frustrations, or from the anguish of losing themselves. This is the spirit of self-preservation which becomes so dominant that it paralyses the flow of a life of relationship.

On the other hand, attraction and repulsion are two sides of the same coin; they arise from the same prompting and are always forms of desire. At the level of acting, for example, they find an outlet in the desire to do or not to do. Then there are people with an intermediate psychological condition: they would like to act, but they don't act. Others would like to refrain from acting, but then they act; they may be the most frustrated, because there is nothing worse than subjecting oneself to a state of stillness, or a state of movement, which is at odds with one's inner condition.

Having assimilated the effective knowledge of what the being is, we would have to go on to resolve attraction/repulsion and also the result of action. Up to a certain point it may be that our realisative journey has been mainly theoretical. We have had the opportunity of clarifying our ideas, of understanding particular things, and of taking bearings on the situation of our psychical mechanisms, with the result that the *guṇas* (qualified energies) have not received the impact of a 'solar force' to set them on a new course. But when one tries to *restrain*, *master*, *direct* and *resolve* the psychological movement, resistances can be noted.

And if the disciple wishes to go deeper, or is obliged to do so by his level of maturity, then he may notice a withdrawal of his energies, a feeling of discomfort, which can lead to restlessness, often to indifference, and even to irrational aboulia; we would say that the psyche, turning back upon itself, misfires, as they say, feels no interest in 'tending towards', lacks motivation. Why is this? It is because, at this point, the fundamental justification which gives the impulse to the action of attraction/repulsion is beginning to be weakened. The driving force which determines *vitality* is bombarded, diminished, reduced. The ego/

ahaṁkāra is undermined, deserts itself in a negative sense, and goes into a state of apathy.

The energies that motivate the (worldly) aim of life become constricted, creating a crisis of non-motivation and disinterest.

At this point, in the case of a disciple rather than a mere aspirant, further shortcomings may show themselves on account of a twofold recognition: the evidence that fundamentally it was not pure Consciousness that was acting and the qualities that were manifesting were not innocence and spontaneity; hence the inevitable resulting disappointment at having believed something that was not so. There can also occur a subsequent crisis of emptiness and the impossibility of proceeding. In other words, he may touch the very depths of the powerlessness/emptiness of the individualised process; he may recognise that, in brief, it is not he, but someone in him, that has until now lived and acted in his stead. He may question all that he has done, and he may come to understand that throughout his life he has never really known, really loved, or really worked.

It is a sensitive moment when the ego turns back upon itself because its existence is being sorely tested. The disciple truly finds himself with his back to the wall and even doubts whether the choice of realisation has been made by this someone within him or by himself in full awareness. The being loses its security, its arrogance; it loses its pride and that particular kind of feeling which characterised its 'happy' days – days which were nevertheless deceptive.

What path can be taken by an individual reduced to apathy and to the acknowledgement of his own emptiness and impotence? What can he do when confronted by a situation like this? Of course, interests of attraction/repulsion could be stimulated once again, causing the old energies to flow back, so that he will slowly return to living as he used to and may come to see it all as a bad dream, a bad period, or some such thing.

But let us assume that he has reached a point where his consciousness will not allow him to return. When he, the true being, no longer allows a return to the world of illusions, what can he do? How can he get out of a situation where everything seems to have collapsed, even the hope of resuming his old habits and his old psychological inclinations? It is a delicate moment, an unfathomable moment, because the 'individualised psychical person' senses deep in his being the odour of death, the smell of a corpse. At this point, of course, there is nothing the disciple can do: he has no strength to act, no reasoning ability, no elucidating light.

Some solutions may be offered, but most of them are external suggestions. So individuality cannot provide solutions; nor can *ahaṁkāra*, for it can offer only its own ways of doing things, ways which pertain to its own nature. The being, therefore, has to turn elsewhere; it must necessarily find help.

When a novice at swimming finds himself in extreme difficulty because he is being overwhelmed by the waves of the sea, the *ahaṁkāra*'s spirit of self-preservation takes fright and is tormented by anguish. Making wild and irrational movements is useless, but there is an optimal position which could save him: that of being 'the dead man afloat', of abandoning oneself, of 'releasing the grip', in an *active*, *conscious* way; then the waves will not only support him but will actually cradle him. In a situation where individuality has been pushed to the extreme limits of survival, what needs to be done is to remain in a quiescent, silent state, as a silent observer, a *conscious state of motionlessness*, while being profoundly *aware* of what is happening. It is only in this way, and gradually – though time counts for little – that dawn begins to break and consciousness may note that a restorative and clarifying light starts to flood the entire psychical space. This is the *albedo* of the alchemical *opus*. If this is what happens, the disciple will find himself in a new and more advantageous set of circumstances which open the way towards the high peak of universal awareness.

'Dying while living' is not for all, but those who dare and succeed will savour a *fullness* which the individualised world cannot even conceive. According to Plato, genuine philosophy is a training in death, but every death implies a new birth.

> 'And so, is this not what is called death, the *release* and *separation* of the Soul from the body?'
>
> 'Exactly,' he replied.'[1]

---

[1] Plato, *Phaedo*, XII. 67c.

DESIRE AND KNOWLEDGE

'One whose actions are freed from the spur of desire, whose actions are consumed by the fire of knowledge, the wise call him the knower.'[1]

From the point of view of *Vedānta*, individuality consists of *ahaṁkāra* (the feeling of ego), *manas* (empirical mind), *kāma* (desire/feeling/passion) and the coarse physical body. Behind this energetic structural complex there is Consciousness as the reflection of the *jīva* (Soul), which, in turn, is the reflection of the *ātman/Brahman*.

Ahaṁkāra is that factor which breaks up the unity of the *jīva*, just as a prism splits the unity of a beam of sunlight, so that the reflected consciousness becomes identified with a particular colour/note. Individuality therefore represents a scissure, a 'cleaving' of universal Consciousness, with the result that one believes oneself to be autonomous, with a will and destiny of one's own. The 'fall' of the Soul is often spoken of, but in the initiatory context it is nothing but this scissure, this dissociation, this fracture, which obviously is not absolute. Hence there arise the various types of yoga, initiatory schools, and so on, which propose the reunion of the individualised consciousness with its universal counterpart. 'I strive to take the divine which is in me back to the divine which is in the universe,' as Plotinus put it.

Once individuality has established itself as an autonomous being (the myth of Narcissus), it has to find all possible means for perpetuating it, and very often it is in opposition to other

---

[1] *Bhagavadgītā*, IV, 19.

individualities which, for their own survival, are pursuing the same egoistic ends. Thus we have many different entities struggling to re-discover completeness/fullness, which they will never be able to find, for the simple reason that the very *nature* of individuality is transient, defective, and limited. Thus, although it may be able to see itself as torn apart from universal Being, it will never be able to be *causa sui*, and will never be able to become so, for in the final analysis it is an accidental element, a marginal factor, when taken in isolation. From this it follows that, precisely because it is not, it *must necessarily desire to be so*, for otherwise it would have no need to desire.

We desire what we do not have, but whatever desire individuality can express and carry to fruition will never be able to make its nature perfect and complete, precisely because this nature is a *deprivation*.

Every individualised action is therefore motivated by the desire which aspires to something good which it lacks and by that profound urge which instigates the search for self-satisfaction; if the urge is right, because the reflection of consciousness is trying to regain its forgotten fullness, the wrong direction is followed. On the other hand, we observe that although individuality may gratify its own desires – and we know that a 'golden calf' society has means and things at its disposal – yet it is not happy and complete. We believe this is clear to everyone.

From this traditional and initiatory truth is born the Platonic Teaching of the Soul which has 'fallen into generation' and which must *recall*, must re-instate in its own awareness (*anámnesis*), what it truly is. To realise this requires *Eros*, as the philosophical yearning for the supra-sensible, and *purification* coinciding with the process of rising to the supreme *knowledge* of the intelligible.[1]

And in his *History of Ancient Philosophy*, Reale states that it is precisely upon this recognised value of purification

---

[1] For further information, see *Initiation into the Philosophy of Plato* by Raphael. Aurea Vidyā, New York.

by Knowledge that we need to reflect in order to appreciate the novelty of Platonic 'mysticism'; it is not an ecstatic and a-logical contemplation, but a cathartic effort of inquiry and progressive ascent to Knowledge/Realisation.

> 'For those whose ignorance (*ajñāna*) is destroyed by knowledge, the latter, like the resplendent sun, reveals the supreme Reality.
>
> 'Those whose impurity is cleansed by knowledge.'[1]

Thus he whose actions are free from the stimulus of desire and passion has overcome the urge to *go outside himself*, because the fire of Knowledge has made him comprehend that fullness resides not outside but within him as the natural reality of the *ātman/noûs*. Knowledge is a factor of purification, a cathartic virtue that imparts *comprehension* in order to Be.

In *Phaedo*, 69a-d, Plato emphasises the similarity of knowledge, virtue, and purification: ' ... and be aware that the only genuine coin – that for which all other things must be exchanged – is knowledge and that, in brief, virtue is only virtue when accompanied by knowledge ... and that virtue is nothing but a purification from all passion.'

And the *Gītā* (IV, 38) says, 'In this world there is nothing so purifying as knowledge ...' (as Plato and Plotinus affirm) '... and one who aspires to perfection in *yoga* will in due course find it by himself in the *ātman*.'

Desire is the child of deprivation (*peras*) or of that 'reckless' act, as Plotinus calls it, which impels Souls to procreate in the world of 'shadows' until they 'end by not knowing themselves or their origin.' By purifying the Soul, Knowledge dissolves the bond with the sensible; thus the Soul, regaining her wings, will be able to be re-united with her divine counterpart.

---

[1] *Bhagavadgītā*, V, 16-17.

VIVEKA AND VAIRĀGYA

'Then the mind turns to discrimination (*viveka*) and has a propensity for *kaivalya*.'

'Non-attachment (*vairāgya*) is the conscious mastery pertaining to one who has ceased thirsting for visible and audible [manifest] objects.'[1]

In these *sūtras* Patañjali enunciates two working procedures which are peculiar to *Vedānta*: *viveka* and *vairāgya*, discrimination or the power to distinguish between the supreme Real and the relative/contingent, between what really is and what appears, and the consequent detachment from what is not or what is mere appearance.

In the state of *aviveka* one is guided solely by 'opinions' and projections of the collective unconscious. The mind is lethargic; it is lived by the different sensory impressions and by a passive involvement coming from the world of names and forms. When the light of *viveka* begins to arise in one's disposition, the whole situation changes: there is an interest in the fundamental problems of existence; there is an act of selection, evaluation, and synthesis with regard to one's own experience and the values of relationships; there is an effort to discover the *Constant* hiding behind the phenomenal flux of forms. This kind of discrimination/*viveka* is not the result of a process of analytic or discursive thought, but of an enlightened condition of the mind.

[1] See *The Regal Way to Realisation* (*Yogadarśana*) by Patañjali, IV, 26 and I, 15. Translation from Sanskrit and commentary by Raphael. Aurea Vidyā, New York.

> 'If, therefore, this is how things are, it must be admitted that there is a (first) factor which is always identical to itself, unbegotten and indestructible, and which never receives anything into itself from outside and never changes into anything else, being invisible and imperceptible by any of the senses. It behoves the intellect to contemplate this.
> But there is a second (factor) with the same name and similar to the first, yet this is perceptible by the senses, generated and in continuous movement; this originates in one place and perishes there, and is apprehended by opinion and with the help of the senses.'[1]

If *viveka* acquires sufficient force, it triggers the action of *vairāgya* (detachment from what we have *understood* to be unreal or contingent and impermanent).

> 'It needs to be kept in mind that *viveka* and *vairāgya* are bound to each other in the closest possible way and are, in fact, two sides of the same coin. *Viveka* implies detachment from the objects which hold the soul in thrall, thus opening its eyes; and the detachment that is thereby developed makes the sight clearer as far as the soul is concerned and allows it to see more deeply into the illusion of life. Therefore *viveka* and *vairāgya* corroborate and strengthen each other and make a kind of virtuous circle which accelerates exponentially the progress of the yogi.'[2]

Vairāgya derives from *rāga*, a word defined by Patañjali as the pleasure that arises in consequence of attraction, and hence repulsion, for some object.[3] Thus *vairāgya* means the absence of any attraction/repulsion whatsoever: a detachment that comes not from an irrational or volitional inhibition as an end in itself but from the awareness/discrimination (*viveka*) that

---

[1] Plato, *Timaeus*, 51e–52a.

[2] I. K. Taimni, *The Science of Yoga*, commentary on Patañjali's *Yogadarśana*, IV, 29.

[3] See *The Regal Way to Realisation* (*Yogadarśana*), especially Raphael's commentary to II. 7-9.

events/objects only imprison us, without solving any problems. Every type of attachment (pleasure/pain) acts as a limit on the freedom of the soul. In other words, *viveka* and *vairāgya* provide the ability to roam freely among the countless processes of life and at the different levels of existence until the attainment of *kaivalya*. Thus *viveka* can be utilised at higher levels when there is a deep discrimination between the individuality or individualised process of the being and the soul or *jīva* that governs this process; or, again, between the *jīva* itself and the *ātman* as pure consciousness of a metaphysical order. If *viveka* has recognised individuality as a factor of 'fall', of separation from the universal context, *vairāgya* can go so far as to cause the objectivised or manifest reflection of consciousness to merge into its original and transcendental source.

These transitions, these acts of awareness and realisation, are the result of *viveka* and *vairāgya*. Their proper use depends, of course, on one's specific position of consciousness and on the aim one wishes to achieve. *Advaita/asparśa* starts with such means and ends by transcending the world of *avidyā/māyā*.

I. K. Taimni writes: 'It is simply necessary to remember that sheer absence of attraction due to the inaction of the body, or to satiety, or to an interest in other things, does not constitute *vairāgya*.' It may happen that 'the attraction is merely suspended, ready to come back to the surface as soon as the necessary conditions obtain. What is needed for a true and proper *vairāgya* is the deliberate destruction of all the pulls and the consequent attachment, together with conscious mastery over desires ... Control over the vehicles by means of which desires are known and awareness of the mastery arising from this control are essential elements of *vairāgya*. To attain this kind of mastery, one would have to have been in contact with temptations of all kinds and to have passed through tests of fire of every variety, emerging not only triumphant but without feeling the slightest attraction. For if one feels any attraction one has not completely mastered the desire, even if one does not succumb to the temptation.'[1]

[1] I. K. Taimni, *The Science of Yoga*, commentary on Patañjali's *Yoga-darśana*, I. 15.

OBEDIENCE

'Obedience' comes from the Latin verb *obedire* and can have more than one meaning, one of which is 'not putting up resistance, following suggestions or commands, complying with or submitting to someone's or something's inspiration, work, or task.'

Obedience is a way of *behaving*, a way of moving, a *habitus*; it may concern the formal aspect of relationship, or the psychological aspect, or even the conscious aspect, depending on where the urge of obedience takes its rise. As a mode of behaviour, it is an effect and can therefore be subject to modification. It is very important to understand that it is a mode of behaviour/an effect, because the fact of being obedient, or not, is referred to a motivating cause which stands behind it.

For example, one may be obedient out of psychological weakness, or because there are specific complexes, or out of ignorance; one may obey as an act of duty, love, or respect for a superior, and so on.

Not only are these types of obedience effects but they also depend on factors which are *external* to the subject; thus obedience is an assent to an authority which is not the actual subject. This implies that as the external object or the external motivation diminishes, so does the obedience.

Let us be clearer: obedience may be the result of a 'command' that comes from within the subject or from outside. We may command ourselves to carry out a particular action; we may obey or disobey this command of ours; but it is a command issuing from ourselves to ourselves. On the other hand, it may be a command which comes from outside and is independent of our own will/decision.

Again, the command may certainly come from outside, but then we make it our own in total freedom, so that it is as if it came from within us.

There may also be a command of obedience which does not originate from a person but from particular circumstances that are quite impersonal. For example, a social body imposes obedience; there is not a specific person who chooses to impose it, but the very necessity of the relational circumstances.

Thus obedience arises from a social order, from particular circumstances, from a person, from ourselves, and, we may also add, from universal nature by way of specific laws. A law, human or divine, implies obedience, imposes a way of behaviour, and is presumed to be the symbol of harmony inasmuch as it imposes an order that is suitable for a social or universal context.

Now our aim as disciples on the Way is to see whether it is possible to find a factor by means of which obedience becomes a 'response of growth', a means (no longer the final effect) by which consciousness awakens to certain recognitions. Let us remind ourselves: a prescriptive norm (juridical or otherwise) aims to produce a type of behaviour which will entail merely a formal aspect or an involvement of our whole being. It depends, as we have said, on the realm from which the norm takes its rise.

So, we may ask ourselves, is there a solution which will establish obedience purely as a means of raising our consciousness?

And whom should the disciple on the way of Realisation obey? It seems obvious to us that, first of all, he should obey the 'voice' of his own conscience; then the Teaching which he considers most suitable for his *sādhanā* (spiritual discipline); and finally his precise *dharma* (duty) of initiate-to-be. Before all else, we must put our trust in the voice that reaches us from the very depths of the Soul: Realisation does not take place as a result of mere curiosity, or because we have been urged on by others, or to please someone, not even to please an Instructor/Initiator.

Realisation is the result of a maturity that is not only of the psyche but primarily of the *consciousness*; it is this consciousness which must feel sufficiently awakened to embark on the Way; we could even speak of *vocation*, and this is an extremely personal matter.

Subsequent to such an act, the other important aspect is the Teaching. There are Teachings at various levels, which presuppose the right qualifications. The Teaching is always one, because Reality is one, but each disciple, according to his development of consciousness, *comprehends*, in time and space, only portions or segments of the whole Teaching.

However to accept a Teaching and then, let us say, not to obey it is something to contemplate carefully. In this case, obedience is something which arises from a *conscious acceptance*, voluntary and free. Now if there is a free acceptance of a Teaching, the result of discrimination and vocation, non-obedience raises a number of perplexing issues. A Teaching is directed at someone and is such if it teaches something; now, if one accepts it because one considers it to be just and appropriate for one's own experience at the time, why does one not obey wholeheartedly? Here obedience is not in the form of an imposition; a spiritual Teaching never imposes, but rather indicates certain possibilities.

The way of the Teaching may also be the way of Silence, some examples of which we find in the *Upaniṣads*; indeed, is there any teaching higher than that of Silence?

Obedience to a choice made consciously means obedience to one's own *dharma*. The word *dharma* has many connotations; we shall use it to designate an individual's 'way of being', the law which he has decided to follow and which he will have to obey. This varies from person to person; the *dharma* of an aspirant is not that of an accepted disciple, or of an initiate, or of a Master. Furthermore, the *dharma* changes in time/space until one comes to embody universal *Dharma*.

Dharma coincides with the being's most immediate *duty*; not to obey one's own *dharma* means to betray the purpose of one's own existence or embodiment; it means not putting oneself in the right frame of relationship of oneself with oneself, of oneself with others, and of oneself with the universal *Dharma*, in which everyone will have to play his own part. Obedience is the conscious assent to the imperative of our Soul and to the Teaching – both of which can provide us with the right conditions for our development – and to a possible Instructor as a living embodiment of the Teaching.

So, to conclude this simple note of meditation, the committed disciple will have to obey

1. The 'voice' of his own conscience.
2. His chosen Teaching.
3. His most immediate *dharma*.

If he succeeds in doing this, it may well be said that obedience will bring tangible fruits for the development of his condition.

HUMILITY

Knowledge teaches humility or, rather, imposes it, because Humility is an indispensable condition for Knowledge. Humility (*bhūmitva*), in the widest meaning of the term, *is* Knowledge itself, and Knowledge is Humility; so that – as happens with knowledge – Humility, too, is susceptible to a gradual comprehension and actuation, and it implicates the being not only in one of its peripheral modes of expression but in the totality of its essential possibilities.

If true Knowledge is not limited to the conceptual acquisition of notions and representations but totally involves the being in a self-determining movement of transformation, re-conversion, and sublimation (this is the Platonic *catharsis*, in which not only does the specific vehicle/instrument avail itself of a given philosophical or metaphysical concept, but the *consciousness* itself is nourished by it, absorbing its essence and realising it through unity/identity); at the apex of this parabolic trajectory and beyond all bonds of inertia (and therefore beyond every possible contingent condition of an instinctive/sensory or emotional/mental character), it cannot but happen that there is revealed a State that is stable within itself, imperturbable and unchangeable, not subject to any modifications as pure Being (*sat*), in which every being and occurrence finds its existence, manifesting itself and expressing in its own cycle one of the countless modalities of life. And it is in this non-condition – which is at the beginning, in the middle, and at the end, which reveals itself only with the *solution* of its own being/knowing in pure Knowledge/Existence (*sat/cit*) – that the value of Humility in its full extent can be comprehended.

Humility comprises not only a virtue that is moral, benign, and bound to the human level, and is therefore of an ethical or religious/emotional nature; and it cannot be said to be simply an intellectual gift, although the Humility of which we have spoken undoubtedly includes these positive qualities.

Humility is a *spiritual symbol*, and as such it encompasses a value that is immense, limitless, because it is the fulfilment of the total renunciation of every *identification*, that is, a renunciation of the entire capability of what is contained in the mind, from gross objects to universal Being (*Īśvara*), and it is therefore the very essence of *renunciation* (*saṁnyāsa*) in its highest form: self-renunciation; that is, renunciation of oneself, renunciation of the *jīva*/the centre of the self-consciousness of 'existing' as a separate entity, and therefore its own dissolution and extinction (*nirvāṇa*) in the Self/*ātman*.

Humility is *self-renunciation*; and the *humble* and all-embracing living expression not only heralds to some extent one's own spiritual elevation but in fact leads on to full Knowledge/Realisation. We would say that it is the 'clear sign' of all-pervading Knowledge, which reveals the Unity of Consciousness in someone who has come to live, truly and totally, his own all-embracing vision.

Since *to comprehend* is to know and to be at the same time, total and unconditioned renunciation (*parasaṁnyāsa*) reveals its own conscious and existential disposition to Be, having comprehended, and therefore transcended, every aspect of the world of becoming.

Thus Humility is the natural consequence of discrimination (*viveka*) and detachment (*vairāgya*) and therefore of non-identification: the *freedom* which this brings is the privilege only of those who have realised their own Identity with absolute Being.

Here there is no room for any kind of sentimental and restrictive interpretation of Humility, since in the meantime its hugely extensive and unlimited connotations and implications reveal themselves.

Self-renunciation/humility, if lived fully, brings with it, not an abasement or degradation of the being, but a boundless enrichment, an unfathomable integration, a true and proper all-inclusive expansion, and thus an endless expansion of *consciousness* to the realisation of the *equivalence/identity* with the unity of the *Brahman* without a second.

Then it is only in acknowledging the true meaning of Humility that there can also be a recognition of the rarefaction, the *purity*, the resplendent *heterogeneity*, of what has been resolved, dispersed, dissolved, like a drop in the Sea of the Self, of That which *is there* no longer inasmuch as it *is*.

Moreover, it is by putting oneself *humbly* into tune, into hearing and waiting, that one can receive the limitless continuous *presence* of That – One without a second – which seems to the mind to be absent in place, form, datum, and so on.

If the *humilitas* of the body and mind pertains to those who perform right action at the right place (*dhārmika karma*), the *humilitas* of the Spirit belongs to one who – being gentle, calm and submissive to everything – has consciously placed himself beyond every external manifestation, every expression with form or without form, manifest or unmanifest, all the contents of the mind, and even beyond the principial Idea of himself, and has re-discovered himself as pure, absolute Being/Knowing, the Substratum and support of all knowledge and existence, and as Absolute, the sphere and place of all relativity, just as the Earth (*humus*) is the support for every living creature.

Humility, then, cannot correspond to an external attitude which becomes exhausted in a mental standpoint which is subject to birth and dissolution; on the contrary, humility must constitute a precise *state of consciousness* from which each and every thing spontaneously emanates and flourishes.

Humility is 'being the substratum of everything', *being Brahman*, or simply Being without a second.

True Humility is therefore an expression of identity with the Substratum; and rather than a condition that has been attained and is transient or, in any case, relative, it is the State *par excellence*, where Equilibrium reigns, stable and everlasting (*sanātana dharma*), transcendent and present both in movement and stillness and, in short, where absolute, unqualified Being reveals itself, the metaphysical foundation of every possible qualification, subsequent relative existence, and the world of becoming itself; hence it is pure metaphysical Reality as non-dual Consciousness (*advaita caitanya*).

The Kingdom of Heaven is for the 'poor in spirit', since it is in non-attachment, non-adherence of the spirit to the objects of the world of *māyā*, that the Soul (*jīva*) merges into the *ātman*, revealing the Freedom (*mokṣa*) which is its very nature and which is proper to *That* which is single and has no duality.

If the *jīva* is the reflection of the *ātman* within the *ātman* itself, the awareness which it expresses is the reflection of consciousness within Consciousness, 'spirit within spirit', and it is on this account that it can resolve itself into the Self by *recognising itself* as the non-dual Self.

And this recognition may coincide with an 'act of deep awareness', provided only that there has been a renunciation of everything, including oneself as an empirical ego, that is, on the condition of having completed an extreme act of total, absolute Humility. It may well be said, then, that Humility is the support of the *sādhanā* as well as the characteristic of those who have attained the Goal: it alone allows that tiny spark which is the *jīva* to re-discover itself as the infinite Light of the Self which illumines beings and events.

It is this Humility which transforms into the *sovereignty* of one who, having renounced everything, really *possesses* everything inasmuch as he is *Everything*. It is the infinite, radiant brightness, aware of the One who has realised the Unity of Consciousness, the One who, having awakened to full awareness of non-dual Reality, lives as Witness (*sākṣin*) of the unlimited pageant of existence and of all that exists.

Humility, in brief, is the *Dignity* of the One who, 'seeing all things in the Self and the Self in all things', is ready and disposed to welcome everything, embrace everything, comprehend everything, share everything; in short, to be *one with everything.*

Blessed is He who, 'humble among the humble', has perfected his true self-renunciation at the level of consciousness, and therefore at the level of existence, and, in the total peace which results from supreme detachment, has resolved the duality of subject and object and the very unity of the self-consciousness of *jīva/Īśvara* by merging into the non-dual Reality as *pure Knowledge*, the substratum of all knowledge/existence.

There is, therefore, a single true Humility, and it is that which is reflected in the *pax profunda* of one who has comprehended each and every thing within himself, one who, having recognised the necessity of realising *at first hand* the non-duality of the Self, has merged into the *ātman* and has rediscovered himself as the unbounded Fullness of Consciousness and Bliss. When the note of Humility has merged into union with that of Knowledge, when this intimate union has brought into conformity with itself the whole spatiality of being, by resolving that which is a mere metamorphosis (becoming) into a true *transmutation*, and that which is imaginary inventiveness into pure Consciousness without contents, then, and only then, will the perfect Silence of the One-Good – the Silence of the Unqualified (*Nirguṇa*), the Fourth (*Turīya*) – be able to establish itself as clear, silent Awareness, all-pervasive like ether.

VESAK

Vesak refers to the festival of the *Buddha*, which normally falls on the day of the full moon in the month of *Vaiśākha* or *Vesak*, which corresponds to the month of May.

The festival of *Vesak* commemorates three events at the same time: the birth of Prince Siddhartha; the Enlightenment of Gautama, who thus became the Buddha, the Enlightened One; and lastly the Buddha's attainment of the supreme *nirvāṇa* (*Paranirvāṇa*).

The events – by chance or otherwise – coincide and fall on the same date.

The teaching and example of the Buddha have remained alive and will always remain alive. The path which leads beyond *saṁsāra*, beyond suffering, is ever open to men of good will, to those beings that dare and die to themselves as separate egos.

Gautama lived in an intellectual climate similar to that in which many *Ṛṣis* of the *Upaniṣads* lived; but since the Buddha, who belonged to the *Kṣatriya* caste, did not recognise the authority of the *Vedas*, and especially the *karman* (Ritual) practised by the *Brāhmaṇa* priests, his teaching was considered heterodox.

However, his teaching and that of the *Upaniṣads* have the same aim, although they start from premises that are different, yet not opposed. Thus the Buddha developed the 'Philosophy of becoming', while the *Upaniṣads* principally developed the 'Philosophy of Being'.

In any case, the intention of the Buddha was not to formulate new metaphysics, but merely to point out to mankind the *way* which must lead to Liberation. We have to agree, however, that if the intention was to indicate a 'way', some questions of a philosophical and metaphysical order have found their way into his formulation.

Let us recall, for example, that the Buddha was interested in the nature of desire, in the nature of suffering, and in that within us which can dispel these defects.

Today we would say that he approached this subject in its psychological and philosophical aspects. And since the purpose of such a teaching is to transcend all that is impermanent and contingent, we can also say that it contains a consequent metaphysical Teaching.

If scientists reveal numerous mysteries about the working mechanics of the phenomena of life, the Buddha reveals the working mechanisms of the processes which lead to suffering, to pain, and to the disorder of the planetary system.

Science provides us with the means to make our empirical life more comfortable – but not that much more comfortable –, offers us advances in knowledge which curtail illnesses at the coarse physical level, and gives us technological developments in the manifold aspects of human activity; but it does not give us the answer to suffering, to conflict, to pain, and to mental disorder. The pain the Buddha speaks of is not, of course, physical or psychical, an end in itself; his intention is not the hedonistic one of fleeing from pain as such. His question is deeper, because it entails the nature of human individuality itself.

The four noble truths of the Buddha – his four postulates – relate to:

1. The existence of suffering (conflict both individual and general).
2. The cause of suffering or conflict.
3. The cessation of suffering.
4. The means which lead to the cessation of suffering (the eightfold path of Buddhism).

We could express these postulates differently, without affecting the Buddhist Teaching:

1. Existence is becoming.
2. The cause which instigates becoming.
3. The cessation of becoming.
4. The means which lead to the cessation of becoming.

In fact, the Buddha declared that all that is located in the field of our experience is *impermanent*, and this field includes both objective/coarse data and subjective/subtle data. There is no *stable* centre or permanent substratum to be found in this becoming/process. In this sense the Buddha developed the theory of *anatta*, the non-self (as a stable *ego*), in contradistinction to the speculations of the *Upaniṣads*, which speak of the Self or *ātman*. However, we need to distinguish between the *ātman* and the *jīva*, and between the *jīva* and the empirical ego.

We may say that the Buddha is referring to the *jīva* (individual soul) and to the empirical ego itself; and we are right, because this is also true for *Vedānta*, and thus there is no contradiction with the *Upaniṣads*.

This becoming/process: is it real or unreal, according to the Buddha?

In fact, this is a question on which the Buddha never made a categorical pronouncement, with the result that there have been many controversies. He contented himself with simply emphasising the experience of *change*, an experience, of course, which cannot be negated; but he did not take a stand either against the idealists or, basically, against the speculation of the *ātman/Brahman* of *Vedānta*.

The Buddha states: 'This world is the expression of two opposite aspects – it is, it is not; but a wise person perceives how, in truth, things are born and thus discovers that there exists nothing in the world of which one can say, "This is not." The wise person perceives how things die and thus discovers that there exists nothing in the world of which one can say

"This is." To declare that in this world "something is" is to put oneself into an extreme position, but to declare that "something is not" is to go to the other extreme. The Truth is found in the middle.'

This Truth is very significant if we bear in mind that *Vedānta* itself maintains that, according to the specific point of view that we hold, the universe *is* and *is not.*

With regard to man, the Buddha portrayed him in five elements (*skandha*, aggregate) which make an organic whole:

1. *rūpa*, physical body;
2. *vedanā*, sensation;
3. *saññā*, perception;
4. *saṅkhāra*, mental process arising from unconscious tendencies;
5. *viññāna*, Knowledge or Consciousness (*vijñāna* in Sanskrit).

Of these five elements, the physical body (*rūpa*) and the element of consciousness (*vijñāna*) play a major role in Buddhism.

Consciousness is the result of countless cognitions which may appear during the course of the embodiment. The body comes into existence when the consciousness organises matter/substance under the influence of the *saṁskāras.*

We can say that the consciousness conceived in this way corresponds to the *jīva* of *Vedānta.* It may also be likened to the conception found in theistic doctrines; it differs from these, however, on account of the fact that this consciousness is itself a compound and so is not a *single element*, because it is characterised by the combination of various factors: sensory contacts, sensations, corresponding perceptions, and so on. The perceptions of the present moment are transferred to the elements which take their birth from another moment: hence the continuity of perception.

Let us repeat that, according to Buddhism, there does not exist an *eternally motionless centre*, which raises the question, How then, can there be memory, continuity of consciousness, knowledge itself, and so on, if there is no stable co-ordinating centre?

It seems to us that Buddhism has hypothesised a mechanistic theory (biological, chemical changes, and so on) of perception itself and thus of sensory knowledge.

Consciousness itself, therefore, is nothing but the combination of various factors which find their nourishment in the *thirst for life*, in the powerful instinct of self-preservation. When this thirst/desire ceases, everything disintegrates; and we might wonder what remains. *Śūnya*: the Void; in the emptiness, where there is no determination or qualification, there is unlimited fullness. Some might conclude that Buddhism is nihilistic and leads to the annihilation of Reality itself as such. To avoid falling into this misconception it would be necessary to have a proper comprehension of the whole Teaching of the Buddha.

The ultimate goal which the Buddha wishes to point out to us is the state of *Being* in which subject and object completely vanish. This is also the goal of *Vedānta*, and especially of *Advaita Vedānta*.

It is not true that the Buddha denied a permanent entity. He denied the conception of a stable entity within the things which constitute the *spectacle*, the becoming of things, a spectacle which, as we have already said, is of an order that is both physical/gross and subtle.

We would say that within becoming there is nothing stable; and if any postulate a *stable entity* within this unceasing movement, they are mistaken.

In the *Upaniṣads* it is said that the field of knowledge can be divided into two paths: the *dṛk*, the observing subject, and the *dṛśya*, the spectacle.

Now it is pointless to look for an absolute substratum/witness from which this polarity originates, because it cannot be an object of perception, nor, therefore, can it be found in the realm of the limited.

In this ultimate and absolute *substratum* the Buddha says he takes no interest in the mind, because, in fact, it is pointless to do so, since it is not an *object of perception*.

Having experienced the temporal process, the Buddha deduced that a permanent/absolute Being could find no place in such a process. Let us repeat that this does not imply the admission of absolute nihilism, as has been stated even by some of his followers and many outstanding figures of Eastern and Western culture. Even *Sāṁkhya* maintains that both *puruṣa* and *prakṛti* exist and that this duality is permanent, but in doing so it does not deny *metaphysical Unity*.

Such are the different perspectives from which the question of Being and non-being can be approached. Some adopt one particular viewpoint, and others a different viewpoint, and both of these viewpoints may be valid.

Thus *Vedānta* has not rejected *Sāṁkhya* but has accepted it, taking it as the base, or *starting-point*, for its own speculation. In other words, that which represents the ultimate goal of *Sāṁkhya* constitutes the 'beginning' of *Vedānta*.

We know how Śaṅkara replied to some nihilistic Buddhists. We can allude to just one of his numerous sayings: 'To affirm that nothing exists, one must be conscious of non-existence, which in turn implies the existence of a being which is affirming this proposition.' In other words, 'We can deny everything except the person who is making the denial.' In denying the one who is making the denial we are implicitly affirming him: two negatives make a positive. This means that to take denial to its extreme is impossible. Śaṅkara is anticipating the days of a specific Western philosophical approach, such as that of Descartes.

Thus the Buddha did not deny the *one who was able to deny*. He said, it seems to us, that Being, the permanent, could find no place in becoming, in non-being. The Buddha refused to recognise that anything presented as an ego can have a permanent value.

Individuality, in its entirety, belongs to the nature of change, the relative, the contingent, and so why speak of an ego which endures? The ego of today is not the ego of yesterday; the ego of one embodiment, with a name and a form, is not the ego of another embodiment. The Paul of today (the present embodiment) is not the Maria of yesterday (a previous embodiment). So if the ego comes and goes, exists and does not exist, how can we speak of a 'philosophy of the ego', a psychology of the ego, as a stable and permanent individuality?

Do I perceive my individual existence? Then, says the Buddha, all that I perceive is impermanent, because it concerns a mere perceivable object or a *spectacle*, and the spectacle/object is a becoming, a process, a prison. All the elements which comprise what we call human individuality must be considered the not-Self, and true Liberation can occur when the being eliminates from its consciousness the false concept of individuality.

In other words, individuality is nothing but a dream. Shakespeare declares:

> 'The cloud-capp'd towers, the gorgeous palaces,
> The solemn temples, the great globe itself,
> Yea, all which it inherit, shall dissolve,
> And, like this insubstantial pageant faded,
> Leave not a rack behind.'

He says the same about man:

> 'We are such stuff as dreams are made on,
> And our little life is rounded with a sleep.'[1]

Ignorance makes us say, 'I am this', while Knowledge makes us acknowledge 'I am not this' (*anatta*, egoic non-existence).

This conception is fundamentally not dissimilar to that of *Advaita Vedānta*. They both aim at resolving the ghost

[1] W. Shakespeare, *The Tempest*, Act IV, Scene 1.

of *saṁsāra*, becoming, phenomenon, or that which is not absolute Reality.

Both conceptions aim to transcend subject and object and every phenomenal duality of *māyā*. They both aim at transcendence: *mukti* according to *Vedānta*, and *nibbana* according to Buddhism. Two sides of the same coin, or the same truth seen from different perspectives.

Thus we find that the teaching of the Buddha is directed principally to recognising the impermanence of the phenomenal world and hence the conflict which may ensue when one wants to halt or crystallise that which is flowing and which cannot be held back and enjoyed permanently.

Ignorance (*avidyā*) produces desire, desire produces the thirst for acquisition, and the thirst for acquisition produces the instinct for perpetuity, preservation, and crystallisation. It is a vicious circle which – unless one tries to break it – can only lead to continuous *saṁsāra*/becoming/pain.

Through the very dynamics of the process, every acquisitive identification leads to conflict/suffering.

Within impermanence nothing can be found that is stable, fixed, homogeneous, which means that the *jīva* itself, of which the empirical ego is a reflection in space and time, is a contingent and transient datum. When we have transcended and resolved the realm of becoming, we shall be outside becoming/conflict and thus, the Buddha says, we shall be in *nirvāṇa*.

Vedānta states that when, by means of *viveka* (intuitive discrimination), we have comprehended that which is not absolute Reality, then we shall be able to do nothing but transcend it, in order to rediscover ourselves in the all-pervading *Brahman*.

At this point we may mention a great philosopher of ancient Greece whose teaching, from certain perspectives, may be close to that of Buddha. This philosopher/master is known as Heraclitus.

Heraclitus, who lived at Ephesus in Ionia between the end of the 6th century and the beginning of the 5th century B.C.

(the Buddha is thought to have been born around 563 and to have died in 483 B.C.), has – as we have hinted – a focus of teaching analogous to that of the Buddha. The speculative genius of Heraclitus is focused on a central idea which is profoundly philosophical: the impermanence of life. 'Everything is in flux,' he states, 'nothing is permanent.' The world consists of a never-ending self-transformation, a continuous, unceasing dissolution and resolution, with an inexhaustible movement. One can never step into the same water twice.

When you believe you have stopped an object, a quality, a phenomenon, in its *being*, you find yourself in front of something different, into which the object has been transformed: something which it *is not* and is therefore its opposite. And if you notice that in some way it continues to *be*, this happens precisely because it has been transformed into something else and has ceased to be (what it was), or, in short, because it *is no longer* (what it was).

Parmenides the Eleatic, by contrast, saw Being, not in becoming, process, and change, but in its *Identity*, in its *static reality*, devoid of all change, relativity, and opposition.

Parmenides says that, according to the Truth of things, everything is eternal and motionless; in fact, it is a complete whole, single, unmoving, and *ungenerated*; and what we call becoming is the effect of our wrong seeing.[1] Some exponents of the Eleatic school totally dismiss generation, because in the world of beings there is nothing which is generated and nothing which perishes: generation or movement is an effect of our representation.

Being *is*, says Parmenides, and how can that which *is not* be?[2]

If there is something other than white, it is not white; if there is something other than the good, it is not good; if there

[1] See Parmenides, *On the Order of Nature*, fragment 8.

[2] *Ibid.*, fragments 6-7.

is something other than Being, it is not Being. But non-being, through the very fact of not being, cannot Be.

We might find ourselves facing two apparently contradictory aspects: on the one hand, Being inasmuch as it is, and if it is it cannot become; on the other hand, becoming, and inasmuch as becoming is process, movement, and change, it cannot *Be*.

Fundamentally this problem, when reduced to its essence, can be conveyed by the binomial 'Being and non-being'. In other words, we have the eternal problem of the polar principle of Life.

Some see Being in its absolute and unmoving *essence*, and others see Being in the continuous ebb and flow of *becoming*. From the viewpoint of reason we can only point out that if we posit the concept or image of movement it is because we also have the concept of motionlessness. One term presupposes the other, just as light presupposes darkness. From this it follows that these statements pertain to what we might call *relational truth*, not epistemic truth. Parmenides, however, does not posit an absolute duality but gives us to understand that becoming, or non-being, represents a mere *appearance/phenomenon* of Being, so that *appearance*/world of form has Being as its metaphysical foundation; and here he comes close to the vision of Gauḍapāda's *Ajātivāda*, and thus to the vision of the *Māṇḍūkya Upaniṣad*.

In its speculative thought, *Advaita Vedānta* also reaches a unitive, harmonising, and resolving unity. It maintains that movement and non-movement, the moving and the motionless, becoming and being, are nothing but a *polar* aspect of *māyā*. They are nothing but dialectical moments of the principial One, two 'electromagnetic' forces: one negative, the other positive, interacting; polarities which vanish at a stroke when the *neutral* transcending *Point* is realised. Thus, at the level of the individual, subject and object are immediately resolved once we enter the state of Silence, just as the two points at the base of the triangle are resolved in the point at the vertex.

According to *Advaita Vedānta*, *puruṣa* and *prakṛti* are re-absorbed into *Saguṇa Brahman*.

Thus *Advaita Vedānta* would seem to say: They are both right: the one who sees Being in its process and becoming (*śakti*), and the one who sees Being in its immobility and stillness.

From this it comes about that this *darśana* is not in opposition to anyone, and a *jīvanmukta* of *Vedānta* comprehends equally movement and stillness, the dynamic condition and the static condition, negative polarity and positive polarity.

> 'On the one hand, being in its eternity which knows not the process of becoming; on the other hand, a process of perennial becoming which never attains being. What is the definition of each principle? The first is intelligible through an act of pure intellection in the company of a rational act: eternal being in its identity of being. The second, by contrast, is conceived by opinion in the company of feeling and in itself is devoid of all rational acts; this becoming, which participates in a never-ending process of generation and dissolution, can never be in all its fullness.'[1]

> 'O Monks, there exists the unborn, the uncompounded, the non-become, the unconditioned. If there were not the unborn, the non-become, the unconditioned, the uncompounded, we would have no way of fleeing from the born, that which becomes, that which is conditioned, and that which is compounded.[2]

What follows is Gautama's *Hymn of Victory*, sung when he attained Enlightenment:

> Many abodes of life
> Have imprisoned me:
> I constantly sought the one
> Who constructed these prisons
> Of senses, built of sorrows!
> Sorrowful was my unceasing struggle.
> But now I know you,

[1] Plato, *Timaeus*, III. 28a.

[2] *Udana*, VIII, 3.

Builder of this Tabernacle!
Never again will you construct
Those walls of grief,
Never will you erect the architrave
Of lies, never will you place
New beams on clay!
Your dwelling is broken,
And its central pillar cut down!
Illusion formed it!
I depart from here
To attain Liberation.

'Let us therefore flee towards the beloved homeland: this is the truest advice one can give.

'But what is the nature of this flight? And how to rise again … ?

'Our homeland is the one whence we have come, and up there is our Father. What, then, is this journey, and what is this flight?

'We need not make it with our feet … there is not even any need to prepare coaches or boats, yet it is necessary to detach oneself from these things and no longer look at them. Exchanging physical sight for another sight, one needs to awaken that faculty which everyone possesses but few use.'[1]

[1] Plotinus, *Enneads*, I. VI. 8.

RAPHAEL

Unity of Tradition

Raphael having attained a synthesis of Knowledge (which is not associated with eclecticism or with syncretism) aims at 'presenting' the Universal Tradition in its many Eastern and Western expressions. He has spent a substantial number of years writing and publishing books on spiritual experience; his works include commentaries on the *Qabbālāh*, Hermeticism, and Alchemy. He has also commented on and compared the Orphic Tradition with the works of Plato, Parmenides, and Plotinus. Furthermore, Raphael has written several books on the pathway of non-duality (*Advaita*). He has also translated and commented on a number of key Vedantic texts from the original Sanskrit.

With reference to Platonism, Raphael has highlighted the fact that, if we were to draw a parallel between Śaṅkara's Advaita Vedānta and a Traditional Western Philosophical Vision, we could refer to the Vision presented by Plato. Drawing such a parallel does not imply a search for reciprocal influences, but rather it points to something of paramount importance: a sole Truth, inherent in the doctrines (teachings) of several great thinkers, who, although far apart in time and space, have reached similar and in some cases even identical conclusions.

One notices how Raphael's writings aim to manifest and underscore the Unity of Tradition from the metaphysical perspective. This does not mean that he is in opposition to a dualistic perspective, or to the various religious faiths or 'points of view'.

An embodied real metaphysical Vision cannot be opposed to anything. What counts for Raphael is the unveiling, through living and being, which one has been able to contemplate.

In the light of the Unity of Tradition Raphael's writings or commentaries offer the intuition of the reader precise points of correspondence between Eastern and Western Teachings. These points of reference are useful for those who want to approach a comparative doctrinal study and to enter the spirit of the Unity of Teaching.

For those who follow either the Eastern or the Western traditional line these correspondences help in comprehending how the Philosophia Perennis (Universal Tradition), which has no history and has not been formulated by human minds as such, 'comprehends universal truths that do not belong to any people or any age'. It is only for lack of 'comprehension' or 'synthetic vision' that one particular Branch is considered the only reliable one. From this position there can be only opposition and fanaticism. What degrades the Teaching is sentimental, fanatical devotionalism as well as proud intellectualism, which is critical and sterile, dogmatic and separative.

In Raphael's words: 'For those of us who aim at Realisation, it is our task is to get to the essence of every Teaching, because we know that, just as Truth is one, so Tradition is one even if, just like Truth, Tradition may be viewed from a plurality of apparently different points of view. We must abandon all disquisitions concerning the phenomenal process of becoming, and move onto the plane of Being. In other words, we must have a Philosophy of Being as the foundation of our search and our realisation.'[1]

Raphael interprets spiritual practice as a 'Pathway of Fire'. Here is what he writes: 'The "Path of Fire" is the pathway each disciple follows in all branches of the Tradition; it is the Way of Return. Therefore, it is not the particular teaching of an individual or the path parallel to the one and only Main Road... After all, every disciple follows his own "Path of Fire", no matter which Branch of the Tradition he belongs to'.

In Raphael's view, what is important is to express through living and being the truth that one has been able to contemplate. Thus, for each being, one's expression of thought and

[1] See Raphael, *Tat tvam asi*, (That thou art). Aurea Vidyā, New York

action must be coherent and in agreement with one's own specific dharma.

After more than 60 years of teaching, both oral and written, Raphael withdrew into *mahāsamādhī*.

* * *

May Raphael's Consciousness, expression of Unity of Tradition, guide and illumine along this Opus all those who donate their *mens informalis* (non-formal mind) to the attainment of the highest known Realization.

PUBLICATIONS

Aurea Vidyā Collection

1. Raphael, The ***Threefold Pathway of Fire***, Thoughts that Vibrate for an Alchemical, Æsthetical, and Metaphysical ascesis
ISBN 978-1-931406-00-0

2. Raphael, ***At the Source of Life***, Questions and Answers concerning the Ultimate Reality
ISBN 979-8-576124-75-6

3. Raphael, ***Beyond the illusion of the ego***, Synthesis of a Realizative Process
ISBN 978-1-931406-03-1

4. Raphael, ***Tat tvam asi***, That thou art, The Path of Fire According to the Asparśavāda
ISBN 979-8-583067-52-7

5. Gauḍapāda, ***Māṇḍūkyakārikā***, The Metaphysical Path of *Vedānta**
ISBN 978-1-931406-04-8

6. Raphael, ***Orphism and the Initiatory Tradition***
ISBN 979-8-539590-78-9

7. Śaṅkara, ***Ātmabodha***, Self-knowledge*
ISBN 978-1-931406-06-2

8. Raphael, ***Initiation into the Philosophy of Plato***
ISBN 978-1-466486-98-0

9. Śaṅkara, ***Vivekacūḍāmaṇi***, The Crest-jewel of Discernment*
ISBN 978-1-931406-08-6

10. ***Dṛdṛśyaviveka***, A philosophical investigation into the nature of the 'Seer' and the 'seen'*
ISBN 979-8-669178-69-7

11. Parmenides, ***On the Order of Nature***, Περί φύσεως, For a Philosophical Ascesis*
ISBN 979-8-698821-95-3

12. Raphael, ***The Science of Love***, From the desire of the senses to the Intellect of Love
ISBN 978-1-931406-12-3

13. Vyāsa, ***Bhagavadgītā***, The Celestial Song*
ISBN 979-8-562809-02-5

14. Raphael, ***The Pathway of Fire according to the Qabbālāh*** (Ehjeh 'Ašer 'Ehjeh), I am That I am
ISBN 978-1-931406-14-7

15. Patañjali, ***The Regal Way to Realization***, Yogadarśana*
ISBN 978-1-931406-15-4

16. Raphael, ***Beyond Doubt***, Approaches to Non-duality
ISBN 979-8-657281-16-3

17. Bādarāyaṇa, ***Brahmasūtra****
ISBN 978-1-931406-17-8

18. Śaṅkara, ***Aparokṣānubhūti***, Self-realization*
ISBN 978-1-931406-19-2

19. Raphael, ***The Pathway of Non-Duality***, Advaitavāda
ISBN 979-8-552322-16-9

20. ***Five Upaniṣads****, Īśa, Kaivalya, Sarvasāra, Amṛtabindu, Atharvaśira
ISBN 978-1-931406-26-0

21. Raphael, ***The Philosophy of Being***, A conception of life for coming out of the turmoil of individul and social conflict
ISBN 979-8-630006-39-4

22. Raphael, ***Awakening***
ISBN 979-8-716953-07-9

Related Publications

Raphael, ***Essence and Purpose of Yoga***, The Initiatory Pathways to the Transcendent
Element Books, Shaftesbury, U.K.
ISBN 978-1-852308-66-7

Śaṅkara, A brief biography
Aurea Vidyā. New York.
ISBN 978-1-931406-11-6

Forthcoming Publications

Śaṅkara, ***Brief Works***,* Treatises and Hymns

Māṇḍūkya Upaniṣad, with the Gauḍapāda's *kārikās* and the Commentary of Śaṅkara

Upaniṣads*

Raphael, ***Essence and Purpose of Yoga***, The Initiatory Pathways to the Transcendent

* Translation from Sanskrit or Greek and Commentary by Raphael.

Aurea Vidyā is the Publishing House of the Parmenides Traditional Philosophy Foundation, a Not-for-Profit Organization whose purpose is to make Perennial Philosophy accessible.

The Foundation goes about its purpose in a number of ways: by publishing and distributing Traditional Philosophy texts with Aurea Vidyā, by offering individual and group encounters, by providing a Reading Room and daily Meditations at its Center.

* * *

Those readers who have an interest in Traditional Philosophy are welcome to contact the Foundation at:
parmenides.foundation@earthlink.net.

Printed in Great Britain
by Amazon

76604057R00193